Luminos is the Open Access monograph publishing program from UC Press. Luminos provides a framework for preserving and reinvigorating monograph publishing for the future and increases the reach and visibility of important scholarly work. Titles published in the UC Press Luminos model are published with the same high standards for selection, peer review, production, and marketing as those in our traditional program. www.luminosoa.org

Beyond the Binary

Beyond the Binary

Gender and Legal Personhood in Islamic Law

Saadia Yacoob

UNIVERSITY OF CALIFORNIA PRESS

University of California Press
Oakland, California

Suggested citation: Yacoob, S. *Beyond the Binary: Gender and Legal Personhood in Islamic Law*. Oakland: University of California Press, 2024.
DOI: https://doi.org/10.1525/luminos.186

Library of Congress Cataloging-in-Publication Data

Names: Yacoob, Saadia, author.
Title: Beyond the binary : gender and legal personhood in Islamic law / Saadia Yacoob.
Description: [Oakland, California] : University of California Press, [2024] | Includes bibliographical references and index.
Identifiers: LCCN 2023043570 (print) | LCCN 2023043571 (ebook) | ISBN 9780520393806 (paperback) | ISBN 9780520393813 (ebook)
Subjects: LCSH: Women (Islamic law)—History. | Persons (Islamic law)—History. | Hanafites—Doctrines. | Islamic law—Interpretation and construction—Early works to 1800.
Classification: LCC KBP526.4 .Y33 2024 (print) | LCC KBP526.4 (ebook) | DDC 342/.167087—dc23/eng/20231005

LC record available at https://lccn.loc.gov/2023043570
LC ebook record available at https://lccn.loc.gov/2023043571

To Ammi, whose love knows no bounds

CONTENTS

ACKNOWLEDGMENTS

I tell students that writing and scholarship constitute a communal exercise, a fact made invisible by the single author's name on a monograph. Similarly, this book has been made possible by a large community of people. It has been many years in the making and has only become a reality through their endless support for which I am deeply grateful.

I'd like to recognize my deep gratitude to my teachers and mentors over the years. To Ebrahim Moosa for his guidance and mentorship over the years. His dedication to his students, even past their graduate study, is an inspiring model. My deepest gratitude goes to Juliane Hammer for her love, support, and mentorship over the years. I will always be indebted to her for instilling in me the confidence and belief in my scholarly potential. She has also been a model for me in navigating the demands and conventions of the academy with a strong sense of ethics and commitment to anti-oppression work. I have also been tremendously fortunate to have Kecia Ali as my mentor. Her sharp and critical eye, coupled with incredible intellectual humility, are truly an inspiration and aspiration. This book would not have been possible without the tutelage and encyclopedic knowledge of Shaikh Ṣalāḥ Abū al-Hājj. I am truly grateful and honored that he took me on as a student.

I would like to express appreciation for my colleagues at the Department of Religion at Williams College: Jacqueline Hidalgo, Jeffrey Israel, Jason Storm, Denise Buell, Georges Dreyfus, Neil Roberts, Rhon Manigault-Bryant, James Manigault-Bryant, and Edan Dekel. They read early chapter drafts as I was beginning to conceptualize the book and their engagement with my work has truly broadened my intellectual horizons. I am particularly grateful to Jacqueline Hidalgo, VaNatta

Ford, James Manigault-Bryant, Meredith Coleman-Tobias, and Julia Kowlaski for introducing me to conversations that became the theoretical framework for this project. This book would not have been possible had it not been for my conversations with them over the years.

I would also like to acknowledge the Muslim feminist scholars whose scholarship has not only shaped my own intellectual development but has also been a source of spiritual and emotional sustenance. amina wadud was my very first teacher and mentor. Her scholarship and intellectual and emotional mentorship has truly been a blessing in my life. Kecia Ali, Juliane Hammer, Riffat Hassan, Azizah al-Hibri, Asma Barlas, Asifa Quraishi-Landes, Laury Silvers, Fatima Seedat, Hina Azam, Aysha Hidayatullah, Ayesha Chaudhry, and Zahra Ayubi; this book could not have been conceptualized without their scholarship. I am especially grateful to Fatima Seedat for her love, friendship, and intellectual companionship over the years.

My thinking on the book project has developed through conversations with a number of different colleagues. I cannot name them all but I am very grateful for their role in making this book possible. A special thanks goes to Kecia Ali, Juliane Hammer, Aysha Hidayatullah, Marion Katz, Sohaira Siddiqui, Mariam Sheibani, and Sohaib Khan for their invaluable feedback on drafts of book chapters. To Atiya Hussain for her sharp theoretical insights that have always pushed me to think beyond my intellectual constraints. To Ali Mian, SherAli Tareen, and Sam Kigar for their intellectual companionship throughout graduate school and beyond.

I would also like to thank those who invited me to present my work at conferences and workshops. There are too many to name but I extend a special thanks to Ebrahim Moosa, Omar Anchassi, Robert Gleave, Jonathan Brown, and Ellen McLarney. I am very much a verbal thinker and I develop my ideas through conversations. The opportunity to present my work in these settings was critical in shaping the argument of the book. I would also like to express tremendous gratitude to Peter Mandaville and the AbuSulayman Center for Global Islamic Studies at George Mason University for supporting this book project through a research fellow affiliation. Much of this book was written when I was on sabbatical during the COVID lockdown, when I had no access to an academic library. Their support made possible access to academic resources without which this book could not have been completed. I'm also grateful to the Hellman Foundation for their financial support for the book project.

I'd also like to thank Eric Schmidt and the staff at the University of California Press for all their work in helping publish this book. I am particularly grateful to Eric for his support, advocacy, and limitless patience throughout this process. This book was written during the COVID lockdown and through a time when I was dealing with a number of health issues; I was deeply touched by Eric's generosity and understanding during this time.

And lastly, no amount of thanks is sufficient for the love, support, and sacrifice of my family. My mother has been the pillar in my life and my inspiration, her support and encouragement are unending. I would not be where I am without her presence in my life. I am also infinitely indebted to her for the time she spent taking care of my daughter during the lockdown when we had no childcare. It is no exaggeration to say that there would be no book without her endless support. To my brother Saad for all his love and support and for graciously humoring his niece with stories so I could get some extra writing time. To my sister, Saima, for her love and support and instant willingness to help whenever I needed it. To my *khalas* Ambreen and Tanveer for all their love and encouragement and my *khalu* Yaqub Mirza for ceaseless care, love and encouragement. To Habiba Mohamed (Aye Habiba) for her love and generosity in taking care of my daughter so I could finish up the book manuscript. Again, this book would have not materialized were it not for her support.

And lastly, words cannot describe how grateful I am to have been blessed with Zaid in my life. His constant words of encouragement and belief in me is what got me through the inevitable rough patches of writing. His self-sacrifice and willingness to support me in every way imaginable has been one of the biggest blessings in my life. To my daughter, Ruqaiya, who patiently sacrificed *Amma*-Ruqaiya time so that I could finish up this book. The many books she wrote in the time it took me to write just this one provided a model and an inspiration for me in self-confidence. And finally and most importantly, *hadha min fadli rabbi.*

Introduction

When I was growing up, I often heard the story of my great-grandmother, Hamida Begum, and her life of veiling and seclusion. My great-uncle, Akhtar Hameed Khan, a prolific author, poet, and social scientist, writes about his mother extensively in his book *Komila se Aurangi Tak* (*From Komila to Aurangi*).[1] He describes his mother as a kindhearted and self-sacrificing person. She was also an avid reader who was deeply attached to books and invested in the intellectual conversations of her time. She was familiar with the works of leading Muslim Indian intellectuals of her time, people like Muhammad Iqbal, Shibli Nomani, Abdul Halim Sharar, Muhammad Ali Jauhar, and Abul Kalam Azad.[2] Family lore has it that because she was well-educated in English, she often composed and edited her husband's administrative letters and memos. Her husband, a police inspector, often practiced his English with her so that she might correct his pronunciation.

She was married at a young age (fourteen) and, like many other Muslim Indian brides in the early twentieth century, she received a copy of the Qur'an and *Bihishti Zewar* (Heavenly ornaments) in her dowry.[3] *Bihishti Zewar*, authored by the eminent South Asian scholar Maulana Ashraf Ali Thanvi, is one of the most influential and widely read Islamic texts in South Asia. Written to impart religious education to Muslim women, it focuses on a wide range of issues—from teaching reading, to the etiquette of letter writing, to basic Islamic legal rulings on rituals and ritual purity. The book also discusses legal rulings pertaining to marriage and divorce and explicitly endorses a social hierarchy in which the wife maintains a subordinate role in relation to the husband. My great-uncle explains that his mother was very earnest and sincere in living out the teachings of this book and devoted herself entirely to serving her husband and caring for her children.[4]

Like many other Muslim women from middle-class families in Northern India, she also practiced seclusion and refrained from going out in public. On the occasion that she did, she would not only cover her entire body and face but also travel in a covered palanquin or horse cart.[5] My great-uncle recounts that as a child, he struggled to understand his mother's seclusion. He felt his mother's practice of seclusion rendered her dependent, because her mobility restrictions made her incapable of doing anything on her own. She could neither go out to the market to purchase things she needed nor travel on her own without a male family escort. Her son's perception of her as dependent was perhaps a sign of social changes well under way in the late nineteenth and early twentieth centuries that made a life of seclusion increasingly difficult. Subsequent generations of women in the family no longer practiced seclusion and went out in public without covering and did not cover their faces or their heads. For my great-grandmother, however, her covering and mobility restrictions were not a sign of dependency but instead of high social status. As a woman from a family of high status (*shurfa*), she had the right not to toil in public and to be provided for financially. You can see the difference in perception of mother and son in a conversation that my great-uncle recounts in his book. He writes that when the family moved to Meerut in 1920, they were neighbors with a Muslim family of cowherders. The women of this family appeared uncovered in public and, for my great-uncle, this was a striking difference from his mother's practice of seclusion. He saw these women as freer because they worked alongside the men of their families, bought and sold in the market, and interacted with men to whom they were not related. His mother clearly saw the lives of these women not as freedom but instead as a disadvantage. When he inquired why they could be out in public but his mother could not, she explained that seclusion was the practice of women of a high social status: "my mother used to tell me that these [uncovered women] are women of low birth [*choti zat*] whereas we are people of noble and high birth [*unchay aur sharif log*]."[6]

This family story powerfully demonstrates the layers of complexity built into social hierarchies. The ways that class and gender intersect in it remind us that women, both historically and around the world, are not united in a shared oppression. My great-grandmother's life of seclusion, a sign of her class status, necessitated the existence of other women who had to emerge in public and perform the labor that secluded women could not do. Seclusion had its own disadvantages, of course. The inability to go out in public frequently or to travel without an escort meant that elite women had to rely on others to fulfill their needs. Tying seclusion to elite status, however, meant that elite women could become invested in their own confinement. I was reminded of this exchange between my great-uncle and his mother as I began studying Islamic law. When I first came across the legal rulings around veiling and mobility restrictions on Muslim women, I was struck by the distinctions made between free and enslaved women. Whereas Muslim jurists insisted that free elite women must cover their entire bodies, remain in seclusion, and not interact with men outside their family, they simultaneously insisted that enslaved women could not cover like free women and their mobility could not be restricted. An enslaved person's primary role was to labor at the command of their enslavers. To restrict the enslaved woman's mobility by requiring veiling as well as seclusion would impinge on the enslaver's rights.

As I read these discussions, the picture drawn of my great-grandmother's life became a window into a world where there was no assumption that legal rulings need apply universally to people because of a shared identity or biology. My great-grandmother's words made clear that veiling and seclusion were practices not of *all* women but of *particular* women. Her assertion was not just a reflection of the social hierarchies of her time but was also borne out in Islamic legal discussions. The distinctions between different categories of women in Islamic law were not confined to matters of mobility and veiling alone. These distinctions can be found in other aspects of the law as well. Free adult women had to consent to a marriage, but a free child or an enslaved woman could be coerced. Similarly, the free adult wife could petition for a divorce, a right that was not granted to a free wife who was a minor until she reached legal majority or an enslaved wife until she was emancipated. As I moved from one aspect of the law to the other, those distinctions based on gender, age, enslavement, social status, religion, and so on appeared everywhere. This observation led me to the realization that gender is neither the sole nor the primary factor in determining an individual's legal status in Islamic law. In fact, neither "man" nor "woman" are functional categories in Islamic law. That is, if we seek to understand what factors shape an individual's legal status and subsequently their ability to claim rights and obligations, we cannot rely on a simple assessment of men as privileged and women as disadvantaged. This male-female binary fails to capture the complexity of how power and status function in legal discourse. This has implications not only for how we understand Islamic law historically, but it also challenges us in the contemporary moment to move beyond a simple gender binary (or other fixed and predetermined categories) in our assessments of power, privilege, and oppression.

The question of women's status in Islamic law has been a burning issue in modern Muslim discourse. From academic to confessional Muslim literature, the arguments about women's status has ranged from proclaiming the progressive nature of Islamic law to a critique of its patriarchal nature and the need for reform. Many modern Muslim thinkers have argued for the progressive aspects of Islamic law and its affirmation of women's rights, particularly in relation to Christianity and Western law. These thinkers largely claim that Islam has already granted women rights such as property ownership and political standing, rights that have only recently been instituted by Western nations. In accounting for gender-differentiated rulings, they argue that these differences reflect a complimentary relation between men and women that is divinely ordained and necessary to maintain social order and harmony.[7] The other argument regarding women's status in

Islamic law is perhaps best articulated by the scholar of Islam and gender, Leila Ahmed. In her highly influential book *Women and Gender in Islam: Historical Roots of a Modern Debate*, Ahmed argues that Islam continued and reinforced an increasingly patriarchal shift that was already under way owing to the Greek, Roman, and Christian periods that preceded Islam.[8] Ahmed's historical account insisted on a tension between an egalitarian impulse in Islam and the developing orthodoxy that was not only hierarchical but also decidedly patriarchal. For Ahmed, the status and autonomy of women were increasingly restricted as Islamic law developed and matured as a legal tradition:

> Orthodox Islam, on the contrary, gave paramountcy, as it elaborated its understanding of Islam into laws, to the practices and regulations Islam had enunciated, paying little heed in elaborating laws regarding women to the religion's ethical teachings, particularly its emphasis on the spiritual equality of women and men and its injunctions to treat women fairly. As a result, the religion's emphasis on equality and the equal justice to which women were entitled has left little trace on the law as developed in the Abbasid age.[9]

Other scholars of gender and Islamic law turned to the positive legal tradition (*furu'*), where jurists engaged in the construction of legal rulings rather than abstract theoretical and methodological conversations, with an eye toward its gender assumptions. In doing so, they nuance Ahmed's historical narrative by interrogating women's legal status and its implications for how jurists developed rulings and institutions.[10] These scholars have explored the juristic assumptions as well as the historical context that informed the law. In interrogating the legal construction of marriage and divorce, Kecia Ali notes the relation between gender and slavery as categories of legal disability in Islamic law.[11] These two categories, she argues, were not independent of one another, as marriage and enslavement were deeply connected in the juristic imagination about human relationships. Both enslaved people and women "were overlapping categories of legally inferior persons constructed against one another and in relation to one another—sometimes identified, sometimes distinguished."[12] Despite the interconnectedness of these two categories, Ali argues that only gender is a permanent and enduring impairment to legal subjecthood in Islamic law, whereas other impediments, such as enslavement and legal insanity, are temporary in nature.[13] Like Ali, Baber Johansen also recognizes the multiple social hierarchies that functioned in shaping an individual's agency in social exchange (i.e., the exchange of noncommodities for goods or monetary values, typified by marriage).[14] Speaking of the distinction between commercial (exchange of commodity for commodity) and social exchange, Johansen argues that while commercial exchange was accessible to all who were deemed to have rational capacity, an individual's admission into social exchange depended on their (or their family's) location within five social hierarchies: religion, gender, kinship, generation, and freedom versus enslavement.[15] While noting these different hierarchies,

Johansen also makes an argument similar to Ali's—namely, that gender stood out as a permanent impediment: "the importance of the gender criterion outweighs that of the difference between free male persons and male slaves."[16]

In her study of women and family in Islamic law, Judith Tucker argues that *woman* as legal subject is a matter of "doctrinal tension."[17] While women's agency in economic matters was largely similar to that of men, in other aspects of the law they were more constrained. She concludes that men's and women's legal status shifted depending on the area of the law. Thus, while women could be independent property owners, as a member of a family a woman was hampered in her agency by the interests of the family and a patriarchal society. This is particularly evident in the diminished legal agency of the woman in matters pertaining to marriage and divorce. Thus, while a woman may contract sales on her own behalf, she does not possess the unrestricted right to contract a marriage or a unilateral right to divorce.[18] Depending on the legal arena, Tucker argues, the tension between the full and impaired legal agency of the woman was resolved by allowing the interests of a patriarchal society to supersede:

> Woman as family member (whose marriage will affect her male relatives and there-fore must be vetted by them) and Woman as part of patriarchal society (whose behavior must be policed and restricted, thereby limiting her knowledge of and activity in the public sphere) trump the Woman as equal legal subject.[19]

These different studies have given us critical insight into gender-differentiated rulings in Islamic law and the tension between gender and other social identities. Yet these scholars have not fully explored the impact these intersecting identities had on gender as a determining factor in women's legal agency in Islamic law. The resultant effect has been a stability of the category "woman" in historical studies of Islamic law, even if differences between women are recognized. As Marion Katz has argued, while gender has a central role in juristic thought, "gender and its attendant legal implications are deeply modulated by reference to other markers of personal and social status."[20] In early Islamic legal discourse, she argues, "woman" was not a homogenous category but was mediated by other factors. Jurists thus assumed that women of different ages and statuses would take on different legal rulings rather than a consistent ruling by virtue of them being women.[21]

In order to more fully investigate the relationship between the law and women as recipients of the law, I attempt to elucidate the archeology of juristic assumptions regarding personhood, the legal subject, and male and female natures.[22] This book contributes to this ongoing scholarly conversation by offering a theorization of how the legal status of individuals was developed at the intersection of different social identities, and what that tells us about gender as a reliable indicator of individuals' legal status. Intersectionality has been a critical framework for thinking about the ways in which these identities shape legal status. In theorizing how gender and other social hierarchies intersect in shaping the individuals' legal status, I also offer a theorization of legal personhood in early Hanafi discourse.

GENDER AND LEGAL PERSONHOOD IN EARLY HANAFI LAW

This book makes a simple but bold claim that neither "woman" nor "man" are legal persons in early Hanafi law. An individual's legal capacity instead depended on a number of social identities, of which gender was just one. These identities included age, enslavement, religion, lineage, and social status, among many others. I focus on three in particular here: gender, enslavement, and age. Concentrating on this particular set of social identities allows me to carefully trace the way they intersected in impacting legal personhood. I argue that legal personhood in early Hanafi law is intersectional and relational, making gender both an unstable category and an unreliable predictor in determining an individual's legal status. My theorization of legal personhood in early Hanafi law gives us a picture of the complex social hierarchy that populated the legal world. Many social identities simultaneously constructed an individual's status as a subject of the law and impacted their legal rights and agency.

In order to understand the construction of legal personhood, I engage in a close reading of a number of case studies that pertain to gender-differentiated legal rulings. These case studies come from varied aspects of the law and cover a number of different legal topics, including sexual intercourse, same-sex sexual intercourse, marriage of children and enslaved people, and bodily covering and gendered prayer postures. Such an approach allows me to trace how gendered legal subjects were formed and reformed within each case and also to demonstrate the intersectional and relational nature of legal personhood. This permits me to reveal the inconsistencies in the law's stated goal regarding gendered norms and the instability and incoherence of the gendered legal subject.

In reading these case studies comparatively within one legal school rather than across different legal schools, I found that gender functioned at different registers in legal texts. At times, Hanafi jurists articulated what appears to be an essentialist notion of masculinity as active and femininity as passive. This normative construction of gender, however, did not entail that gender identification determined an individual's legal personhood. On the one hand, there are stated beliefs about the gendered dispositions of men and women; on the other hand, there is the impact on these gender assumptions when they intersect with different social identities. Noticing the multiple ways in which gender was articulated and functioned in legal thought, I decided to put these case studies in conversation with one another. The case-studies approach not only demonstrates how normative constructions of gender functioned in legal reasoning but also throws into relief the dissonances and ruptures in these stated conceptions of gender. The gendered narrative shifted as gendered subjects were reformulated in individual case studies.

The book makes three main arguments regarding gender and legal personhood in early Hanafi law. The first is that legal personhood was constructed at the intersection of a number of social identities rather than gender alone. Comparing the different case studies shows that some legal persons in early Hanafi law were unable to fully inhabit gendered norms. Enslaved men and male minors, for example, could not occupy the autonomy or social dominance that was a critical element of masculinity. Similarly, while the free woman, the enslaved woman, and the female minor were all characterized by passivity, the free woman possessed greater autonomy and legal agency than other female subjects as well as enslaved men and male minors. In noting the inability of different male and female legal persons to occupy the normative constructions of masculinity and femininity, we can see that these gender constructions serve a hermeneutical role in justifying particular legal rulings but do not map onto the law's designation of sexed bodies. Thus, focusing on gender as the sole determiner of individuals' legal status in Hanafi law would give us an incomplete picture of the complexity of legal personhood.

The second argument of the book is that legal personhood is relational. The legal person of early Hanafi law was neither abstracted nor singular; that is to say, there was no single, abstracted, universal person that the law assumed as its subject. There were instead a multiplicity of legal persons who acquired their status at the intersection of their different social identities. Legal personhood, then, was not defined by the gender identity of the individual but instead by their relations; that is, the rights and obligations that pertain to the legal person were tied to the social relations in which the individual was embedded. For Hanafi jurists, legal persons did not exist outside their social relations. The individual in Islamic law is a fundamentally social being. The relational nature of legal personhood meant that an individual's legal agency was fluid and constantly shifting. Thus, an individual acquired different legal rights and obligations or exercised different legal agency depending on different aspects of the law—from commercial to criminal or familial aspects of the law. An individual's legal status also shifted depending on their relation to other individuals. As a minor child moved into adulthood or a free adult woman became a free wife, their legal personhood was reconstructed, either increasing or decreasing their legal agency. The focus on relations also allows us to see that a particular individual could occupy multiple constructions of legal personhood owing to their multiple relations. A free wife did not carry her legal impediment owing to her status as a wife in all aspects of the law. As an enslaver, for example, she could exercise power and dominion over other individuals despite herself being subject to her husband's dominion. Similarly, an enslaved man acquired dominion (albeit a limited one) over his wife once he became a husband, despite his status as an enslaved person. The relational nature of legal personhood meant that individuals did not have a singular construction of legal personhood that followed them throughout the law. Depending on their particular relations, as well as the particular aspect of the law, individuals could exercise different modes of legal agency.

Given the intersectional and relational nature of legal personhood, the third argument of this book takes on the utility of gender as a category of analysis in the study of premodern Islam. The juristic discussions around gendered legal rulings reveal that gender was neither the sole nor the primary determiner of an individual's legal personhood. The normative construction of gender along the active/passive binary was also not an overarching logic of the law. Normative gender emerged at particular moments to justify a ruling that established the school's legal precedent. However, at other times this normative gender construction was set aside, or even overturned, when it intersected with other social identities or conflicted with particular juristic concerns. These observations point to the instability of gender as a determiner of legal status, as well as its instability as a signifier. Gender did not carry a fixed meaning as a legal incapacity; that is, being a female legal subject did not mean all females carried the same impairments to their legal capacity owing to their shared gender identity or sexed body. The instability of gender as a signifier also meant that gender did not have a fixed legal capacity when it intersected with other social identities. Instead, we will see that each social identity—gender, freedom/enslavement, and age—took on particular signification at their intersections. As Ash Geissinger has argued in relation to the Qur'anic exegetical tradition, there was no singular gender script but instead a multitude of gender constructions that Muslim exegetes drew on.[23] Fatima Seedat has similarly argued that femininity as a signifier in legal discourse is inconsistent. It is instead a "mobile concept that seldom coincides in all respects with any singular physical woman."[24] These observations demonstrate that gender in early Hanafi law was not tied to some juristic idea of biological sex. Rather than demonstrating a binary of male and female subjects, early Hanafi law was populated by a diversity of gendered subjects who took on a number of legal roles.

MAPPING GENDER AND SEX IN EARLY HANAFI LAW

A primary concern of this book is an investigation into gender and its role in constructing an individual's legal personhood. As such, both the terms "gender" and "sexed body," as I use them in this book, require clarification. Scholarship on gender in the premodern Islamicate context has made critical interventions in the field of Islamic studies, a male-dominated field that is largely inattentive to gendered power dynamics. In employing gender as a category of analysis, however, this body of scholarship has largely left their own assumptions about gender—and particularly the universality and naturalness of the gender binary—unexamined. The resultant effect of such an approach has not only made invisible the diversity of gender and sexed bodies in the premodern world but has also naturalized the very binary construction that scholars seek to dismantle. Gender has been interrogated alongside categories like slavery and social status; however, the relation between these identities and how they intersect has not been adequately considered or theorized. Given this, scholars largely analyze whether gender trumps or is subsumed by these other categories.[25]

An increasing body of scholarship has challenged this binary conception of gender in the premodern Islamicate context. The studies cited below have looked at homoerotic relations, intersexuality, and nonbinary gender (those neither masculine nor feminine) to demonstrate the diversity of sexualities and gendered and sexed bodies that characterized the premodern world. The work of Everett Rowson, for example, has demonstrated that gender roles were not tied to sexed bodies in the premodern Middle East but instead to the performance of a gender role in public.[26] As such, the presence of men who appeared feminine (and subsequently took on the submissive role in sex with adult men) was tolerated because they had abandoned their position of dominance. The dissonance between the sexed body and the publicly performed gender role was of little consequence as long as the sex/gender/sexuality matrix aligned.[27] Dror Ze'evi's work on sexual discourses in the Ottoman Middle East also highlights the recognition of human sexual and gender diversity.[28] He argues that Ottoman medical treatises saw the human body as a one-sex body in which the sex organs identified as female were seen as inversions of the male. The difference between male and female, then, was about quantity rather than a diametrical opposition. In relation to sexual diversity, both Dror Ze'evi and Khaled el-Rouayheb have argued that the premodern Middle East had no conception of a binary that would distinguish people based on the object of their sexual desire (i.e., heterosexuality vs. homosexuality).[29] Indira Gesink's recent work extends the conversation on gender and sex in Islamic history by focusing on intersexuality in Islamic law and medical discourse.[30] Through a discussion of intersex people (*khuntha*) in Islamic legal and medical discourses, Gesink demonstrates that these discourses recognized sex ambiguity and were willing to consider and accommodate nonbinary sex embodiments.

This scholarship illustrates the sexual and gender diversity of premodern Islamicate societies and has been critical in demonstrating the complex nature of the historical relation between gender and the sexed body. Building on these studies, this book further problematizes the relation between gender and the sexed body by examining how the law imagined the relation between gender identity and corresponding gender roles—that is, did the law expect all individuals with a shared legal gender to perform similar gender roles? In exploring this connection, the book interrogates whether the law insisted on a congruence between the legally ascribed gender and the gender role that an individual was expected to perform. I argue that despite the law's recognition of intersexuality (*khuntha*) and nonbinary genders (*mukhannath*), it both recognized and relied on an idea of a male and female sexed body in certain rulings; that is, they established male and female as two polar ends, with other genders sitting in a liminal space in between. This dual-ity, however, did not mean that either man or woman were stable categories. They were instead disrupted by the intersection of gender with other social identities. In that sense, my reading of early Hanafi law is informed by Geissinger's argument that premodern Qur'anic exegetes constructed, negotiated, and reconstructed gender, demonstrating the fractured nature of these gendered norms.[31]

As I discuss in chapter 1, early Hanafi law certainly spoke of gender in dual-istic language in some texts where jurists articulated masculinity as active, self-determining, and socially dominant. Femininity, its foil, was then constructed as passive and subordinate. This normative construction of gender, however, gets dis-rupted by other social identities like enslavement, age, and social status. Manuela Marin urges historians to look beyond any absolute category of "woman" in the Islamic textual tradition, arguing that even if Muslim authors articulate an essen-tial category of "woman," historians must consider the many differences between categories of women that were also drawn out in these texts.[32] Speaking to Islamic law in particular, Marion Katz has argued that "woman" does not act as a mono-lithic or stable category in legal discourse.[33] Judith Tucker has similarly noted that women's legal subjecthood shifts depending on the different areas of Islamic law.[34] This book likewise takes an intersectional approach to demonstrate that juris-tic articulations of a normative gender construction were disrupted when they converged with different social identities. That is, the normative constructions of masculinity and femininity that were sometimes expressed by jurists were not seen as an essential aspect of being identified as a man or woman.[35] What this reveals, then, is that premodern Islamic law's recognition of sex and gender diversity was not limited to intersexuality and nonbinary gender alone. Even within the catego-ries of male and female, the jurists conceptualized a diversity of gender roles. Legal identification of male and female did not correspond to an essentialized idea of gender but instead marked multiple constructions of masculinity and femininity. This diversity makes apparent that there is no congruence between gender identi-ties and gender roles in early Hanafi law. Rather, the law considered a number of intersecting social identities in establishing the gender role that an individual was expected to perform.

. . .

A brief note on language and terminology: throughout the book, I use the terms "sex," "sexed bodies," and "gender." I recognize that these terms have long been complicated. Recent literature has made a compelling argument for the instability of the human body and the constructed nature of both gender and sex.[36] The book follows this genealogy of critique by showing the instability of these categories in a historic tradition like Islamic law. It is important, however, to recognize that the contemporary distinction between sex/gender emerges from a history and gene-alogy that is not shared by the early Hanafi legal discourse that is the subject of this book.[37] Thus, I use the terms "sexed bodies" and "gender identity" to reflect the conversations that I encounter in the works of early Hanafi legal jurists who are my interlocutors in this book. My intent in using these terms is not to make a normative claim about a biological reality of sex or gender but instead to reflect early Hanafi legal discourse.

I also use the terms "sex" and "gender" interchangeably here because I find that early Hanafi jurists did not distinguish between them. While the terms "male" (*dhakar*) and "female" (*untha*) certainly appear in legal discourse, there is no master category of sex. The term *jins*, which has come to mean sex and sexual desire in contemporary Arabic, did not carry the same meaning in early Hanafi legal discourse. When early Hanafi jurists used the term *jins*, it meant "genus," not a biological sex.[38] As I note in chapter 2, where early Hanafi jurists do employ the term *jins* in relation to sexual duality, they are not speaking of a biological essence but instead about a difference in legal status. The genus distinction also depends on the particular subject or ruling under discussion rather than a master category reflected across the various gender-differentiated rulings in Islamic law. At times, early Hanafi jurists assumed a correspondence between the body and gender roles. At other times, they recognized the instability of the body as a marker of gender and often ascribed a number of gender roles to bodies that were sexed the same in the law because of the intersection of a number of social identities. There is thus no distinction between sex and gender in early Hanafi legal discourse. While Muslim jurists recognized both the nuances and complexity of reading the human body for stable markers of sex, they did have a notion of the sexed body that was used to assign gender identity to the individual. Their recognition of intersexuality was always within a homosocial social order that necessitated the sexing of most individuals into male and female. I thus use the language of gender and the sexed body to reflect the assumption of Muslim jurists.

WHY LOOK AT LEGAL PERSONHOOD IN POSITIVE LAW?

This book examines how individuals were assigned legal rights and obligations in early Islamic law. As Judith Butler has argued, the subject of the law does not stand *before* the law but is instead *produced* by the law itself; this subject is then presented as natural in order to conceal the process of subjectivation by which this subject was produced: "Juridical power inevitably 'produces' what it claims merely to represent . . . In effect, the law produces and then conceals the notion of 'a subject before the law' in order to invoke that discursive formation as a naturalized foundational premise that subsequently legitimates the law's own regulatory hegemony."[39] To understand, then, how the law determines individuals' legal capacity and agency, we must consider not just what rights and obligations are granted to the individual but instead how the granting of rights and obligations, or indeed exclusion from them, produces a subject of the law.

The idea that the legal person is a creation of the law is a central inquiry of feminist jurisprudence as well. Legal theorist Nagaire Naffine has argued that a feminist critic of law must analyze the very conceptual categories that the law uses to authorize itself. Such an approach allows feminists to step away from critique centered on individual male bias or the desire to maintain patriarchal privilege and instead consider the fundamental priorities and orientations of the law.[40] Interrogating the law's imagination of the abstracted legal person, Naffine argues, is critical for challenging the law's presentation of itself as objective, impartial, and fair. While Naffine is speaking to feminist legal theorists' critique of the modern liberal legal system, it offers important insights for feminist critiques of Islamic law. As Kecia Ali has argued, rather than focusing on what legal rulings might be beneficial for women, feminist critiques of Islamic law need to interrogate its internal logic and question its foundational assumptions regarding gender.[41] While Ali is attuned to the gendered logic of Islamic law, I read her assertion as one that ties to Naffine's argument about the necessity of interrogating the very conceptual categories that organize legal discourse. In analyzing the construction of the legal person in early Hanafi discourse, this book asks who are the subjects of law imagined by Hanafi jurists? How are these individuals constructed as legal persons? What factors do the jurists consider in assigning rights and obligations to individuals? And lastly, what role does gender play in the construction of different legal persons?

The question of legal personhood in Islamic law is a complicated one that has not been extensively explored. While there are a few articles that look at legal capacity (*ahliyya*) in Islamic law,[42] to date only Seedat has offered a careful theorization of the construction of the female subject of law.[43] I contend, however, that a focus on legal personhood is critical if we are to understand how individuals acquired legal rights and obligations that have been the subject of significant scholarly inquiry in the past several decades.

Perhaps the closest discussions on legal personhood in Islamic law are those related to legal capacity (*ahliyya*) that often appear in legal theoretical works (*usul al-fiqh*). In Islamic law, all people, by virtue of their humanity, are obligated to follow God's law (the creation of this obligation indicating their legal capacity). The Hanafis in particular divide legal agency into the agency of obligation (*ahliyat al-wujub*) and agency to act (*ahliyat al-ada'*).[44] This distinction allows them to grant legal agency to all human actors (agency of obligation) while maintaining that not all individuals are full legal agents in terms of acting on their obligation.

The Qur'an describes this covenant in the following verses:

And whenever thy Sustainer brings forth their offspring from the loins of the children of Adam, He [thus] calls upon them to bear witness about themselves: "Am I not your Sustainer?"—to which they answer: "Yea, indeed, we do bear witness thereto!" [Of this We remind you,] lest you say on the Day of Resurrection, "Verily, we were unaware of this"; (172) or lest you say, "Verily, it was but our forefathers who, in times gone by, began to ascribe divinity to other beings beside God; and we were but their late offspring: wilt Thou, then, destroy us for the doings of those inventors of falsehoods?"[45]

For Muslim jurists, this covenant conferred on all humanity the obligation to obey God's law. This capacity was granted to each individual at the point of ensoulment (believed to happen at forty or one hundred and twenty days) and ended at a person's death. While all humans, by virtue of their humanity, carry the capacity of acquiring this obligation, it is the capacity of execution that requires an individual to follow the divine law. This capacity of execution is acquired in stages and can be hindered by different impediments (*'awariḍ*). Thus, this distinction between the capacity of obligation and the capacity to execute those obligations allowed jurists to recognize the full humanity of all individuals—a conception embedded in the primordial covenant—while granting them differentiated legal capacities.

Legal capacity was of particular concern because it determined who was morally and legally accountable for an individual's actions. A full legal agent in legal theoretical texts is understood to be one who is free, sane, and of legal majority—that is, after the onset of puberty. The ability to reason is a fundamental aspect of acquiring legal capacity of execution. In *Usul al-Fiqh al-Islami*,[46] Wahba al-Zuhayli argues that a child acquires a partial legal capacity of execution when they reach the age of discernment (*tamyiz*).[47] At this age, the child is not required to perform any of the obligatory rituals and may not engage in any financial transactions that carry financial risk, regardless of their guardian's approval. The child may, however, engage in financial exchanges that are of benefit to them as long as the transactions are ratified by the guardian. This diminished legal capacity ends at puberty, when the child acquires full legal capacity of execution.[48] The full capacity of execution, however, can also be hindered by impediments that are both natural (*samawi*) and acquired (*muktasib*). Among the impediments beyond an individual's control are insanity, legal minority, unconsciousness, forgetfulness, illness, enslavement, menstruation, lochia, and death. Acquired impediments include ignorance, drunkenness, jest, foolishness, travel, and coercion.[49]

The juristic discussions on legal capacity that I describe below speak in the abstract about the particular factors of impediments that might hinder or impair an individual's ability to act. This book's interrogation into legal personhood is in conversation with the juristic category of *ahliyya* but also considers how these discussions functioned in the creation of a legal person. I am particularly interested in the role that gender played in an individual's legal status. Interestingly, Hanafi discussions on *ahliyya* do not consider "femaleness" to be a hindrance to an individual's legal capacity. While legal minors, enslaved individuals, and the legally insane were categories of people who had impaired legal capacity, there is no comparable category of "female" impairment. As Seedat has argued, legal theoretical discussions do not differentiate between male and female legal capacity.[50] The absence of femininity as a legal incapacity in legal theoretical texts, however, should not lead us to conclude that the legal person in Islamic law is ungendered. To fully understand the role of gender in the construction of the legal person in Islamic law, we must also consider positive law (*furu'*), where jurists engaged in the construction of legal rulings rather than abstract theoretical and methodological conversations. Much more voluminous than theoretical texts, positive legal texts are also a rich repository for mining the religious and social ideals held by the jurists.[51] Positive law gives us a rich picture of how jurists constructed individuals' legal rights and obligations. As the case studies explored in this book demonstrate, however, gender's role cannot be understood apart from the numerous other social identities that jurists were attuned to. It is only through tracing the interactions between these different social identities and how they impacted legal capacity that we can begin to understand how Hanafi law produced its subjects.

READING ISLAMIC LAW THROUGH
INTERSECTIONALITY

My reading of Islamic law is deeply informed by intersectional theory, which has given me a language and framing for the construction of social hierarchy through multiple intersecting social identities. The scholarship of Kimberlé Crenshaw, Patricia Hill Collins, and Jennifer Nash fundamentally reshaped the lens through which I read for gender in Islamic law.[52] What Crenshaw describes as a single-axis approach—one in which subordination and discrimination are analyzed through a single category such as gender or race[53]—fails to account for the experiences of individuals (in her study, Black women) and their subordination when it sits at the intersection of different categories. Crenshaw proposes an intersectional lens for analyzing how different systems of power interlock and intersect, offering the metaphor of traffic at a four-way intersection. If we think about discrimination as traffic, then we can recognize that an accident at an intersection will likely be due to cars travelling from many different directions rather than from just one. In this manner, if we analyze discrimination intersectionally, then we understand that an incident of discrimination can be the result of multiple intersecting factors rather than one alone.

Since the beginning of the twenty-first century, intersectionality has been taken up by scholars across different fields, as well as by activists and policy advocates. The term has also been the subject of significant controversy, with many articulating critiques of intersectionality in what Nash calls the "intersectionality wars."[54] Despite its prominence, however, there is little coherence around what the term means and what constitutes an intersectional analysis. For the purposes of this book, I use Patricia Hill Collins's and Sirma Bilge's definition of intersectionality:

> Intersectionality investigates how intersecting power relations influence social rela-
> tions across diverse societies as well as individual experiences in everyday life. As an
> analytical tool, intersectionality views categories of race, class, gender, sexuality, class
> [*sic*], nation, ability, ethnicity, and age—among others—as interrelated and mutu-
> ally shaping one another. Intersectionality is a way of understanding and explaining
> complexity in the world, in people, and in human experiences.[55]

For Collins and Bilge, intersectionality's core insight is that the vulnerabilities of individuals and communities are created through different power relations that function together and build on each other.[56] As a tool for critical inquiry, intersectionality is useful for thinking about how Islamic law makes determinations about the legal capacity and agency of individuals.

I recognize that intersectionality most directly addresses the intersections of the categories of race and gender in modern scholarship. Yet intersectionality theory's critique of White feminism's sole attention to gender as the central category through which women experience discrimination has opened up my own readings of Islamic law. Rather than thinking about gender as the sole or even primary factor in determining legal personhood, an intersectional analysis gives us a complex picture of the multiplicity of social identities at play in the granting or curtailing of legal agency. Intersectionality is also open-ended with regard to the social identities through which power functions. This flexibility provides a space to attend to the particular social identities that create vulnerabilities and form the nexus through which power is exercised.

Beyond the intersection of different social identities, intersectionality has also been a helpful framework for "thinking about the problem of sameness and difference in relation to power."[57] If we consider, for example, the enslaved adult woman as a legal person in Islamic law, we can see that her vulnerabilities and the constraints on her legal personhood cannot be understood through femininity alone. Both the free adult woman and the enslaved adult man had varying levels of legal autonomy in relation to one another, but both had greater legal autonomy than the enslaved woman. Thinking intersectionally allows us not only to note the relation between age, gender, and enslavement in the construction of the legal personhood of the enslaved adult woman but also to recognize that the intersection produces a new subjectivity altogether.

As a metaphor, intersectionality allows me to chart the complex social world created by Hanafi jurists. As we see throughout the book, the legal world is populated by a multitude of legal persons existing at the intersection of a variety of social identities. If we consider the identities of gender, age, and enslavement alone, we can observe the proliferation of different legal persons who are created and recreated as various identities converge. The legal personhood of an enslaved adult woman is different from that of an enslaved female child. Similarly, the legal personhood of a free adult woman differs from that of an enslaved adult man or a free male child. The identities of age, enslavement, freedom, and gender are also interdependent and mutually constructed. Enslaved status is worked out in relation to freedom, legal majority in relation to legal minority, and masculinity in relation to femininity. Employing an intersectional lens allows us to see the complex legal terrain in which legal persons were both produced and recognized. Such a complex and vast landscape of interconnected social relations can be mapped out and conceptualized through the metaphor of the intersection. As Patricia Hill Collins has noted, "using intersectionality as a metaphor provided a ready-made yet open-ended framework for making meaning of the social world."[58]

One might ask whether thinking of gender, age, and enslavement as social identities is an anachronism. Can we speak of identities in the construction of subjects in the premodern past? This question has gotten a lot of attention in the history of sexuality, a conversation animated by Michel Foucault's claim that sexual identity is a modern construction.[59] Identity is also an important dimension of intersectionality, given the latter's attention to how structures make identities the vehicles for exercising power. As Stuart Hall has argued, identity is neither a fixed attribute nor an unchanging essence of an inner self; identity is instead "a constantly shifting process of *positioning*."[60] Thought of in this way, identity is not something that we are but instead what we are in the process of becoming. Intersectionality's understanding of identity as both intersecting, performative, and constantly shifting has been helpful for me in mapping the shifting landscape of social identities in the construction of legal personhood.[61] In the context of early Hanafi legal discourse, one notes that legal rights and obligations are defined through collective social identities rather than through or for an abstracted individual. To put it more clearly, a person acquires legal recognition not as an abstracted and universal individual (as with a liberal legal system) but as free adult men, enslaved adult women, free female children, and so on. My understanding of social identities as they play out in constructing legal personhood in Hanafi law is thus not a static and unchanging notion of identity but one that is shaped and reshaped by social relations. As an individual's position in the life cycle shifted from legal minority to legal majority or from enslavement to freedom, that individual acquired different legal capacities, since these social identities were not essential or reflective of an inner self but instead relational and constantly shifting.

SOURCES AND PERIODIZATION

As I began my research looking at gender and other social hierarchies that affected legal personhood, I found myself focusing on many different aspects of the law. As I tracked cases where jurists were adjudicating legal personhood, I moved from the books on marriage and divorce to those on criminal law and rituals. In tracing these discussions, I found it most effective to focus on a single legal school in order to adequately address the depth and breadth of these conversations across the legal texts. I have therefore focused specifically on the Hanafi school's construction of legal personhood in Islamic law.

Much of the feminist scholarship on Islamic law has taken a comparative approach across the different Sunni legal schools rather than focusing on a single one, allowing scholars to provide a close reading of different aspects of the law. Such an approach has given us a detailed account of gender norms at play in legal discourse. For instance, Kecia Ali's study looks at the construction of marriage in the formative years of the Sunni legal tradition.[62] Her comparative approach demonstrates that despite their methodological differences, the three major Sunni legal schools shared a gendered cosmology that shaped their understanding of marriage. She additionally shows that these legal schools used slavery as a model for thinking about the marriage relationship. While they might differ on particular points about the rights and obligations of spouses within the marriage or on matters of divorce, they did not differ in their fundamental approach to the marital relationship. Carolyn Baugh similarly looks at three major Sunni legal schools in the formative period of Islamic law, tracing the development of legal discourse on the marriage of minors.[63] Marion Katz's work offers a comparative, longitudinal study that explores the view of Sunni jurists on women's mosque attendance. She demonstrates that despite jurists' shared suspicion regarding women's nature and right to mobility, they did not always share the same notion of gender. Katz contends that early jurists distinguished between younger and older women, restricting the mobility of younger women more severely than that of older women.[64] Judith Tucker looks at both Sunni and Shi'a legal discourse, arguing that Muslim jurists constructed woman as legal subject differently depending on the aspect of the law.[65] Hina Azam's study of sexual violation in Islamic law compares the Hanafi and Maliki legal schools, showing how the Islamic legal tradition combined older Near Eastern proprietary ethics regarding female sexuality with the emerging theocentric ethics upheld by the Qur'an and the Prophetic example. Her comparative approach allows us to see how these two competing ethical approaches to female sexuality led to differing attitudes towards regulating and punishing sexual violation.

The comparative approach of these different scholarly studies has offered us a rich understanding of gender across different legal schools, and shared juristic attitudes toward women but also places of divergence that could lead to very different legal rulings. This book also takes a comparative approach; but, rather than focusing on multiple legal schools, I compare cases across different aspects of a single school. Such an approach allows me to explore how jurists made different determinations around gender when confronted with different sets of social identities and to note dissonances and instabilities in the juristic construction of gender across varied aspects of the law.

I have also focused this study temporally, looking at Hanafi legal texts from the early formative period to the end of the classical period—that is, the eighth to twelfth centuries. The question of periodization is always a complicated one for historians, with significant disagreement on the movement from one period of development to another. The same is true in the study of Islamic law. While some scholars have argued that the formative period of the Hanafi legal school ended in the early eleventh century, others have placed it almost a century earlier.[66] Despite these disagreements about the precise dates for shifts in legal discourse, we can see that the early centuries in the development of Islamic law were marked by significant diversity of legal opinions but no clearly established legal schools. By the early tenth century, however, the legal schools had begun to form; and, by the end of the century, the constitutive features of Islamic law had emerged.[67] At this point, the doctrines of the legal schools were systematized, methods clarified, and coherency given greater importance.[68] Talal al-Azem has argued that the eleventh to the thirteenth centuries in the Hanafi legal school were a period of *tarjih*,[69] a process by which the legal rules of the particular school were determined. The jurists between the tenth and twelfth centuries focused their attention on the justification of the school's already developed legal doctrine.[70] Speaking to the Hanafi legal school in particular, the early period began with the writings of the eponymous Abu Hanifa's two main disciples, Muhammad b. al-Hasan al-Shaybani (d. 189/804) and Abu Yusuf Ya'qub (d. 182/798). These were followed by a number of prominent books in the formative period, among them the writings of the Hanafi jurists Abu Ja'far al-Tahawi (d. 321/933), Abu Bakr al-Jassas (d. 370/981), and Abu'l-Layth al-Samarqandi (d. 373–75/983–5). The classical period in the development of the Hanafi legal school saw greater proliferation of writings by jurists such as al-Quduri (d. 429/1037), 'Ala' al-Din al-Samarqandi (d. 539/1144), Muhammad b. Ahmad al-Sarakhsi (d. 483/1090), 'Ala' al-Din al-Kasani (d. 587/1191), and Qadi Khan (d. 592/1196); it ended with Burhan al-Din al-Marghinani's (d. 593/1197) *al-Hidaya*, a book that continues to have significant prominence for contemporary Hanafi jurists.

For this study, I focus on the legal texts written by these prominent jurists in this four hundred-year period in order to clarify the legal conversations around gender and legal personhood as the Hanafi legal school moved from a diversity of opinions to greater standardization and authoritative judgments. I also consulted the *Musannaf* collections of 'Abd al-Razzaq al-San'ani (211/826) and Ibn Abi Shayba (d. 235/849), two early compendia of reports from the generation of Muhammad's companions and Meccan authorities. Taking this approach has allowed me to trace shifts in the legal positions of the Hanafi school and note changing justifications offered by jurists. I am thus able to offer some reflections on changing social conditions that adjusted the parameters of acceptable rationalizations of legal rulings. The two texts I have relied on most are the expansive, thirty-volume *Kitab al-Mabsut* by the eleventh-century jurist al-Sarakhsi and *Badai' al-Sana'i'* by the twelfth-century al-Kasani.[71] Both these texts are noted not only for their breadth but also for their extensive rationalization of legal rulings. Al-Sarakhsi's text is particularly interesting, since it is organized around points of dispute in the law, regarding which al-Sarakhsi presents the positions of different authorities. He then reasons through the evidence to arrive at what he considers to be the authoritative judgment on the issue.[72] Moreover, al-Sarakhsi and his teacher al-Halwani (d. 1056–57) were towering figures in the intellectual genealogy of the Hanafi legal school. Al-Sarakhsi's legal texts, as well as those of his students, were so influential that they came to define the Hanafi school in the centuries that followed.[73] Al-Kasani's *Badai' al-Sana'i'* is less concerned with intraschool disputes but is similarly focused on justifying the legal doctrines of the Hanafi legal school. Given the breadth of information, detailed legal argumentation, and extensive rationalizations for legal rulings that characterize both of these texts, I have relied on them significantly in unpacking the juristic considerations and sensibilities that shaped legal personhood.

STRUCTURE OF THE BOOK

This book argues that the legal status of individuals in Islamic law must be understood not through gender alone but at the intersection of a number of social identities and relations. As such, the chapters of the book build a cumulative argument, demonstrating the intersecting relationships between the social identities of gender, age, and enslavement. Throughout these chapters, I argue that despite juristic articulation of gender essentialism, this narrative did not form the hermeneutical framework for determining the legal status and legal agency of individuals. The jurists instead considered the particularities of an individual's social location and positionality, as well as their relations to other individuals.

Chapter 1 traces normative constructions of gender in early Hanafi legal discourse. Through a focus on legal discussions about illicit sexual intercourse, covering of the female body, and gendered prayer postures, this chapter argues that masculinity in Hanafi legal discourse is characterized as active, self-determining, and socially dominant. Femininity functions as a foil, characterized by passivity and subordination. This normative gendering along the active/passive binary often serves the role of justifying legal precedents. The chapter also notes where this binary construction breaks down by focusing on instances where Hanafi jurists make arguments that contravene this narrative. In demonstrating these dissonances in gender constructions, the chapter contends that this abandonment of the gender binary opens up the possibility of questioning the hermeneutical role occupied by gender in juristic discourse, a question that animates the rest of the chapters in the book.

Chapter 2 turns to enslavement as a category that impairs legal personhood in Hanafi law. The chapter focuses on two main case studies: legal coercion in the marriage of enslaved people and the forced bodily exposure of enslaved women. Through these case studies, the chapter demonstrates that enslavement impaired the legal personhood of enslaved persons by subjecting them to the dominion of male and female enslavers alike. In exploring the intersection of enslavement and gender, we can see that the active/passive binary could be flipped not only in rendering certain male subjects passive and subordinate but also by granting some female subjects power and dominance over certain male subjects. Exploring the intersection of these two social identities also demonstrates that enslavement impaired the legal personhood of individuals differently depending on whether they were men or women. Enslaved men and women thus occupied different legal personhoods despite their shared status as enslaved individuals.

Chapter 3 turns to the intersection of gender and legal minority and their combined impact on legal personhood. Through a close reading of the legal discussion on the marriage of minors, it demonstrates that legal minority functioned to diminish the legal personhood of children, depriving them of autonomy, subjecting them to the will of the father as patriarch as well as to their legal guardians. This chapter reveals that minor male subjects could also occupy the status of passivity and subordination that Hanafi jurists otherwise associated with femininity.

Chapter 4 engages intersectional theory and decolonial feminist theory to argue that legal personhood in Islamic law was constructed at the intersection of multiple social identities. Through an intersectional reading, this chapter contends that legal personhood was not determined based on an individual's gender; that is, individuals did not share legal status based on a mutually assigned and legally ascribed gender identity. Gender thus carried no stable meaning in legal discourse. Instead, legal personhood was determined by the intersection of a number of different social identities. These identities took on particular meaning only in relation to one another. The rights and obligations acquired by an individual were also tied to their relation to other legal subjects. An intersectional legal personhood meant that individuals occupied multiple legal identities simultaneously and could exercise different forms of legal agency depending on the relation. Legal personhood in Islamic law was not confined to the gender binary but was instead fluid and constantly shifting. The chapter concludes that a biological, essentialist gender binary is neither natural nor universal and did not exist in premodern Islamic law.

The last chapter brings the six case studies discussed throughout the book together to theorize about gendered legal personhood in early Hanafi law. I have written this chapter with the intention of it being a stand-alone chapter. Chapters 1–3 are interconnected, and the book's argument is built through the exploration of case studies in these three chapters. These chapters are best read alongside one another. Chapter 4, however, is written in a manner that summarizes both the case studies and the argument and analysis built up throughout the book so as to be accessible without needing to read the other chapters. As such, the introduction and chapter 4 can be assigned together to give the reader a full sense of the book's argument and analysis.

1

Gendering the Legal Subject

Masculinity and Femininity in Legal Discourse

In his 1940 book *Purdah from a Social and Legal Perspective*,[1] the South Asian scholar Abu'l A'la Maududi argues for a hierarchical relationship between men and women as authorized by the Islamic social system.[2] In making a case for this hierarchy, however, Maududi does not begin with the nature of the sexes but instead with a theory of nature. Likening God to a master engineer, Maududi argues that God has created and ordered the entire universe (likened to a machine) on the principle of pairing (*zawjiyyat*). All that exists in the universe is thus in a paired relationship, and all that one can see in this world is the resultant effect of the interaction of these pairs.[3] Maududi calls this interaction between the pairs the "law of sex" (*qanun-e-zawji*).[4] His conception of the relationship between men and women is therefore set within a broader cosmological framework where the necessity of the active/passive binary relation is not only divinely ordained but also natural. This is perhaps most evident in Maududi's insistence that all created pairs function within this sexual principle, which entails that the parties must be defined through difference, granting them different roles. Indeed, it is the interaction between their different roles that is generative. A divinely ordained and harmonious relationship between the pair is only possible if one partner acts on the other and must be structured along this hierarchical ordering of active and passive.[5] Maududi writes:

> Activity [*fi'l*] in its essence is superior to passivity and receptivity [*qabul o infi'al*]. This superiority does not mean that there is honor [*izzat*] in activity vs. humiliation [*zillat*] in passivity. It is rather due to the fact of possessing dominance, power, and activity [*athar*]. A thing that acts upon something else does so precisely because it carries the power to dominate, to assert power, and to act. And the thing that receives [the active party's] act is acted upon, the reason for its receptiveness and passivity is precisely because it is

dominated, weaker, and inclined to receive the effect of an act . . . Then, the nature of the active partner in a pair [*zawjayn*] requires that it have the qualities of dominance, power, authority—which is understood as masculinity [*mardangi*] and manliness [*rujuliyyat*]—as this is necessary for it to fulfill its service as a part of the machine. In contrast to this, the passive nature of the other party demands that it be characterized by softness, delicacy, elegance, and reception—referred to as femininity [*unuthat nisaiyat*]—because these qualities alone can help it perform its passive role successfully.[6]

This utility of the active/passive binary in the construction of gender roles becomes more apparent once Maududi begins to talk about marriage and family, both of which he considers to be crucial building blocks of society and thus subject to regulation and scrutiny. In regulating the marriage relationship, Maududi argues, Islam has established equality between men and women to the extent possible. Islam does not endorse a notion of equality that violates the laws of nature, however;[7] the husband maintains a certain superiority to the wife. As the active subject, the husband takes charge of the family (*qawwam*), serving as its protector and watching over the virtue and conduct of the family members.[8] The wife and children, in turn must obey the husband/father, setting them in a passive position that they must take on in order for him to fulfill his role.

When describing the woman's role in society, Maududi explains a number of legal restrictions on her mobility and access to her as a matter of honor and respect for the woman. Given that she is freed from the obligation to earn a living or providing for the family, she is the "queen" of the household and responsible for its management.[9] Because of this responsibility, she does not have to attend communal prayers in the mosque, the weekly Friday prayer, or funeral prayers. In describing this easing of obligations, Maududi vacillates between a language of relief from obligation and prohibition.[10] The woman is not obligated to go for *jihad*, but she is prohibited from traveling without the escort of a male family member.

For those familiar with Hellenic philosophy, Maududi's insistence on the active/ passive binary ordering creation will sound quite familiar. His argument about the creative and generative abilities of the active/passive pair resonates with Aristotle's theory of nature. For Aristotle, nature was a composite of form and matter, in which form is associated with activity, directive agency, and the masculine, and matter with passivity, reception, and the feminine. In this relation between form and matter, it is form that directs matter toward a purpose.[11] Feminist philosophers have made a similar criticism of the gender hierarchy embedded in Western philosophy. In critiquing Aristotle's theory of hylomorphism, feminist philosophers have argued that matter and form are gendered notions: as form and matter are not equal (i.e., form is better than matter), this sets up a gendered hierarchy in Aristotelian metaphysics.[12] Connecting Aristotle's metaphysis to his cultural context, Susan Okin argues that Aristotle's functionalist theory served as a means for justifying the hierarchical social order of Athens, in which enslaved people and women were subordinated to free men.[13] Elizabeth Spellman argues similarly that

Aristotle's political theory depends on a gendered conception of the soul. Aristotle's assertion that men are by nature rulers over women is based on the theory of the relationship between rationality and irrationality in the human soul. As the irrational element in the soul overpowers the rational more easily in women, men, with their greater control over their irrational element, are more suitable to rule over not only women but also enslaved people and children.[14]

Maududi's insistence on the active/passive binary as a necessary and essential aspect of the cosmos finds resonance in early Hanafi legal texts as well. While legal texts are rarely explicit about their philosophical assumptions, there are several instances where early Hanafi jurists justify gendered legal rulings by appealing to the active/passive binary. Like Maududi, these jurists insist that masculinity possesses the power and ability to act on the passive element. This understanding of masculinity translates into the public visibility of men and a bodily disposition that exhibits power and dominance.

In this chapter, I explore case studies where this gender norm appears in rationalizations in defense of the legal school's precedence. In doing so, I utilize R. W. Connell's theorization of hegemonic masculinity in order to draw out idealized conceptions of gender norms.[15] Connell describes hegemonic masculinity as the form of masculinity that legitimates unequal gender relations in society. Hegemonic masculinity, then, is understood in relation to emphasized femininity, the construction of femininity that accommodates and adapts to legitimize hegemonic masculinity. For Connell, gender is inherently relational; that is, ideas of masculinity and femininity do not exist outside their contrasting relation to one another.[16] To study hegemonic masculinity, then, one must consider the processes and relationships that both construct and legitimate these gendered constructions.[17] I find this relational approach particularly useful for my exploration of gender in Islamic law, as it points out the ways in which the jurists always conceptualize masculinity and femininity in relation to one another, requiring each to act in particular ways in order to legitimate the gendered norm. Connell's focus on nonhegemonic masculinities is also useful for demonstrating how Hanafi jurists did not have a singular construction of masculinity. In fact, hegemonic masculinity may very well be what only a minority of men are able to enact, especially in relation to nonhegemonic masculinities. Hegemonic masculinity, then, is not hegemonic because it is the only form of masculinity; rather, it is instead what is considered normative, the ideal conception of what it means to be a man.

This chapter explores idealized gender constructions in early Hanafi law by thinking through the relation between hegemonic masculinity and emphasized femininity. Exploring this relation shows the asymmetry between masculinity and femininity in the social order. What I find particularly useful about Connell's theorization of hegemonic masculinity is that it does not need to correspond to the lives of a particular group of men.[18] As I will argue throughout this book, the construction of hegemonic masculinity and emphasized femininity is disrupted by the intersection of numerous social identities in legal personhood. This gendered norm articulated by the Hanafi jurists does not point to a particular group of men who take on the most privileged status in society but is instead an idealized notion of gender that makes an appearance when needed in order to justify unequal relations in the social hierarchy. The first section of this chapter explores a case study on illicit sexual intercourse and the conceptions of criminal culpability that hinge on this gender norm. As sexual autonomy is a foundational aspect of masculinity, the first section will look at how masculinity was enacted through a reading of bodily practices in sexual intercourse. Through an exploration of legal discourses on illicit sexual intercourse and the conception of the marriage contract, I demonstrate that an asymmetrical gender relation was used to justify the law's construction of marriage and sexuality. In the second section, I turn to legal discussions on the distinctions between vaginal and anal sexual intercourse. Among the Sunni legal schools, the Hanafis were the only school to insist that anal penetration did not constitute sexual intercourse and thus would not require the punishment for illicit sexual intercourse. The legal rationalizations for this position rely again on the conception of masculinity as active, acting on a receptive subject. The last section of the chapter then turns to juristic discussions on gendered prayer postures and bodily coverage to trace the gendered dispositions and bodily practices that gave meaning and legitimation to these idealized gender norms. While this chapter outlines the early Islamic definitions of hegemonic masculinity and emphasized femininity, it also notes the moments where legal precedence countered such a gendered narrative.

HEGEMONIC MASCULINITY AS ACTIVE AND EMPHASIZED FEMININITY AS RECEPTIVE

> He [al-Sarakhsi] said: If an insane man coerces a sane woman and commits illicit sexual intercourse with her, there is no *hadd* punishment on either one of them. As for the woman, this is because she is coerced, and it is impossible for her to be willing. As for the man, this is because he is insane and not liable for punishment. If a sane adult woman invites [*da'at*] an insane man or a male child, and he commits illicit sexual intercourse with her, there is no *hadd* on her according to us [the Hanafi legal school].[19]

The scenario presented above is part of a longer discussion in the *Book of Hudud* by the eminent eleventh-century Hanafi jurist Muhammad b. Ahmad al-Sarakhsi. In providing these hypothetical cases, al-Sarakhsi engaged in an exercise to determine which cases meet the requirement for *hadd* punishment. In the excerpt I have translated above, he considers two cases of illicit sexual intercourse (*zina*) between a legally insane man and a legally sane adult woman. In Islamic law, sexual intercourse between a man and a woman is deemed licit based on the legal relationship between the individuals. More specifically, sexual relations are deemed lawful only if the man possesses usufructuary right over the sexual commodity of the woman. Thus, if the two are married or the enslaved woman is a concubine, then intercourse between them is considered licit. The punishment for illicit sexual intercourse, referred to as *hudud*, is either lashing or stoning, depending on the marital and sexual status of the individuals. If a man and a woman willfully engage in sexual intercourse outside the bonds of marriage or slavery, both of them are to be punished. As the punishments are severe, the standards for evidence are stringent, requiring four male witnesses to attest to the act of penetration. In addition to the high bar for evidence, punishment was also avoided in cases where doubt (*shubha*) existed about the illicitness of the act or whether the parties were aware that they were committing an illicit act.[20] There are numerous circumstances that provide grounds for doubt in the case of illicit sexual intercourse, circumstances that could subsequently exonerate the accused. For example, if a man had sex with his wife's female slave or his son's female slave under the mistaken belief that he was her enslaver, then he was not punished for engaging in illicit sexual intercourse.[21] In cases with reasonable doubt, penalties could be reduced to lighter discretionary punishments (*ta'zir*) or dropped altogether.[22]

Here, al-Sarakhsi considers cases of illicit sexual intercourse where one of the individuals is not legally liable. If the man is legally classified as insane, he is exempt from punishment because of the impediment to his legal capacity. The adult woman of the second case, on the other hand, is culpable, as she possesses all markers of legal capacity: she is both of legal majority and of sound mind. As a free person of legal majority, she is a full legal agent and thus should be liable for punishment. What we find, however, is that neither party is punished.

In rationalizing the Hanafi position in this scenario, al-Sarakhsi relies on the legal construction (similar to what we saw in Maududi earlier) of masculinity as active and femininity as passive. He argues that in sexual intercourse, man is the acting subject (*al-fa'il*) while the woman receives the act (*maf'ul biha*).[23] Alternative terms used to describe the man's penetrative act carry similar connotations: he is the principal agent in the sex act and the effective cause.[24] The woman, on the other hand, is described as following the man's action by enabling the sexual act (*al-tabi'ah*).[25] In such a conception of sexual intercourse, the man's act of penetration not only constitutes his culpability in an illicit sexual encounter but also brings the act into legal existence. As the passive party in the sex act, the woman serves as a receptacle (*mahal*). Her culpability is understood as the *enablement* of the act by willfully making herself available for penetration.[26] In the scenario with the insane man, since the acting subject is not legally culpable, his penetrative act does not constitute sexual intercourse under the law. Subsequently, in both cases, the woman acts only to enable the man by making herself available as a receptacle. Her action, then, has no bearing and is legally insignificant.

This construction of hegemonic masculinity and emphasized femininity along the active/passive binary appears in legal justifications for other cases of illicit sexual intercourse as well. When considering a case of illicit sexual intercourse with a minor girl, al-Sarakhsi argues that the child is of legal minority and thus exempt from punishment. The adult man, however, should be punished, as he played his role as an active, penetrating subject and fulfilled his sexual desire illicitly.[27] In this case, since the girl takes on status as receptacle and receives the penetrative act, the issue of legal significance is not her legal capacity but her desirability. As long as the minor girl is of an age that is considered desirable, she is legally recognized as a receptacle where a man's desire can be licitly or illicitly fulfilled. Thus, she can serve as a receptacle, completing the illicit sex act, despite the fact that she is not legally culpable.[28]

Al-Sarakhsi adopted this position from earlier Hanafi texts. He recounts that Abu Yusuf and Muhammad b. al-Hasan al-Shaybani, two of the three most prominent students of Abu Hanifa, the eighth-century jurist and eponym of the Hanafi legal school, differed on the conclusion of this scenario. Abu Yusuf held that the woman in the second such situation, where she has intercourse with a boy or an insane man, should be punished, whereas al-Shaybani argued the opposite. Abu Yusuf supposedly argued that illicit sexual intercourse is by definition any act of sexual intercourse that occurs outside of a marital contract or enslavement (i.e., concubinage). Sexual intercourse between an insane man or minor male and an adult woman fulfills the legal definition of sexual intercourse. The male party exemption from punishment is owing to his insanity, and not because the sex act did not occur. Thus, the woman is culpable and should receive punishment, since she fulfilled her sexual desire in an illicit manner when she willingly made herself available for penetration.[29] Al-Shaybani, however, argued that if a minor male or an insane man commits illicit sexual intercourse with a woman who willingly submits to his sexual advances, neither party should be prosecuted.[30] Al-Shaybani's legal compendium formed some of the most authoritative texts in the Hanafi legal school, and thus his legal ruling won over that of Abu Yusuf's in this matter. By the time al-Sarakhsi was writing in the eleventh century, this opinion had become the well-established position of the school.

Al-Sarakhsi wrote to justify this Hanafi position against those of other legal schools. The Shafi'i legal school, for example, held that a woman who engages in illicit sexual intercourse with a man who is not legally liable would still receive *hadd* punishment. They judged the culpability of each party to be independent of the other. As proof for their conclusion, the Shafi'i jurists cited a Qur'anic verse that refers to the woman who commits illicit sexual intercourse as the active party (*al-zaniyah*).[31] Linguistically, the terms used in the verse confer subject status on both genders, negating al-Sarakhsi's assertion that only men are active parties in intercourse. Anticipating a Shafi'i critique that the Hanafi position defied scriptural evidence, al-Sarakhsi turned again to idealized masculinity and femininity for legitimization. He argues that although the verse might linguistically indicate that a woman, too, is an active subject, what is intended in meaning is the passive participle: *mazny biha*—that is, one who receives the sexual act.[32]

How could Hanafi jurists argue for the opposite meaning in a verse that clearly describes women as active participants in sexual intercourse? Such a reading of the verse might also raise major theological and hermeneutical issues. How could Muslims be assured that the common sense and apparent meaning of words in Qur'anic verses were in fact the intended meaning? If a word can carry both its apparent meaning and its opposite, this would leave the Qur'an open to innumerable interpretive possibilities.

To explain why the word *zaniya* in verse 24:2 necessarily means the opposite, al-Sarakhsi relies again on idealized gender norms, arguing that it is the construction of femininity as passive and receptive and masculinity as active that serves to adjudicate how we read the Qur'anic verse. The commonsensical meaning of referring to a woman as an adulteress could only be that she is one who receives the act, rather than one who actively commits it herself.

Such a conception of masculinity and femininity along the active/passive binary was not unique to the Hanafis alone. The prominent thirteenth-century theologian and exegete Fakhr al-Din al-Razi (d. 606/1209), for example, argued that anal intercourse between two men is repugnant, because masculinity is characterized by activity.[33] In ascribing activity to masculinity and passivity to femininity, only vaginal intercourse is conceptualized as natural and desirable along the active/passive binary. Anal intercourse, then, becomes repugnant because of its disruption of this foundational binary.[34] Hadith literature also presents male and female sexuality in similar ways. As Ash Geissinger has shown, male sexuality is depicted as active and assertive while female sexuality remains, even in paradise, passive and receptive.[35]

Al-Sarakhsi's argument became popular among Hanafi jurists of the classical period. Two prominent Hanafi jurists of the twelfth century, al-Kasani and al-Marghinani, both made similar arguments. Arguing in defense of the Hanafi position on this issue, al-Kasani followed an analogous structure of argumentation to al-Sarakhsi's. He asserted that a woman is punished for illicit sexual intercourse not because she is the one who commits the act but because she enables it. If the one who commits the act is the male but his act does not constitute illicit sex, then her enablement also carries no legal significance. The Qur'anic reference to the woman as an adulteress, he concludes, is only metaphoric.[36] In his well-known and highly influential text *al-Hidaya fi Sharh Bidayat al-Mubtadi'*, al-Marghinani also follows the exact same pattern, arguing both for her status as enabler rather than acting party as well as the metaphoric meaning of adulteress in the Qur'anic verse.[37]

This conception of masculinity as active and femininity as passive is not limited to the Hanafi legal imaginary alone. While the Shafi'i legal school held that male and female subjects' culpability in illicit sexual intercourse was independent of one another, they nonetheless exhibited a similar construction. Like other Sunni legal schools, the Shafi'i conception of marriage relies on this construction of gender where masculinity confers subject status, granting one party control and dominion over the other party. In justifying this conception of the marriage contract, al-Shafi'i stated quite emphatically that man is a penetrator (*al-nakih*) and woman is penetrated (*al-mankuha*).[38] As both Ali and Katz have demonstrated, the Shafi'i school certainly employed a similar understanding of hegemonic masculinity in legal reasoning, sometimes even using it as a defense for abandoning clear textual evidence.[39]

EMPHASIZED FEMININITY AS RECEPTIVE: WOMEN, SEX, AND DOMINATION

Nowhere is the construction of hegemonic masculinity as a subject position of control and dominance and emphasized femininity as receptive and submissive clearer than in the Hanafi construction of the marriage contract and female sexuality. Marriage in Islamic law is understood as a form of dominion (*milk*) that the husband asserts over the wife. This idea of marriage does not emerge clearly from the textual sources of the Qur'an and Prophetic traditions, being instead a construction that formed early in Islamic law and that cuts across the different legal schools. As Ali notes, in Islamic law, "licit sex was possible only when a man wielded exclusive control over a particular woman's sexual capacity."[40] Marital claims were differentiated along gendered lines, granting husbands the right to sexual access and control of the wife's mobility and wives the right to financial support and companionship.[41]

Hanafi jurists recognized that such a construction of marriage put women, particularly free women, in a precarious position. In order to fulfill her sexual desire and have children, something that jurists considered not only a desire of all humans but also a free wife's right in marriage, she would have to compromise her freedom (and, by extension, her legal autonomy as a free subject) by allowing her husband to acquire dominion over her.

Among the different legal schools of thought, the Hanafis were perhaps the most attuned to this predicament. As al-Sarakhsi states explicitly, "The establishment of dominion [of marriage] over the woman is a form of humiliation."[42] Quoting a Prophetic tradition, al-Sarakhsi draws an analogy between marriage and slavery.[43] This status of the wife analogous to an enslaved person is an ethical conundrum for al-Sarakhsi owing to another Prophetic tradition that prohibits any free Muslim from humiliating themselves.[44] Furthermore, while Islamic law permitted slavery, it recognized freedom as both the fundamental condition of each human being, as well as the preferred means of social existence. That is, Muslim jurists held that freedom grants individuals a dignity that they should not abandon. It is for this reason that individuals were encouraged to emancipate enslaved people as a means of reparations for sins. With such a legal construction of marriage, al-Sarakhsi had a pressing need to rationalize why the free woman should justly curtail her freedom.[45] In other words, why is it permissible for free Muslim women to enter into a relationship of dominion, and thus humiliation, in the form of marriage?

Hanafi jurists answered this ethical conundrum by appealing to a narrative of social order and harmony that necessitated unequal gender relations. Al-Sarakhsi argues that human sexual desire is essential to the fulfillment of the divine command for the continued existence of humanity. Marriage is the primary legitimate means by which humans are to fulfill their sexual desire and procreate, as it carries multiple religious and social benefits and wards off social discord.[46] Innate sexual desire and the necessity of procreation could be fulfilled through rape or illicit sexual intercourse, but both of these are of course undesirable methods: rape, because it would cause great social discord (*fasad*), and illicit sexual intercourse because it would entail the destruction of patrilineality.[47] The only means by which humans can then fulfill their sexual desire, procreate, and yet maintain a harmonious social order is within an institution that allows a husband to establish dominion, sexual exclusivity, and control over his wife. This dominion also ensures that the lineage of children can be ascribed to the father, who is then obliged to provide for them financially. For al-Sarakhsi, men's financial responsibility is essential for maintaining social order. He argues repeatedly that women have little means to provide for themselves. In fact, to require them to financially provide for themselves and their children would create social discord, as they would turn to sex work.[48] Al-Sarakhsi concludes, then, that marriage allows for the protection and financial maintenance of the free wife, despite the reduction of her autonomy as a free subject, because she would otherwise be forced into sex work in order to provide for herself and her children.[49]

Al-Kasani makes a similar argument about the social and individual benefits of marriage that are only possible if the husband acquires dominion over the wife. He argues that marriage offers tranquility and love to the individual, allows for licit procreation and abstinence from illicit sex, and gives the wife financial maintenance. All these benefits of marriage, he argues, are only possible through the imposition of dominion over the wife.[50] While the free adult woman is a free subject and thus entitled to self-determination and relative autonomy, social order and harmony necessitate that in her role as a wife, she yield aspects of her freedom.

The conception of gender along the active/passive binary was not unique to Islamic law but permeated the Near Eastern world more broadly. Historical studies of gender and sexuality in Greek and Roman civilizations have made similar observations regarding the active/passive binary that was understood not only as a matter of biology but also held cosmological significance.[51] Masculinity was granted subject status and femininity object status. This subject/object dichotomy was fundamental to how those societies understood sexual behaviors and identities.

As feminist historians and philosophers have argued, Aristotle's biological and philosophical concepts of sexual difference, which saw masculinity as active and femininity as passive, was partly based on Aristotle's notion of humors, according to which males have greater heat in their bodies than females.[52] As the male-generated sperm was the seed from which the embryo grows, the male thus became the active, generative sex. Woman contained raw material that was activated by the man's action. The male was form, the female matter.[53]

Craig Williams argues that ancient Romans closely associated masculinity with an penetrative role and femininity with a receptive role. Free Romans of both sexes were granted sexual integrity; that is, one could have sex with free Roman women only through marriage, and sex between free Roman men was unacceptable.[54] However, while free Roman women were largely confined to sex within marriage, free Roman men could engage in sexual intercourse not only with their wives but also with male and female slaves, as well as sex workers of both genders. Sex with male slaves and noncitizen male sex workers did not call the free Roman man's masculinity into question as long as he could maintain the appearance of being in the penetrative role: "the distribution of physical roles was at least notionally aligned with the power-differential between master and slave: the master must be seen as playing the active role and the slave the passive role."[55] It was not biological sex but gender that determined people's social status in Roman society. While masculinity was defined by impenetrability and femininity by penetrability, not all men inhabited hegemonic masculinity; young boys and enslaved men were penetrable.[56] Williams describes this system as a phallic masculinity, where free adult Roman males were understood to be penetrators, and women, enslaved men, and sex workers were understood to be penetrated.[57]

The Islamic intellectual tradition that developed in the broader milieu of the Near East incorporated the hierarchical worldview that was characteristic of both Hellenic and Sasanian thought. The eleventh-century Islamic philosopher Ibn Sina (d. 428/1037; known in the West as Avicenna), for example, conceived of human reproduction as a result of the active/passive binary. He held that both males and females have sperm but that, while reproduction happens with the mixing of the two, it us is the male sperm that acts (*al-fa'il*) on the female sperm.[58]

In her work on early Islamic thought, Louise Marlow explores the tension between hierarchy and egalitarianism in Islamic thought from the seventh to the thirteenth centuries. She argues that early Islam carried with it an egalitarian impulse, as the idea of one God put all members of humanity on par with one another as part of a collective family. The tribalism of pre-Islamic Arabia also emphasized communitarianism rather than the kingship that was more common in the empires surrounding seventh-century Arabia. This egalitarian impulse, Marlow argues, can be found in the Qur'an and Prophetic sunnah, which deride class and tribal hierarchy. Marlow cites several hadith in wide circulation in the first century of Islam, including the statement, "The nobility of this world is in riches, the nobility of the next world is in piety, you are male and female, your nobility is your riches, your high birth your piety, your inherited merit [*ahsab*] your moral characteristics [*akhlaq*], your genealogies your deeds,"[59] which deliberately rejects the importance of lineage and tribal affiliation in individuals' societal status. The Qur'anic verse 49:13, "Human beings, We created you all from a male and a female, and made you into nations and tribes so that you may know one another. Verily the noblest of you in the sight of Allah is the most God-fearing of you. Surely Allah is All-Knowing, All-Aware," can also be read as leveling many of the social hierarchies that existed in a tribalistic system, giving all people the opportunity to cultivate personal dignity and social esteem regardless of their tribal or class background.[60] Marlow argues, however, that this egalitarian potential of early Islam was eventually superseded by a more hierarchical orientation. The early Muslim conquests brought with them significant wealth and power and an established elite who were invested in a stratified society. The conquests also led Arab Muslims to settle in Syria and Egypt, places with a long tradition of social hierarchies centered on heredity, occupation, and intellectual aptitude. These hierarchies were seen as necessary for social harmony. Muslim interest in Hellenic thought and the translation of Greek texts in the 'Abbasid period further solidified this hierarchical orientation, providing Muslim scholars with a philosophical framework for justifying a hierarchical social order.[61]

More recently, Elizabeth Urban's book on the conquests and imperial expansions in early Islamic history explores how the tensions between spiritual equality and social hierarchy in the Qur'an developed during this period.[62] By focusing on enslaved and freed people in early Islam, Urban notes the shifts taking place in the newly forming Muslim empire as it moved from a less hierarchical pietistic movement to one that favored a hierarchical social order in the model of the recently conquered Byzantine and Sassanian Empires. This shift, however, was not without resistance, as enslaved and free populations negotiated a place for themselves in the increasingly hierarchical social order.

Leila Ahmed's work has similarly argued for a gender egalitarian impulse in early Islam that was superseded by a gender hierarchy.[63] For Ahmed, Islam continued and reinforced an increasingly patriarchal shift that was already under way owing to the Greek, Roman, and Christian periods that preceded Islam.[64] Despite an early egalitarian impulse, the status and autonomy of women was increasingly restricted while Islamic law developed and matured as an intellectual tradition.

This gender hierarchy, according to which hegemonic masculinity was ascribed subject status and emphasized femininity object status, was pervasive throughout the different genres of the Islamic intellectual tradition. As Ash Geissinger has demonstrated in their survey of the premodern exegetical tradition on the Qur'an, commentators from the formative and medieval periods constructed gender in a manner that presented the free Muslim male in the abstract as embodying human intellectual, physical and spiritual potential in its most complete form. Such emblematically masculine completeness is constructed in these texts over and against the deficiencies and weaknesses in intellect, linguistic expression and body as well as religious practice that supposedly typify femininity.[65]

Geissinger argues that this gender trope remained compelling in the exegetical tradition because it was bolstered by similar gender constructions in other genres, such as the legal tradition.[66]

In her expansive exploration of pre and postcolonial Qur'anic exegetical tradition, Ayesha Chaudhry shows the power of this unequal gender system in shaping the interpretation of Qur'anic verses. Building on amina wadud's earlier work, Chaudhry refers to this gender hierarchy as a patriarchal idealized cosmology,[67] a vision of the world with an ontological ordering of society with God at the top. In such a conception of the world, men not only sit above women but they also mediate the relationship between women and God.[68] This is particularly evident in the marriage relationship, where the husband is charged with overseeing the wife's moral well-being.[69]

The conception of gender along the active/passive binary existed in Islamic philosophical literature as well. In Zahra Ayubi's close reading of the ethical treatises of Abu Hamid al-Ghazali (d. 505/1111), Nasir ad-Din Tusi (d. 672/1274), and Jalal ad-Din Davani (d. 907/1502), she argues that these ethicists' hierarchical worldview demonstrates a "construction of femininity as inferior, instrumental, and irrational, and the construction of masculinity as powerful, authoritative, and rational."[70] In marriage and the home, men were counseled to have dominion over the wife and other members of the household in order to live a virtuous life and flourish.[71] In this understanding of masculinity, women were instrumentalized, as control over them was linked to the man's ethical refinement.[72] In describing the ethicists' gendered assumptions, Ayubi points out the fundamental tension in their discourse. At one level, they believed that both men and women shared equally in their humanity and were thus metaphysically equal. On the other hand, they considered man to have greater control of his emotions and possess a more complete rational capacity. Thus, while men and women may be metaphysical equals, the focus on rationality in ethical refinement gendered the ethical discourse male and centered man as "the primary ethical subject."[73] Islamic ethics, she argues, is

> based upon concepts of being, ontology, and metaphysics that are actually not egalitarian at all, but rather starkly gendered and hierarchical in nature. That is, women of all classes, men of lower classes, and enslaved people are excluded from the discipline of ethics on the assumption that they are less rational or less human.[74]

This section has demonstrated that the conception of gender along the active/passive binary rendered emphasized femininity as necessarily receptive and passive in its role and therefore opposite to the conception of hegemonic masculinity as active and dominant. This construction of emphasized femininity is reflected in early Hanafi legal discourse and was shared by the Islamic intellectual tradition more broadly.

HEGEMONIC MASCULINITY AS PENETRATIVE: CAN MEN BE PASSIVE?

Hanafi jurists made emphatic claims about the relational nature of hegemonic masculinity and emphasized femininity, according to which hegemonic masculinity is construed as necessarily penetrative and emphasized femininity is construed as receptive. This insistence raises the question as to whether Hanafi jurists could recognize and conceptualize situations where sexual activity challenged this active/receptive binary, as the realities of human sexual expression are far more complex than the mode of sexual intercourse imagined in the discussions on illicit sexual intercourse. How, then, might Hanafi jurists understand and narrate sexual encounters where the man takes on a receptive role? To explore this further, I turn to the regulation of what the law identifies as anal intercourse between two men (*liwat*). Same-sex sexual intercourse serves as an interesting case for two reasons: firstly, the law's recognition of the fact that male bodies are also penetrable serves as a challenge to the understanding of masculinity as active and impenetrable. Secondly, the shifting opinion on anal sex among the first generation of Hanafi jurists demonstrates that the juristic deliberations on this gendered norm took on a hermeneutical role in determining legal rulings.

In Islamic law, the legal term *liwat* refers to an act of anal penetration, although jurists disagreed over whether this pertained to the anal penetration of men alone or both men and women.[75] Between the four Sunni legal schools and the Shi'i Ja'fari legal school the main debate was whether anal intercourse was equal to penetrative vaginal intercourse. The Hanafi legal school concluded that anal intercourse was unlike vaginal intercourse; thus, acts of anal penetration were not to be punished as illicit sexual intercourse. In this, the Hanafi jurists diverged from the other three legal schools of Sunni Islam and the Shi'i Ja'fari legal school, all of which held that sodomy was to be classified as illicit sexual intercourse.[76] Early Hanafism, however, was not united on this distinction between anal and vaginal penetration. Whereas Abu Hanifa held that they were two distinct sexual acts, his disciples disagreed. They argued instead that both the vagina and anus were conducive to male sexual pleasure. Eventually, however, Abu Hanifa's opinion won out, and the Hanafi legal school defined sexual intercourse as exclusively a vaginal penetrative act. In al-Sarakhsi's rationalization of the eventual Hanafi position on anal intercourse, we can observe the ways in which the penetrative role of masculinity and the receptive role of femininity came to play a central role in justifying the school's opinion.[77]

The central disagreement between Abu Hanifa and his two disciples centered on the definition of illicit sexual intercourse (*zina*), and whether anal penetration legally falls into that category. Abu Hanifa's two disciples, Abu Yusuf and Muhammad al-Shaybani, argued that since anal and vaginal sexual intercourse are both penetrative activities, anal intercourse and illicit sexual intercourse should receive the same punishment. Foundational to the position of the two disciples was the argument that both anal and vaginal penetration fulfill male sexual desire. Figuratively, they argued, illicit sexual intercourse refers to any act carried out with the explicit goal of "illicitly inserting a genital organ into another with the intent of ejaculation."[78] Anal penetration fulfilled this definition, as both the vagina and the anus come under the broad category of genital organs. The disciples' argument rested not only on the fact that according to Islamic law both vagina and anus require covering as *ʿawra* (parts of the body to be covered) but also that the vagina and the anus are "naturally desirable"[79] as marked by their shared physiology—that is, they are both characterized by "suppleness and warmth."[80] In this, penetration of both the vagina and the anus facilitates male ejaculation.

Abu Hanifa, on the other hand, argued that anal and vaginal penetrative intercourse are fundamentally different acts. This distinction between the two is embedded not only in a linguistic difference but also in normative claims about appropriate objects of desire. Abu Hanifa asserted that in everyday language, anal and vaginal intercourse are distinguished linguistically. Whereas the term *zina* denoted illicit vaginal penetrative acts, *liwat* specifically designated anal penetration. For Abu Hanifa, language was not arbitrary but instead signified essences. Thus, the inability to refer to anal intercourse as *zina* linguistically marked it as an essentially different act that could not be subsumed under the same ruling as *zina*.

These differing opinions also rested on the question of the "naturalness" of anal intercourse. For the disciples of Abu Hanifa, men's sexual desire was expressed in their penetration of a genital orifice with the goal of ejaculating.[81] As this was achieved by the penetration of either a vagina or an anus, they argued that anal intercourse between men was an act of illicit sexual intercourse. Abu Hanifa, on the other hand, was concerned not only with the act of penetration but also the object of desire. In reconstructing his argument about the unnaturalness of anal penetration, al-Sarakhsi claimed that Abu Hanifa was of the opinion that men naturally desire not just penetration but specifically vaginal penetration. In an instance of anal intercourse, the man who is penetrated should not desire to be in a receptive role. If he does in fact incline toward being penetrated, then such an act can only be understood as a deficiency (*nuqsan*). Al-Kasani made a similar argument about the unnaturalness of desire for anal intercourse. Illicit sexual intercourse, he contends, is punished as deterrence, since it is a very prevalent sexual act. Anal intercourse, on the other hand, is not prevalent and thus not punished as a form of deterrence. To justify this latter claim, al-Kasani makes an argument similar to Abu Hanifa's about the naturalness of vaginal penetration. Whereas both parties desire the penetrative act in vaginal sex, in anal intercourse, al-Kasani argues, there is no desire on the part of the man who is penetrated.[82]

While the disciples and Abu Hanifa differed on the desirability of anal penetration, both agreed that the man who is penetrated acted against his nature.[83] In *How to Do the History of Homosexuality*, queer theorist and historian of sexuality David Halperin argues that in the ancient Greek world, sexual identity was determined by a person's gender and social status, not identified as a pathological condition.[84] In ancient Greece, the *kinaidos* was an adult male who preferred to take on the receptive role in sexual intercourse. The offense caused by his behavior, however, was defined more centrally in relation to gender than to desire. It was common in the ancient Greek world for a man to desire other men and seek them out for sexual encounters. Thus, as long as men maintained their proper penetrative sexual role, they were acting in accordance with their nature. It was his abandonment of his proper gender role and the desire for the passive role that marked the *kinaidos*'s sexual deviance.[85]

In the Islamicate context, scholars like Everett Rowson, Dror Ze'evi, and Khaled El-Rouayheb have similarly observed that premodern understandings of same-sex sexual acts have some discontinuities with the idea of sexuality as an orientation. They point out that Islamic law is largely inattentive to an individual's desire and more concerned with classifying the licit or illicitness of sexual acts.[86] We see this in a juristic discussion of male-male anal intercourse in which both al-Sarakhsi and al-Kasani assert that it is the male that takes on the passive, receptive role who acts against his natural disposition.[87] For Hanafi jurists, gender roles, rather than the sexual object, determine the naturalness of sexual inclinations. The man who willingly assumes the passive role and desires to be penetrated is censured for violating the fundamental conception of masculinity as penetrative. What is censured in same-sex sexual encounters, then, is not the sexual object choice but instead the violation of gender roles. Daniel Boyarin has made a similar observation regarding the rabbinic prohibition against male-male anal intercourse in late antiquity. He argues that while in the Roman context, it was role reversal or "gender deviance" that was problematized, in the Talmud it was concern around "mixing of the kinds."[88] Talmudic concerns centered on the man in the receptive role taking on the position of the female, rather than with him degrading his status as a free adult male.[89]

Despite their different positions regarding anal intercourse's classification, early Hanafi jurists were united in their understanding of masculinity as penetrative and femininity as receptive. The discussion was not about the gender of the partner as much as about the desirability of the anus for the male penetrator in terms of its physiology.[90] They did not argue that some men desired to take on a receptive role. Abu Hanifa, on the other hand, naturalized male sexual desire as wanting penetration of the vagina alone, arguing that men not only desire the penetrative, dominant role but also penetration of a particular genital organ. Both parties also shared the conclusion that anal intercourse between men was an illicit sexual activity, even if it did not meet the strict legal definition of illicit sexual intercourse. For the Hanafis, anal intercourse was to be punished by discretionary chastisement (*ta'zir*) rather than the more stringent *hadd*.[91] In the Hanafis' rationalization of this position, we see the solidification of the legal construction of gendered personhood along the active/passive binary. The Hanafi legal construction of anal intercourse as "not sex" establishes men as the only penetrative subject.

SATR AND *'AWRA*: HEGEMONIC MASCULINITY AND EMPHASIZED FEMININITY AS BODILY DISPOSITIONS

Hanafi jurists constructed hegemonic masculinity in a manner that legitimated and justified unequal gender relations. Hegemonic masculinity in this legal discourse is associated with dominance and control. Emphasized femininity enables and accommodates hegemonic masculinity, thus defining it as passive and dominated. This construction is most evident in the law's conception of the gendered body as evinced in legal rulings pertaining to sexuality. In this section, I will explore how these gendered notions shape the conception of emphasized femininity as not only submissive but also concealed, giving us insight into the law's bolstering of hegemonic masculinity as associated with control and dominance and also with visibility. Exploring hegemonic masculinity and emphasized femininity as a *relation* allows us to see the interdependence of the gender-subject construction. To this end, this section will focus on Hanafi legal discussions on the covering of the human body and gendered prayer postures.

In a discussion of bodily covering and the legal parameters of the desirous gaze, al-Sarakhsi states: "From her head to her feet, a woman is *'awra*."[92] The term *'awra*, which al-Sarakhsi uses here to describe the default condition of women, refers to the parts of the human body that must remain concealed from sight. In Islamic law, men also have *'awra*; that is, even a man has parts of his body that must be concealed.[93] However, in al-Sarakhsi's categorical statement, it is not that woman has *'awra*, but that she *is* *'awra*. Whereas men have parts of the body that must remain covered, women in their very being and existence must be concealed.[94]

In Islamic law, looking on the human body is only permissible within certain boundaries and relationships. A man could look at the bodies of his wife and concubine, desirously or otherwise, without much restriction, since this was the only relationship in which the fulfillment of desire can be licit.[95] With unrelated free women, enslaved women owned by others, and even female relatives, there were greater degrees of restriction around bodily exposure.[96] For the law, the fundamental conception of femininity was that it must remain concealed from the male gaze. This construction of the female body as *'awra* is produced through the male gaze, which views the female body as always potentially desirable. Here, hegemonic masculinity is the consumer of female sexuality. For the Hanafis, male desire was all pervasive and potentially present in any relationship between men and women. Marion Katz has argued that early Islamic law saw the desirability of women largely through their life cycle.[97] Postmenopausal women had significantly fewer restrictions on their covering and mobility, as they were seen as beyond the age of desirability.[98] Katz argues, however, that by the eleventh century, these life-cycle distinctions had largely collapsed.[99] Al-Sarakhsi, for example, does not consider women of any age to be beyond desirability. He even mentions the possibility of incestuous desire for female relatives.[100]

Given this presumption regarding women as always a potential source of temptation and desire, the legal implication would be that any amount of bodily exposure of women should be categorically prohibited, except where desire can be fulfilled licitly (i.e., with a wife or concubine). Al-Sarakhsi explains the exceptions to this principle by appealing to social necessity. That is, there are certain exceptions in which the male gaze is permissible.[101]

What emerges most clearly from this discussion of covering is the legal construction of hegemonic masculinity as not only visible but also as the desiring subject, on the one hand, and emphasized femininity as desirable and in need of concealment, on the other. While al-Sarakhsi certainly recognizes that men must also cover parts of their bodies and that women might also experience desire while looking on a man,[102] the legal discussion of covering and the desirous gaze is extensively and disproportionately concerned with male desire. It is his desirous gaze that falls upon her. This gendered assumption structures the entire section on the gaze. Whereas al-Sarakhsi's rationalization of the legal precedent regarding the covering of the female body centers on male desire, the discussion of the female gaze has no such consideration of female desire. The parts of the male body that must be covered are deemed so owing to legal precedent, not because of their desirability. In the discussions of the male gaze upon the male body, desire does not arise as a concern at all. For al-Sarakhsi, men are not a subject of desire in relation to other men.[103]

Concealment and visibility were not confined to matters of clothing alone. Concealment was seen to be a condition so essential to femininity that it had to be embodied by women in all aspects of their existence. This is most evident in the legal distinction between the body postures of men and women in prayer. While prayer postures are largely the same for everyone, there were some minor distinctions that were motivated by legal assumptions about masculinity and femininity. In general, Hanafi jurists argued that women should pray in a manner that reflects the concealment that characterizes femininity.[104] While men were encouraged to pray while maintaining separation between their limbs and other parts of their bodies, women were advised to pray in a compact manner. While standing in prayer, women are supposed to place their hands on their chests, while men place them lower, by their navel. In bending over to perform the *ruku'*, men are to flatten their back, placing their hands on their knees and spreading their fingers. Women, on the other hand, are to only bend slightly, so that their fingertips reach the top of their knees. They are also advised to keep their knees slightly bent, to not spread their fingers, and to pull their arms in close to their torso. In prostration (*sujud*), men should maintain distance between their torso and their thighs and place their elbows above the ground. Women are to prostrate in a manner that takes up less space, placing their hands close to their ears, their forearms and elbows on the ground, and flattening their stomach on their upper thighs. Men raise their hands to their ears in the opening invocation to God for prayer (*takbir*); Hanafi jurists differed regarding this stipulation for women. While a report attributed to Abu Hanifa held that women should also raise their hands to their ears, another opinion held that women should only raise their hands to their shoulders, "because this is more concealing of her and the matters concerning women are established on the basis of concealment."[105]

In their article on the gendering of the body in prayer postures, Geissinger has argued that the discussions of gendered prayer postures demonstrates the concern with maintaining and marking hierarchical difference even in a space that should largely transcend difference.[106] The concern here, Geissinger explains, is with making sure that an individual's position in the social order is marked even as her or she prays. Such concern with marking gendered difference and hierarchy through bodily practices is not unique to Muslim debates alone. Feminist analysis of bodily and nonverbal behavior has long noted the gendered ways in which people occupy space. Writing about feminist campaigns on social media that target manspreading,[107] Emma Jane argues:

> women and men's different sitting styles have close and complex relations with power. Open and expansive body positions, for instance, are characteristics of dominant individuals, while submissive people take up less space by contracting their postures, sitting with closed arm and leg positions, and using diminutive, if any, gestures . . . Furthermore, embodied cognition research reveals that adopting an expansive or "power" posture *stimulates* rather than merely *reflects* a state of dominance. In other words, the links between expansive body posture and power are co-constitutive.[108]

Feminist critiques of gendered postures are useful for thinking about the Hanafi legal discussion of gendered dispositions and comportment. We saw that femininity was considered to be fundamentally a condition of concealment. While free adult Muslim women were expected to cover their entire bodies, the assumption was that other categories of women were exempted from this essential feature of femininity owing to impediments to their legal agency, such as age and enslavement. Men, on the other hand, were expected to be public, visible, and establish their presence in the spaces they occupy. While the differences in prayer posture are mostly minor, they reflect a juristic effort to locate and enact the construction of hegemonic masculinity and emphasized femininity in bodily practices.

As R. W. Connell has noted, gender constructions are not only discursive but also enacted bodily practices through which men and women find their place in the gendered social order.[109] Masculinity is thus expressed and maintained through bodily postures and increased bodily visibility and mobility. Such a disposition reflects power and control not only over oneself but also over others and public spaces. Bodily dispositions attached to femininity, on the other hand, reflect meekness, concealment, and submission.

This performative and acquired aspect of gendered dispositions is also apparent, for instance, in al-Sarakhsi's discussions of custody and parenting of children in the case of divorce. In Hanafi law, a mother gains custody of girls younger than twelve and boys younger than seven. After this age, the girl and boy return to the father's household, which maintains guardianship over them. In explaining why a boy must leave the mother's care at a younger age than a girl, al-Sarakhsi insists that a boy of that age needs to maintain the company of men (i.e., be parented by the father). If he were in the company of women for too long, al-Sarakhsi argues, the boy would be socialized into a feminine disposition, which would affect his mannerisms and speech, causing him to become effeminate.[110]

CONCLUSION

In a discussion of guardianship in marriage, al-Kasani, like other Hanafi jurists before him, argued that a free adult woman can marry of her own will. The other Sunni legal schools disagreed, arguing that a free adult virgin woman needed the consent of her guardians to contract a marriage. Anticipating the argument about women's deficient intelligence, al-Kasani devotes a lengthy paragraph to addressing this point. The argument about women's deficient intellect comes from a hadith in which the Prophet is reported to have said that women are inferior in both their intellect and their religion. When the women inquired about the specificities of this deficiency, the Prophet responded that the fact that two women witnesses are required in the place of one man is evidence of their intellectual deficiency. The deficiency in their religiosity is evident in the fact that women can neither pray nor fast while menstruating.[111]

The argument about women's intellectual deficiency emerges here and there in legal texts, often to justify particular restrictions on the agency of female subjects. Al-Kasani argues, however, that the form of intellectual deficiency that women suffer from does not prevent them from understanding the benefits and purpose of marriage. Women—that is, free adult women—he claims, have the requisite legal capacity to engage in commercial transactions and thus have control over their own wealth. They also carry the legal capacity to confess, to receive punishment, and to be held accountable as a subject of the divine law. Given that in all these matters their intellect is not deemed insufficient, then women have sufficient intellectual abilities to choose their spouse.[112]

The appearance of the argument about women's intellectual deficiency is always interesting to trace in legal reasoning. Here we see that the Hanafis challenge Shafi'i jurists on their use of the deficiency argument to deny women the right to contract their own marriages. In justifying the legal precedence of his school, al-Kasani disagrees with the deficiency argument. He insists that an adult woman has no limitations on contracting commercial transactions and disposing of her property as she wishes, and therefore the argument that she is deficient in her intellect with regard to contracting a marriage makes little sense. In the case of divorce, however, we see this deficiency claim appears to justify the legal ruling that deprives the mother of the legal right to custody. A woman's intelligence is lacking and thus she cannot be trusted to make sound decisions regarding her children. One could argue that if she has a sound enough intellect to make decisions for herself, then she can make sound decisions on behalf of her children. Certainly, a woman who is of legal majority, a mother and a matron, should not be expected to rely on her male relatives to make decisions on her behalf. Instead of making this argument, however, Hanafi jurists use the deficient intellect argument to justify their school's legal precedents. At no point is women's intellectual deficiency defined. The intellectual deficiency of femininity is instead a convenient tool of legal argumentation that aids in justifying the curtailment of free adult women's legal agency and autonomy in certain areas of the law.

I conclude this chapter with this discussion of women's intellectual deficiency because it helps us reflect on the hermeneutical role played by these normative constructions of hegemonic masculinity and emphasized femininity along the active/passive binary. As I have demonstrated throughout this chapter, early Hanafi jurists articulated a gender relation in which masculinity was endowed with power, control, and dominion, and femininity with meekness, submissiveness, and concealment. While at times this gender relation was used as a justification for a legal precedence, the above discussion indicates that it was not actively at play in all gender-differentiated aspects of the law. The Hanafi legal school, for example, held that free adult women could serve as a judge, a position of significant public authority, in cases where they were permitted to serve as witnesses.[113] They also allowed a free adult woman to contract her own marriage, thereby granting a recognition of her legal autonomy not given by other Sunni legal schools.[114] A free mother could contract the marriages of her minor children, and a free adult woman who had the financial means acquired authority and dominion over enslaved people, both male and female. These dissonances in legal discourse indicate that the jurists did not expect all men and women to embody and enact hegemonic masculinity and emphasized femininity in all situations. We see in al-Kasani's discussion, for example, that hierarchies other than gender come into play in determining the individuals' legal agency. Al-Kasani's discussion of the right of the woman to contract her own marriage is not concerned with women as a monolithic category but with free adult women—that is, a legal personhood constructed around three social identities: freedom, legal majority, and gender. These intersecting social identities meant that hegemonic masculinity and emphasized femininity were not the only constructions of gender in the law. At the intersection of numerous social identities, men and women as legal subjects occupied a number of nonhegemonic masculinities as well as non-emphasized femininities. Geissinger notes precisely this point in their discussion of bodily postures in prayer: the concerns around gendered prayer postures show a distinction not only between men and women but between men and nonmen, free men and enslaved men, and free women and enslaved women.[115] The hierarchical social order of gender in early Islam was not a binary, but a spectrum.[116] While this chapter has focused on explicating the construction of hegemonic masculinity and emphasized femininity in Hanafi legal discourse, gender was not the only hierarchy that informed Islamic law's conception of a just social order. This was not a social order in which all men were granted a privileged status above all women. Nor were all women unable to occupy a privileged social status. Other factors like enslavement and age played a role in constructing a complex social order in which there were multiple masculinities and femininities.[117] There are hints of these complex distinctions in some of the legal discussions that I have engaged in this chapter. We see, for instance, that the concealment of the body is not permitted to the enslaved woman. While she is still gendered female in legal discourse, she is not allowed to embody the concealment that is so essential to femininity. The enslaved woman is permitted to pray with significant bodily exposure, as her ʿawra is deemed to be similar to a man's.[118] These legal rulings pertaining to the enslaved woman raise critical questions as to the stability of this gender hierarchy. In the following chapter, I consider enslavement as one of the other axes on which a hierarchal social order is established through legal rulings. In doing so, however, I will look specifically at how gender intersects with enslavement in the creation of legal subjects. Looking at the intersection of enslavement and gender allows us to see the ways in which the categories of "man" and "woman" that are so essential to the gendered narrative are disrupted and displaced when they intersect with enslavement as a legal institution.

2

Gender and the Construction
of Enslaved Subjects

In a discussion of sales contracts, al-Sarakhsi discusses a scenario where a buyer purchases an enslaved person with the understanding that they are male but then discovers that they are female. The legal question of concern here was whether the difference in the enslaved person's gender was a significant enough factor to nullify the sale contract. Al-Sarakhsi stated that the sale was indeed nullified (*fasid*) because enslaved men and women were fundamentally different commodities and not interchangeable in a purchase:[1]

> Human males and females, with regards to legal rulings, are two different genera because the purpose [*al-maqsud*] of the one cannot be actualized in the other. The purpose of [purchasing] the enslaved female [*jariyah*] is concubinage [*istifrash*] and reproduction [*istilad*], and some part of this cannot be actualized in [purchasing] an enslaved male [*ghulam*].[2]

In Islamic law, the assigned purpose (*maqsud*) of a commodity was one of the most critical criteria employed to determine the commodity's genus.[3] Establishing the commodity's genus was thus of utmost importance in commercial exchange, particularly in deciding whether a sale was valid or licit. There were several considerations that determined genus, among them the commodity's origin (*asl*), name, form (*hai'a*), and method of production (*san'a, minhaj*).[4] Among these, however, purpose was a key criterion. In this scenario, we see al-Sarakhsi center purpose in determining whether this sale can be nullified. In explaining that the reason for which enslaved men and women are purchased is significantly different (i.e., enslavers make sexual use of enslaved women in a manner that they cannot with enslaved men), he creates a distinction between human males and females as separate genera. At first glance, this statement reads similarly to the ones we saw in chapter 1, where jurists articulated an essentialist understanding of gender to justify a particular legal ruling. We might read al-Sarakhsi's statement here as affirming that gender is the most fundamental difference between humans—so fundamental that it trumps enslavement and other social distinctions. If we look more closely, however, we realize that al-Sarakhsi's claim is not about a difference between all humans gendered male and female but specifically in relation to enslaved men and women. The genus difference between enslaved people, then, is based on the law's assertion that licit sexual and reproductive use can only be made of enslaved women, and not enslaved men. This differentiation is reflected in Islamic law's permissive attitudes toward concubinage and the rejection of a parallel institution for enslaved men. As Kecia Ali has demonstrated, early Islamic sources mention that female slave owners attempting to claim sexual rights over their enslaved men were immediately chastised.[5]

Baber Johansen has argued as follows: "Where slavery is combined with the gender difference it destroys the unity of the human kind. With regard to human genders, the commercial and social exchange produce, in fact, different genera of human bodies."[6] Contrary to Johansen's claim, I read al-Sarakhsi's argument about a gender-based genus differentiation not as a statement about humanity but instead as a statement about the gender-differentiated legal personhood of enslaved people. Enslaved men and women were fundamentally different legal persons, and what constituted enslavement in Islamic law was different for the enslaved man and the enslaved woman. In purchasing an enslaved woman, the enslaver acquired ownership not only over her bodily labor but also her sexual and reproductive labor. Since the enslaved status of a child depended on that of the mother, the reproductive use of enslaved men and women had different ramifications for the enslaver. In purchasing an enslaved woman, the male enslaver not only had the right to make sexual use of her; any children she had would also be born into slavery (provided they were not the enslaver's offspring). The enslaved man's sexual and reproductive labor was, of course, also the purview of the enslaver. Islamic law only allowed an enslaved woman to be used sexually by her enslaver; however, if we expand our conception of the sexual violence endured by enslaved people beyond concubinage, we can see that the law allowed enslavers to inflict certain forms of sexual violence on enslaved men as well by allowing for their sexuality to be transacted in coerced marriages.[7] Thus, the difference between enslaved women and enslaved men was marked by the particular forms of sexual violence (concubinage) that could be inflicted on one (enslaved women) that could not be licitly inflicted on the other (enslaved men). Furthermore, an enslaved man's children would not acquire his enslaved status or automatically become the property of his enslaver. Only the enslaved woman's child might increase the size of the enslaver's holdings.

Given these legal ramifications, we should read al-Sarakhsi's statement here less as a reflection of some fundamental ontological difference between human males and females and more as an indication of the difference in the legal personhood of enslaved people. Enslaved men and enslaved women were not the same commodity.

I begin this chapter with the statement by al-Sarakhsi to demonstrate that while Muslim jurists do indeed make essentializing assertions about gender, their claims cannot be read as an organizing principle that determined an individual's status under the law. If we read these statements alongside particular cases where jurists were actively constructing individuals' legal capacities, we see a complex matrix of social identities that shaped an individual's legal personhood. Neither gender nor enslavement alone shaped the legal personhood of an individual, nor did an individual's legally assigned gender consistently receive greater weight over other social identities. We must explore the intersections of these social identities in order to grasp the process of subjectification by which the subject of law was produced.

In order to understand this process, I focus in this chapter on a few case studies where gender and enslavement were both factors that Hanafi jurists considered in determining the legal capacity of enslaved people. An enslaved man's ability to marry and the enslaver's right of coercion were both issues that early Hanafi jurists weighed as they navigated the privileged status of masculinity alongside the powerlessness of enslavement. As we saw in the previous chapter, Hanafi jurists argued that hegemonic masculinity was characterized by autonomy and self-determination, giving men not only a privileged status as a legal subject but also greater control over their own persons. Simultaneously, Hanafi jurists saw femininity as a marker of passivity, of being dominated and subjected to the will of another. However, as I noted at the end of chapter 1, these essentialist articulations of masculinity and femininity often break down in different aspects of the law. In looking at the legal personhood of enslaved people, this chapter demonstrates that the law was populated with male subjects who were unable to inhabit the autonomy and self-determination that characterized hegemonic masculinity. We also see different types of female subjects, since the passivity and powerlessness of femininity were inhabited differently by enslaved women and free women. In the discussion of marriage, as well as of the covering of enslaved women's bodies, we can see that for the enslaved woman as legal subject, enslavement intersected with femininity to further compound her vulnerability. The free woman, on the other hand, held a greater level of autonomy and bodily integrity in relation not only to enslaved women but also to enslaved men. Thinking at the intersections of gender and enslavement also allows us to see that the enslaved person was not a singular legal subject; that is, enslavement did not entail a set of static and predictable legal impairments that were shared by all enslaved people. Instead, we see that the gender and enslavement intersected to produce different configurations of legal capacity. Enslaved women and enslaved men, in other words, were different legal persons.

WHAT DID IT MEAN TO BE ENSLAVED IN ISLAMIC LAW?

In Islamic law, freedom is understood to be an essential aspect of the human condition. The statement "al-asl huwa al-hurriya" (the fundamental condition is freedom) appears often in legal texts.[8] In explaining the shared humanness of both the free and the enslaved, al-Sarakhsi argued that the original condition of the human is freedom, after which slavery enters as an accident (*'arid*).[9] Unlike the Aristotelian notion that slavery was part of the enslaved person's nature, enslavement in Islamic law was understood to be a temporary condition. Once enslavement was removed as a legal impediment, the individual would return to their original state as a free subject.[10] The broader Near Eastern world at the advent of Islam recognized multiple avenues through which a person could be enslaved. Capture in warfare was one of the most common ways; the selling of oneself or one's wife or children into enslavement or debt bondage were also recognized as legal avenues for enslavement. Hammurabi's Code, for example, allowed for a husband to sell a dishonest wife into slavery and also regulated the enslavement of abandoned children in situations of warfare or famine.[11] Slavery could also be conferred through birth; that is, a child born of one or both enslaved parents was also considered to be enslaved.[12]

While borrowing heavily from preexisting empires, the early Islamic movement enacted some fundamental changes to these older systems of enslavement in the broader Near East. One of the most critical changes was the drastic reduction in the avenues for enslavement. The Qur'an and Sunnah permitted enslavement only through capture in warfare. With regard to enslavement conferred through the womb, Sunni and Shi'i jurists differed. While Sunni jurists followed the Roman legal principle *partus sequitur ventrem* (that which is brought forth follows the belly) and held that enslavement was conferred from enslaved mother to child, Shi'i jurists held that a child was free at birth if either (or both) of its parents were free.[13]

Religion was also a key factor in determining enslavement, as only non-Muslims could be enslaved in warfare.[14] Non-Muslims living within the Muslim empires, however, were granted protection; their acquired status of *dhimmis* meant they could not be enslaved. Treaties also often specified that a recently conquered population would not be subjected to enslavement. In the early conquest of Syria, for example, the treaty stipulated that the Syrians could continue their lives undisrupted provided they agreed to pay *jizya* and *kharaj*, two forms of taxes paid by non-Muslim subjects of the Muslim empires.[15] While tribal or ethnic identities were not initially a consideration in enslavement, the second caliph 'Umar prohibited the enslavement of Arabs, introducing not only a religious but also an ethnic element to slavery laws.[16] Bernard Freamon argues that this prohibition shifted the Qur'anic conception of enslavement, which had not previously been perceived as a demeaning condition. In prohibiting Arabs from being enslaved, he argues, 'Umar turned enslavement into a humiliating and debased condition to which certain ethnic groups (in this case Arabs) could not be subjected.

These factors—the prohibition against enslaving Muslims, Arabs, and *dhimmis*— led to the development of a system where early Muslim empires acquired enslaved people from the areas on their borders. With the conquest of Iraq, the new Arab Muslim rulers took over the trade routes of the Sasanian Empire, through which they acquired enslaved East Africans, known as *zanj*. Unlike other enslaved people in the early Muslim Empire who did domestic labor in urban households or in the caliphal and royal households, *zanj* were condemned to the horrifying conditions of labor in agriculture or on the marshes.[17] The conquest of Egypt also led to a treaty with the bordering Nubian kingdom. Unlike Syria, where the local population was neither enslaved nor required to provide slaves, the treaty with the Nubian king stipulated that he would provide a fixed number of slaves every year.[18] The armies of the newly established Abbasid caliphate also entered into Eurasia, enslaving people from those areas and bringing them back to the caliphal palace.[19] The Abbasid caliphs also shifted the makeup of the caliphal armies from free Arab soldiers to enslaved Turkic soldiers. Increasingly anxious about the ever-present possibility of disloyalty from free Arab commanders, the Abbasid caliphs felt greater security with an army of enslaved people foreign to the local communities. Their family and kinship ties had been destroyed by enslavement, so they were beholden and loyal to no one other than the caliph. This shift began a long-standing market for Turkic boys from the Asian steppes who were captured, enslaved, and sold in the Muslim empires. These military slaves were an elite group who often acquired a significant amount of power and wealth and developed political interests of their own, at times even becoming a threat to the caliph.[20] Several centuries after the advent of Islam, the slave trade was a thriving industry in the Muslim empires, bringing enslaved people through the Persian Gulf, India, East Africa, Southeast Asia, and China. Ibn Butlan's eleventh-century guidebook to purchasing slaves, for example, lists enslaved people from over twenty places.[21] With the exception of *zanj* and Slavs, most of these enslaved people came from just outside the Muslim empires.[22]

While Islam certainly did not abolish slavery, it encouraged an emancipatory ethic.[23] Manumission was considered a pietistic act and was highly encouraged. Islamic law also established other mechanisms, such as *mukataba* and *tadbir*, which facilitated emancipation. *Tadbir* granted an enslaved person their freedom upon the death of the enslaver. An enslaved person who received this grant of enfranchisement took on the legal status of a *mudabbar(a)*. *Mukataba* described contractual enfranchisement, whereby the enslaver guaranteed the enslaved person freedom in return for an agreed-upon sum. The Qur'an counsels enslavers to enter into such a contract with people they have enslaved.[24] An enslaved person who entered into such an agreement was known as a *mukatab(a)* and was granted certain legal rights not given to other enslaved people. The *mukatab* could not be sold by the enslaver, and an enslaved woman who acquired this contractual agreement would no longer be used sexually by her enslaver.[25] If an enslaved person was able to provide this sum of money, often in installments, they usually received this amount back from the enslaver after emancipation.[26] While contractual enfranchisement was theoretically gender neutral, it was possibly less accessible to enslaved women. The monetary nature of the agreement meant that the enslaved person would need to find gainful employment. It is quite possible that opportunities for employment would have been more restricted for enslaved women; indeed, this possibility is reflected in the juristic discouragement of entering into a contract with an enslaved woman who did not have a licit source of income.[27] In her historical account of women and enslavement in the late Ottoman Empire, Madeline Zilfi notes this gendered dynamic in enslaved women's possibilities for emancipation.[28] Women, she argues, seldom had the financial resources or opportunities to be able to negotiate for their freedom. While enslaved men had different employment opportunities, licit and socially respectable employment for enslaved women was largely limited to the household economy. This gendered disparity among enslaved people bears out in legal opinions from the late Ottoman period as well. Several legal opinions pertain to situations where a *mukataba* was unable to fulfill the terms of the agreement and her contract was rendered null or void.

The welfare of enslaved people and other vulnerable segments of society is also a central concern of the Qur'an, which urges believers to act kindly toward enslaved people.[29] Several hadith also cautioned the enslaver to be mindful of their power over enslaved people. The Prophet famously referred to enslaved people as brethren of free people and outlined the enslaver's obligations:

> Your slaves are your brothers; whom God has put under your command. So whoever has a brother under his command should feed him of what he eats and dress him of what he wears. Do not ask them [slaves] to do things beyond their capacity [power] and if you do so, then help them.[30]

Several hadith also chided enslavers for striking enslaved individuals and discouraged them from using naming practices that would remind the individual of their enslaved status.[31] In assessing this Qur'anic and Prophetic ethos regarding slavery, Bernard Freamon argues that in its early days, Islam upheld an ideal that abandoned existing hierarchies and distinctions and instead emphasized a pietistic egalitarianism.[32] It was this egalitarian and emancipatory piety that rejected social hierarchies, Freamon argues, which attracted so many enslaved people and other vulnerable populations in Arabian society to Islam.

Islam's emancipatory ethic was reflected in Islamic law not only in its recognition of freedom as an essential condition of humanness but also in the recognition of the enslaved person as a (limited) rights-bearing subject.[33] While the different Sunni legal schools held varied opinions on the particular legal rights of enslaved people, they agreed that enslaved people had the freedom to choose and practice their own religious beliefs. Thus, enslaved Muslims could not be prevented from performing their daily obligatory prayers, and enslaved non-Muslims could not be forced to convert to Islam or be prevented from fulfilling their religious obligations. Islamic law also permitted enslaved people to take on certain positions of authority, provided that this position was administrative and not political in nature. Marriages of enslaved people were legally recognized but required the permission of the enslaver. The rights and obligations of a husband and wife are very much gendered in Islamic law, and so granting enslaved people the right to marry also required jurists to work out what legal status they could occupy as enslaved husbands and wives. The juristic tendency to halve the rights or obligations placed on an enslaved person played out in marriage as well. Islamic law granted both free and enslaved husbands the unilateral right of divorce. However, the enslaved husband held only two pronouncements of divorce rather than the three granted to the free husband. Similarly, the waiting period after a divorce was calculated at three menstrual cycles for a free wife but only two for an enslaved wife. In the case of a divorce, Hanafi law granted the free mother the right to custody (*hadana*) of her young children, but no such right was granted to the enslaved mother. An enslaved mother, however, could not be separated from her young children (up to the age of seven) by her enslaver. Hanafi jurists in particular discouraged separating prepubescent enslaved people from their close blood relatives.[34] Enslaved people had a right to life and could not be killed extrajudicially without some form of punishment accruing to their killer.

While the enslaved person was a rights-bearing subject, enslavement certainly hindered an individuals' agency. With the exception of the Maliki legal school, which allowed an enslaved person to acquire property if the enslaver permitted, the other legal schools did not grant enslaved people any ownership rights.[35] Nor could enslaved people give testimony (the one exception in this regard was the Hanbali legal school, which nevertheless restricted such testimony to non-*hadd* cases).[36] Enslaved people also could not acquire or confer *ihsan*, a status acquired by free individuals through sexual intercourse in marriage.[37] Enslavement was also a sufficient cause for voiding religious and legal obligations on enslaved people. This was done primarily in the interests of securing the rights and authority of the enslaver over the enslaved. Thus, while Muslim men are required to attend Friday prayer services, enslaved men were not so obligated because their primary role and duty was to perform labor for the slave owner. Obligating them to attend prayer services would impinge on the rights of their enslaver. Similar arguments were made with regard to the mobility and modesty of enslaved women. Sunni jurists often argued that to restrict an enslaved woman's mobility would impose on the right of the enslaver to make use of her labor. Similarly, preventing men from looking on or touching her body would impinge on the purchasing right of enslavers.

The legal status of enslaved people put them in a liminal space between person and property. The juridical construction of freedom as an innate human condition meant that humans were theoretically protected from being transacted as a commodity. For the Hanafis, freedom granted an individual dignity (*karama*) and the right of inviolability (*hurma*). Given this, allowing a human to be subject to commercial exchange would entail a profanation (*ibtidal*) of the sanctity of humanness.[38] The enslaved person, however, was subject to commercial exchange by virtue of their enslaved status. Despite freedom being an innate human condition, the opposite is true of the enslaved person, who, al-Sarakhsi argued,[39] is an owned commodity.[40] This status between legal subject and property is evident in the many aspects of the law where enslaved people are mentioned alongside animals.[41] Juristic formulations, for example, often discuss enslaved people alongside livestock. Similar terminology is often also used to describe reproduction. The birth of an enslaved child, for instance, is described as the "fruit" (*ghalla*) of the mother, the same term used for animals. In the same vein, the *muhtasib* ensures that people treat their animals and slaves well. And, like livestock, enslaved people could be jointly owned by multiple enslavers.

The equating of enslaved people with property led to a number of dissonances, however. Unlike livestock, there were much greater restrictions placed on the return of an enslaved person based on certain redhibitory vices (*'aib*).[42] The law also recognized the immediate kinship relations of enslaved people, prohibiting the enslaver from separating an enslaved mother from her young children. Additionally, the Hanafis held that if an enslaved person was a direct relative of the enslaver, they were to be automatically emancipated.[43]

The question of what constitutes slavery in Islamic law has been a subject of significant scholarly conversation. Different forms of human bondage and dependent relationships were a normal part of life in the premodern world, including premodern Islam, and even continue to exist in many forms in our world today. Moses Finley, a historian of the Greco-Roman world, has argued that any historical study of slavery must carefully account for what the terms "slave" and "slavery" mean in one's particular historical context.[44] He correctly points out that there are many relationships in the premodern world that might looks like slavery to us that were in fact not understood as such in their original contexts. Indeed, if we do not critically analyze our own assumptions about slavery, we are likely, as scholars, to gloss over or misunderstand certain forms of enslavement. In writing about slavery in medieval Scandinavia, for example, Ruth Mazzo Karras argues that it is "difficult to create a definition of slavery comprehensive enough to cover all social institutions generally classified as slavery yet sufficiently clear to distinguish it from other forms of dependence."[45] And in speaking to the particular context of Islamic law, historians have similarly disagreed on definitions of slavery. Franz Rosenthal has claimed that freedom in Islamic law is defined as the absence of slavery.[46] Bernard Freamon has contended, on the other hand, that Islamic law's definition of slavery was rooted in the idea of property; enslaved people thus occupied a liminal status between person and property.[47] Criticizing Orlando Patterson's argument that it was power and not ownership that defined the enslaver-enslaved relationship, Freamon says that ownership is a critical dimension of slavery, as this legal concept allowed enslavers to convince both the enslaved and society in general that they had the right to exercise power over enslaved individuals.[48] Critiquing most existing definitions and attempts to categorize slavery, Jonathan Brown prefers the term *riqq* to speak of Muslim histories of enslavement. He argues that enslaved people in Islamic law were rights-bearing subjects, similar to other dependent subjects in society, such as legal minors and wives.[49]

While the precise definition of slavery in Islamic law might be useful for understanding the legal mechanisms by which jurists granted certain individuals power and dominance over others, it does not help us understand what was entailed by enslavement in Islamic law. What constitutes freedom and unfreedom is indeed complicated. As Brown puts it, no person is truly autonomous and free in a way where they do not live in some form of dependency on other individuals.[50] Karras showed that in medieval Scandinavian society, while the nobles might be perceived as free by others in their society, they were in fact dependent on the king for the privileges and freedoms that defined their status.[51] Freedom and enslavement, then, are not absolutes but instead *relational*.[52]

Elizabeth Urban has argued that the concept of "unfreedom" is more useful in studying enslaved people in early Islam. "Unfreedom" not only allows us to step away from definitional understandings of enslavement; it also brings our focus to its relational aspects.[53] To bring this concretely to Islamic law, the social and legal status of the enslaved person was created through the granting and restricting of rights to them and to others. In making these determinations, jurists were also always considering the rights of free people. This chapter thus focuses on the legal personhood of the enslaved person rather than definitions of slavery to account for what constitutes enslavement in Hanafi legal discourse. An exploration of legal personhood allows us to observe that freedom and enslavement were mutually constituted; that is, what it meant to be enslaved was defined through its difference from freedom.

THE ENSLAVED MAN: BETWEEN MASCULINITY AND ENSLAVEMENT

Marriage is a particularly useful case study, as it demonstrates the process by which the enslaved man's legal personhood was constructed at the intersection of gender and enslavement. Jurists dealt with the enslaved man as both a male and an enslaved subject. These two aspects, however, were not distinct juridical categories that either gave the enslaved man greater autonomy (owing to masculinity) or decreased capacity (owing to enslavement). Instead, jurists engaged in a complex and contested process, considering the enslaved man's different social identities in a manner that constructed a legal personhood that was particular to him and not shared with other enslaved people who were female or intersex.

The marriage of enslaved people in Islamic law was a complicated issue. Enslavement significantly impaired legal agency, and this impacted marriage in multiple ways. Unlike free adult individuals, enslaved people did not have the right to enter into marriage of their own accord. Any enslaved person wishing to marry had to first garner the permission of their enslaver, for whom the marriage had particular implications. For example, if an enslaved man married, the enslaver was obligated to pay the dower (*mahr*) and financial maintenance (*nafaqa*) to the free wife because enslaved people had no right to property and wealth ownership (except if the enslaver permitted this), and so the enslaved husband would have no wealth of his own to keep his wife. Moreover, since a male enslaver had the right to make sexual use of his enslaved woman, if she were to marry, he would have to agree to give up his sexual access to her. This was why marriage was seen as a "defect" when purchasing enslaved people and could reduce their value.[54] Given these conditions, jurists made the marriage of enslaved people contingent on the enslaver's permission.

As mentioned in chapter 1, marriage in Islamic law was understood to be a transactional exchange in which access to the wife as a sexual commodity came into the husband's exclusive possession. Such a construction of marriage, however, would only allow men who had the legal right to own property to marry, putting enslaved men's very ability to marry in peril. This legal inability to own property created a significant problem for the enslaved man, as marriage was his only avenue to participate in licit sex. In Islamic law, fulfillment of sexual desire was available to men through two avenues: marriage and concubinage. Hanafi jurists were insistent that an enslaved man could marry but could not take on a concubine.[55] In this they differed from the Maliki legal school. The Maliki position was founded on the similarities between marriage and concubinage as forms of ownership over sexual access to women. If the enslaved man retained the legal capacity of ownership in marriage, then he should also retain that in relation to concubinage. The Maliki permission for enslaved men to take on concubines, however, was not without its limitations. The eminent Hanafi jurist al-Shaybani argued that while Maliki jurists allowed an enslaved man to take on a concubine, they did not allow him to acquire ownership over her. This is evident in the fact that he had no right to emancipate her, sell her, or gift her without the enslaver's permission. It was thus the enslaver and not the enslaved man who had ownership of the concubine.[56] For the Hanafi jurists, in order for the enslaved man to take on a concubine, he would have had to acquire the legal status of an enslaver, which they held was a legal contradiction.[57]

This left marriage as the only licit avenue through which an enslaved man could engage in sexual intercourse. However, given that Hanafi jurists insisted that the enslaved man had no right to ownership and marriage was a transactional exchange, how could an enslaved man marry? This conundrum was resolved by distinguishing between patrimonial (*malkiyyat al-mal*) and nonpatrimonial (*malkiyyat ghayr al-mal*) forms of ownership.[58] This distinction allowed Hanafi jurists to give enslaved people the right to administer property (a role often taken on by elite enslaved individuals) and also lay claim to possession of property without having the right to full ownership.[59] The distinction between patrimonial and nonpatrimonial forms of ownership allowed the enslaved man to marry while still preventing him from acquiring the mode of ownership necessary for concubinage.

The debate between the Maliki and Hanafi jurists on this position reveals the contradictions present in legal discourse, as Muslim jurists worked out how much of the rights, agency, and privilege granted to the free adult male could be acquired by the enslaved male. For Hanafi jurists, the legal conundrum was worked out through negotiating the enslaved man's status between the juridical construction of an idealized masculinity and enslavement. If the jurists elevated masculinity over enslavement and granted the enslaved man the right of ownership, they would be granting him the social power and privilege of property rights, which would contradict the very definition of enslavement. It is this that al-Sarakhsi is alluding to when he argues that granting the enslaved man the legal capacity to marry not only diminish the right of the enslaver but also begins to erode the enslaved status of the individual by increasing his legal capacity.[60]

Conversely, to insist that the enslaved man had no ability to make use of a commodity would leave him unable to marry. This would deprive him of the ability to licitly fulfill his sexual desire and also to have progeny, a right that jurists took seriously not only as a fundamental part of God's divine plan but also a basic human desire. In accounting for the existence of sexual desire in humans, al-Sarakhsi argues that divine will has decreed the continued existence of humanity, which is only possible through procreation.[61] The desire for progeny was also understood by the jurists to be an innate human desire. It is for this reason that jurists prohibited husbands from practicing coitus interruptus without a wife's consent and also allowed for the annulment of marriage to an impotent husband, as this would deprive the wife of children.[62] To prevent the enslaved man from marriage, then, was seen by the jurists as a significant injustice. So important was the fulfillment of sexual desire and the right to progeny to the legal idea of masculinity that al-Sarakhsi hinges the resolution to this conundrum on precisely this point: the law allows him this form of dominion owing to the necessity of fulfilling his sexual desire and preserving his lineage.[63]

Once Hanafi jurists found themselves past the legal dilemma of an enslaved man's ownership rights in marriage, they had to consider whether an enslaved man could be coerced into marriage by the enslaver.[64] Sunni jurists in general required that the enslaver consent to the marriage of an enslaved person. Yet, while they were agreed on the right of the enslaver to coerce the enslaved woman into marriage, only the Hanafi legal school allowed for the enslaved man to be coerced into marriage. In explaining the Shafi'i discomfort with coercing an enslaved man into marriage, Kecia Ali explains that "a certain irreducible masculinity prevented an adult male slave from losing the right to sexual self-determination for Shāfi'ī."[65]

The early generation of Hanafi jurists took different positions on this issue. Like al-Malik and al-Shafi'i, Abu Hanifa reportedly held that the enslaver could not marry off an adult enslaved man without his consent (*ridahu*). In providing his rendition of Abu Hanifa's reasoning, al-Kasani argues that the enslaver has no right to the sexual commodity of an enslaved man. Given this, the enslaver cannot make decisions for the enslaved man in matters that pertain to his sexuality without his consent. The same is true, al-Kasani contends, in other modes of enslavement where the enslaved person has acquired the status of a *mukatab*, a contractual agreement to purchase their freedom, because here the enslaver has agreed to relinquish some of their ownership rights.[66]

Other Hanafi jurists disagreed with Abu Hanifa's position and in fact abandoned his precedent. Defending the dominant opinion adopted by the Hanafi legal school allowing the enslaver to coerce the enslaved man into marriage, al-Kasani returns to the legal status of the enslaved person as property. The right of ownership (*milk*), he argues, not only grants the enslaver full ownership over every part (*ajza'*) of the enslaved person; it also entails the right to transact and make use of the commodity without concern for the property's consent.[67] He argues further that every property owner (*malik*) has the right (*wilayah*) to make use of their property, particular in matters where they stand to benefit (*maslaha, fa'idah*). Preventing the enslaver from compelling the adult enslaved man into marriage, then, would not only hinder the enslaver's ability to make use of their property as they wish but also deprive them of the benefit they might receive from arranging such a marriage. Among the potential benefits to the enslaver that al-Kasani lists is an increase in the number of enslaved people owned by the enslaver through reproduction. Marriage would also ensure, he argues, that the enslaved man will not resort to illicit sexual intercourse to fulfill his sexual desire, a defect that would decrease the property value of the enslaved person.[68]

As we will discuss in the next chapter, Muslim jurists granted the patriarchal head of household (father and paternal grandfather), as well as legal guardians, the right to compel other nonnormative legal subjects into marriage. Marriages of children, both male and female, could be contracted by the patriarchal head of household as well as by their legal guardians; moreover, while legal majority granted the adult woman the right to contract her own marriage under Hanafi law, her male kin could challenge her choice of spouse. The power granted to the patriarch over his dependent subjects (wife, children, and enslaved people) was embedded in a paternalistic ethic of care that imagined a father or paternal grandfather would make decisions in the best interest of the dependent. This paternalistic ethic of care did not raise much concern for the jurists.[69]

The jurists assumed a similar paternalistic ethic of care in the enslaver/enslaved relationship. In premodern Muslim societies, particularly in early Islam, enslaved people were considered to be a part of the broader household of the enslaver. While they were by no means integral members of the natal family, they were incorporated into the household and its kinship networks. Enslaved people were expected to be loyal to their enslavers and act in a manner that preserved the interest of the enslaver and his household.[70] This connection between the manumitter and the freed person continued even after emancipation, through a system of patronage that gave the manumitter access to the estate of the freed person and also obligated the manumitter to pay blood money. This relationship of patronage was similar to other kinship connections in Islamic law in that the manumitter could not relinquish his duties; nor, however, could the freed person decide to change their patron. The patronage connection also continued intergenerationally, passing on to the children of the patron.[71]

Given this relation between enslaver and enslaved, jurists assumed that enslavers would act in the best interest of those they had enslaved, thus granting them significant power over the marriage of enslaved people. This power of coercion was granted not only to the male enslaver but also to the female enslaver. Sunni jurists disagreed on whether the female enslaver could contract the marriage herself. As Hanafi jurists recognized a free adult woman's right to marry without the consent of her guardian, this legal capacity to self-determination in marriage carried through in her capacity as an enslaver. Maliki jurists, on the other hand, required the female enslaver to delegate a male representative to contract the actual marriage. Shafi'is were even more particular, requiring the female enslaver's own marriage guardian to contract the marriage of her enslaved woman.[72] The juristic discussion of the female enslaver's ability to coerce enslaved people into marriage is an interesting case study on the intersections of freedom and gender in their impact on legal capacity. As Ali has noted, femininity could indeed intervene to prevent the female enslaver from exercising ownership rights similar to male enslavers.[73] In making this point, Ali speaks specifically of an instance in which the second caliph 'Umar adjudicated a case where a female enslaver was making sexual use of her male slave. The woman claimed that she had the right, just as male enslavers did, to make sexual use of her enslaved man. 'Umar judged otherwise, stating that she had engaged in illicit sex and commanded the family to sell the enslaved man in an area that was beyond the woman's control. Here we see the status of the enslaver as a woman limiting her from exercising the same property rights as a male enslaver. In the case here of the female enslaver's right to coercion, however, femininity does not necessarily intervene to limit her. Despite their disagreements on how exactly she could exercise that right, all the Sunni legal schools maintained that the female enslaver had the same right as a male enslaver to coerce enslaved people into marriage. For the jurists, then, emphasized femininity did not always function in a similar and predictable manner in constraining the legal capacity of female legal subjects.

Despite the fact that the dominant Hanafi position allowed the enslaver to compel an enslaved man into marriage, the enslaved man subsequently had full control of the rights of a husband. He had ownership over sexual access to his wife and the right of unilateral divorce. Ali notes similarly that the law insisted on the sexual agency of the enslaved man and did not turn him into a sexual object. Once the enslaved man became a husband, the enslaver could neither compel the enslaved man to divorce his wife nor could he have sexual access to her, because she was now the wife of another man.[74] These rights acquired by the enslaved man as husband were quite obvious to the jurists. In fact, Abu Hanifa's reasoning for not granting the enslaver the power of compulsion was the recognition that the enslaved man could simply exercise his power of divorce. There was essentially no point in the right of compulsion if the enslaved man could exit the marriage of his own accord.[75]

The vulnerability of enslavement could, of course, keep the enslaved man from exercising a husband's rights. In fact, his inability to contract a marriage without the permission of the enslaver constrained his unilateral right of divorce. Al-Kasani was clearly attuned to this point. In responding to Abu Hanifa's reasoning that the enslaved husband's right of divorce effectively negated any meaningful compulsion into marriage, al-Kasani claimed:

> Indeed, desire for women is in the nature of a virile man [*fahl*]. What is evident is fulfillment of sexual desire particularly in the absence of obstacles—i.e. the forbidden-ness [of sexual intercourse]—and what is also evident is that the condition of an enslaved person is such that he would refrain from rejecting the actions of the enslaver out of respect and in this way the marriage would continue and the full benefit of marriage will be actualized.[76]

If an enslaved man desires licit sexual intercourse with a woman, then he must marry. However, as marriage requires the permission of the enslaver, he becomes beholden to the good will of the enslaver for the fulfillment of his sexual desire. For al-Kasani, being caught in such a bind forces the enslaved man into a calculus whereby he might not exercise his right of divorce in a forced marriage because this might be his only avenue to fulfill his sexual desire. To exit a marriage the enslaver favored not only risked angering his enslaver but potentially risked their refusal to let the enslaved man marry again. While theoretically the enslaved man retains the divorce rights of a free husband, the vulnerable and dependent status of enslavement restricts his ability to fully exercise these rights.

The three legal discussions I have covered in this section—(1) the enslaved man's legal (in)capacity to marry, (2) coercion into marriage, and (3) his right of divorce—all provide insight into juristic reasoning on legal personhood. In all three discussions, we see Hanafi jurists navigate between idealized masculinity and enslavement. As we saw in chapter 1, Hanafi jurists articulated an idealized masculinity that was characterized by autonomy, self-determination, and the ability to exercise power over others. Enslavement, on the other hand, was a legal impediment that entailed the loss of autonomy and self-determination, subjecting one to the will of their enslaver. In determining the legal personhood of the enslaved man, Hanafi jurists engaged in a complex process of reconciling these two contradictory legal capacities. The negotiation between idealized masculinity and enslavement produced a male legal subject who was significantly different from other male legal subjects. Unlike the free adult man, the enslaved man was subject to the will of his enslaver and could be coerced into marriage. In fact, his very ability to marry came into question because the marital contract was imagined through idealized gendered norms that could not be inhabited by the enslaved man. Even after Hanafi jurists resolved this conundrum by granting him the ability to marry through a distinction between forms of ownership, his capacity in marriage (as in other aspects of the law) was halved. Instead of the simultaneous four wives permitted to free men, the enslaved man could only marry two. Similarly, while he retained the right of divorce, he could only take his wife back after one pronouncement of divorce rather than the two available to the free man.

While this section has largely noted the different constructions of free and enslaved men as legal subjects, it is important to consider that enslavement was also not a shared legal status between all enslaved people. Enslavement was certainly a legal impediment for both enslaved men and women. However, what was entailed by that impediment differed significantly. Just as the enslaved man's legal personhood was constructed at the intersection of idealized masculinity and enslavement, the enslaved woman's personhood was constructed at the intersection of idealized femininity and enslavement. In the following section, I focus on juristic discussions about the marriage of enslaved women to demonstrate that the intersections of femininity and enslavement produced significantly different legal capacities for enslaved men and women.

THE ENSLAVED WOMAN: BETWEEN FEMININITY AND ENSLAVEMENT

In addition to the marriage of enslaved men, Hanafi jurists also gave considerable attention to the marriage of enslaved women. Interestingly, however, the legal issues raised in relation to the enslaved woman's marriage rarely mirrored those discussed in the case of the enslaved man. For one, there was little juristic concern over her coercion into marriage. As I discussed in chapter 1, the jurists understood the fulfillment of women's sexual desire only within a framework of dominion. Hanafi jurists were perhaps most explicit about this, arguing that free women were in an odd bind since the fulfillment of their sexual desire always had to come at the expense of their self-determination.[77] Unlike free women, who had to surrender themselves to the dominion of the husband in order to fulfill their sexual desire and have children, enslaved women had no ability to surrender, as Islamic law allowed enslaved women to be used sexually by their enslavers. This permissive attitude toward the sexual use of enslaved woman was by no means unique to Islamic law. The institution of concubinage was prevalent in the late antique world in which Islam came into existence. In Roman society, for example, a male Roman citizen could make sexual use of any people he enslaved, including young boys and enslaved men.

While Islamic law continued both slavery and concubinage as institutions that were prevalent in the broader Near East and the Arabian Peninsula, it prohibited the sexual use of enslaved men by male or female enslavers.[78] Islamic law's abandonment of this Roman practice meant that gender became a differentiating aspect of enslavement. Enslaved men retained some of the sexual autonomy that was so critical to masculinity. They could be coerced into marriage, but doing so put them in a position of gaining sexual access to a woman. Enslaved women, on the other hand, shared with free women the commodification of their sexuality but did not have to the same sexual agency as the latter group. The legal debates I discussed in the previous section on the enslaved man's marriage were animated by the masculinity of the enslaved man. For the enslaved woman, her legal status was negotiated in relation to femininity.

In the Hanafi legal school, free women had the legal agency to contract their own marriages. Although Hanafi jurists preferred that free women still be married off by a guardian, this appearing to have been the norm in practice as well, they nonetheless had the right to arrange marriages themselves. A free adult woman also had the autonomy to resist marriages that she did not desire: as she was seen as owner over her sexuality, her male kin could not compel her into marriage.[79] The other Sunni legal schools prioritized not just age but also sexual status in the acquisition of legal agency of free adult women. For them, a virgin adult woman could also be compelled into marriage by her father and paternal grandfather. For the Hanafi jurists, legal majority and freedom granted the free woman greater legal agency and autonomy than the enslaved man.

Conversely, the law did not recognize an enslaved woman's ownership over herself as a sexual commodity. In fact, the permissive attitude of Islamic law toward concubinage meant that enslavement for women necessarily entailed a loss of ownership over their sexual availability and that the enslavers held the right to compel them in sexual matters. As Ali notes, "in contrast to the male slave and the free female, sexual and marital self-determination was never available to an enslaved female."[80] This right, however, had particular restrictions. Unlike the Roman law, whereby an enslaver could force enslaved woman into sex work, the Qur'an expressly prohibited such a practice. If an enslaved woman was co-owned by several men, they could not all demand sexual services from her. Additionally, if the enslaved woman became pregnant by her enslaver, Sunni jurists agreed that she acquired the status of *umm walad*. The *umm walad* could no longer be sold and was emancipated at the death of the enslaver. Gaining the status of *umm walad* allowed an enslaved woman some mobility in her legal status, since she thereby moved from the legal status of an enslaved woman toward that of a free wife.[81]

The sexual use made of enslaved women was also not limited to male enslavers. While female enslavers could not licitly engage in sexual intercourse with enslaved women, they could still transact the sexuality of enslaved women. Historical accounts tell us that female enslavers often gifted their husbands enslaved women in an effort to acquire his goodwill or favor.[82] Female enslavers who trained singing girls (*qiyan*) often did so in the hopes that they would make a profit through their sale.[83] Male enslavers, like their female counterparts, also transacted the sexuality of enslaved women but were additionally given the right to make sexual use of them personally. The enslaved woman had effectively no legally recognized means of offering consent, since she had no control or ownership over her sexual commodity.

The question of the coercion of enslaved women into sexual intercourse is one that has been the subject of significantly scholarly disagreement. Some scholars of Islamic law contend that the Qur'an does not permit the enslaver to make sexual use of the enslaved woman unless she consents. They argue that in legitimizing sexual intercourse between an enslaver and the enslaved woman, Islam grants her a status akin to the wife.[84] Sexual use of the enslaved woman for these scholars was a means by which kinship ties were created and the enslaved woman incorporated into the household of the enslaver. Ali has noted, however, that the jurists do not really discuss the issue of an enslaved woman's consent.[85] The legal status of an individual was so significant in determining their sexual autonomy that the jurists could not conceive of the enslaved woman as a legal subject who held the autonomy to offer consent. Granting her such a right could undermine the jurists' very conception of the legal subjecthood of an enslaved woman.

It is precisely because of this recognition of her inability to offer meaningful consent that the law gave her a right of annulment (*khiyar al-'ataqah*) of marriage after emancipation—that is, when she came into possession of herself as a sexual commodity. This right of annulment has precedents in Prophetic practice. A hadith often quoted in legal texts is that of an enslaved woman by the name of Barira, who, after being emancipated, decided to end her marriage. Mughith, the husband, still desperately in love with his wife, was deeply distressed by her decision. Al-Sarakhsi described the love-stricken Mughith, crying profusely while he followed his wife around town. But she was insistent in her rejection of the marriage. The Prophet intervened in this situation, hoping to change Barira's mind, urging her to remember that this was her husband and the father of her children. She, however, was adamant and, after confirming that the Prophet was only offering counsel and not commanding her to remain with Mughith, she chose separation. The language used in the hadith to indicate the woman's right to choose emancipation is couched again in the language of ownership and dominion, as the Prophet told Barira: "You have come into ownership of your genital organs so choose [to remain or separate]."[86] Whereas the free woman has ownership over her own body and sexuality, which she transacts to the husband in marriage, the enslaved woman acquires that ownership only through emancipation.

The jurists differ on precisely why an enslaved woman was granted the choice of annulling a marriage at emancipation. Shafi'i jurists held that the annulment was only granted when the husband was also enslaved. While they were compatible (*kafa'a*) as spouses when they were both enslaved, as a free woman she now rises in social rank above her husband. To force her to remain in such a marriage would thus cause her harm (*darar*). Hanafi jurists, however, center the newly acquired sexual autonomy of the emancipated wife in justifying the right of annulment. The harm is not the status difference between the couple but instead the increase in his power (through the marital bond) over the wife. After emancipation, the enslaved woman moved from the legal status of enslaved wife to free wife, which increased the number of divorces the husband could pronounce (from two to three) before an irrevocable divorce. This move also increased her remarriage waiting period from two to three menstrual cycles. It would cause harm, the Hanafi jurists argued, to inflict this on the recently emancipated wife, regardless of whether she had been married off by her enslaver or had chosen to marry with their consent. The option at emancipation was granted to her precisely because of the dominion entailed by marriage. Once freed, she could not be forced to endure the resultant effects of a form of dominion that was placed on her during enslavement, when she could not offer meaningful consent. Al-Kasani states quite explicitly that to keep the emancipated wife in such a marriage would also result in the uncompensated and coercive use of a free woman's sexual commodity by the husband. A free woman, he argues, enters of her own consent into a marriage contract with the agreed on exchange (i.e., the dower) for her sexual commodity. In the marriage of an enslaved woman, it was not the enslaved woman but the enslaver who both negotiated and received the dower (*mahr*) amount.[87] As a free woman, she became owner of her own sexual commodity; she also acquired the legal agency to make decisions regarding her own person and to protect herself from the infliction of harm.[88] The sexual autonomy of legal subjects, then, was set on a spectrum from those who retained full sexual autonomy (free adult men) to those who had very little (enslaved women).

While Hanafi jurists allowed for an enslaved man to be compelled into marriage as well, a similar right of annulment was not granted to him after emancipation. Since marriage meant that the enslaved man came into ownership over the wife's sexual commodity and he held the unilateral right of divorce, Hanafi jurists saw no apparent harm inflicted on the enslaved man when he was compelled into marriage. Despite the fact that the sexuality of the enslaved man was transacted in marriage, the resultant effect of this was not the sexual use of him but rather the acquisition of the right of sexual use. As we saw in the debate around the consent of the enslaved man to marriage, the Hanafi jurists' understanding of masculinity made it very difficult for them to recognize compulsion of men into sexual intercourse.[89]

Given the broader construction of femininity as passive and as the object of male desire, the juristic discussions of the coercion of enslaved women into marriage were not concerned with the enslaver's right of compulsion or her ability to marry. While the legal discussions around the enslaved man were concerned with justifying how and why a male subject could be coerced into marriage, the discussions around the enslaved woman were concerned with the legal implications of the right over her sexual commodity that she acquired after emancipation. Juristic concerns in this case revolved around the dominion of the husband over the wife and the fact that the freedwoman could no longer be subjected to that particular form of dominion if she had not chosen to enter it of her own will. Despite the fact that both the enslaved man and the enslaved woman shared in their status as enslaved persons, enslavement had different implications for their legal capacities. The legal personhood of the enslaved woman was negotiated between idealized femininity and enslavement, which together only compounded her vulnerability, negating her legal agency and autonomy. Gender intersected with enslavement to configure enslaved men and women as different legal persons.

COVERING THE FEMALE BODY: FRAGMENTED GENDERED LEGAL SUBJECTS

Just as the implications of being enslaved were different for men and women, the implications of being female differed for free and enslaved women. This section will focus on juristic discussions of bodily exposure and the modesty of enslaved woman to trace how jurists conceptualized these two classes as different female legal subjects.

In the previous chapter, I considered al-Sarakhsi's discussion of the fundamental condition of women as concealed subjects. Although men must also cover parts of their body in many circumstances, it is women whose entire bodies must be concealed and their presence in public spaces minimized. The inclusion of this discussion under al-Sarakhsi's chapter on juristic discretion (*istihsan*) is perhaps most indicative of the situation-dependent conception of women's bodies as in need of concealment. This statement about women being *'awra* does not mean that the law actually holds that all women must be fully concealed in all circumstances. Rather, this is a categorical statement about the default condition of women that simultaneously recognizes the practical exceptions that allowed different groups of women to expose their bodies to varying degrees both publicly and in certain relationships.[90]

While men could look on certain parts of the body of their wives, concubines, and female relatives, their ability to look at women not related to them in these ways was restricted to their faces or, depending on the legal school in question, only the eyes. Enslaved women, however, were subjected to significant bodily exposure. Despite the categorical character of the statement about the need for women's concealment, it did not, in fact, apply to enslaved women. Across the Sunni legal schools, clothing marked the distinction between free and enslaved women, the latter of whom were prohibited from covering their head or face lest they resemble free women.

The practice of using covering to distinguish between enslaved and free women takes its precedent from the companions of the Prophet, in particular the second caliph 'Umar. Hanafi jurists recount that 'Umar strongly rebuked an enslaved woman who veiled her face (*mutaqanni'a*), threatening to beat her and ordering her to remove the veil, saying, "Remove the head covering from yourself, you stinking one!"[91] Early sources, however, seem conflicted on the covering of the enslaved woman's body. The *Musannaf 'Abd al-Raazaq*, for example, narrates that Hassan al-Basri would order married enslaved women or those who had been taken on as concubines to cover their heads.[92] A few other texts recount that during the Prophet's life, enslaved women veiled their heads during prayer.[93] Another recounts that the scholars of Madina held that enslaved women should cover their heads but not wear an outer cloak (*jilbab*) when venturing outside.[94] Malik b. Anas holds that it is preferable for the *umm walad* to pray with her head covered and that she make up her prayer if she had done so with her head uncovered; he did not, however, require her to cover her head as a free woman must.[95] The only reports that indicate an explicit prohibition against enslaved women veiling their heads or faces all return to the second caliph, 'Umar b. al-Khattab. We can see in the report above—the report most cited by Hanafi jurists—that an enslaved woman who dressed in a manner that concealed her body was severely rebuked by 'Umar for doing so. In the *Musannaf ibn Abi Shayba* we receive another account of 'Umar's attempt to mark the difference between free and enslaved women through clothing:

'Ali b. Mashar told it to us from al-Mukhtar b. Fulful from Anas b. Malik who said: An enslaved woman entered upon 'Umar and he knew her to be enslaved by one of the Emigrants [*muhajirin*] or Helpers [*ansar*]. She had an outer cloak [*jilbab*] over her with which she had covered her face [*mutaqanni'atan bihi*]. So he ['Umar] inquired: "Have you been emancipated ['*utiqti*]?" She responded in the negative. He said: What's with the cloak? Take it off your head, the outer cloak [*jilbab*] is only for free women from the women of the believers. [The enslaved woman] hesitated so he struck her with a switch[96] until she took it off her head.[97]

The caliph 'Umar's need to maintain a clear differentiation between enslaved and free women conflicted with the practice of other people, including the wives of the Prophet, who did not see such a distinction as necessary. For instance, in a text recounted in the *Musannaf 'Abd al-Razzaq*, 'Umar rebukes his daughter Hafsa, one of the wives of the Prophet, for permitting an enslaved woman working in her home to dress in the manner of free women.[98] As these different narrations demonstrate, the issue of enslaved women's covering was a conflicted and contentious issue among the early generation of Muslims. Early reports seem to indicate that enslaved Muslim women were asserting their right to bodily dignity and integrity by covering their bodies as free women would. They were met, however, with physical violence and forced to expose their bodies in a manner that marked their enslaved status.

Many societies have used clothing to mark difference and status distinctions. In writing about Ottoman sartorial laws, Madeline Zilfi has observed that often apparel was more indicative of social place in Ottoman society than housing, transport, or alimentation.[99] The use of veiling to mark social distinction among women was not particular to the Arabian context but had earlier precedents. Assyrian law, for example, carefully delineated which women could veil. Wives, daughters, and concubines had to veil, as did married women who had previously been sacral sex workers. All other sex workers, as well as enslaved women, were prohibited from veiling and would be severely punished for doing so.[100] Veiling in the early generation of Muslims was a physical marker of the social and legal hierarchy separating enslaved and free women. The enslaved woman's decision to cover her head blurred this distinction between those women who were sexually available through concubinage as opposed to through marriage. This distinction is made clear in another report where 'Umar expressed his frustration with a covered enslaved woman whom he mistook for a free woman such that he desired to have sex with her.[101]

Veiling and the bodily exposure of women marked not only the status between free and enslaved but it also conferred certain social protections to free women from male harassment. Al-Sarakhsi mentions, for example, that it was a common practice among pre-Islamic Arabs to engage in jestful banter (*mumazaha*) with enslaved women. It was in the context of this social practice, al-Sarakhsi argues, that the Qur'anic verse ordered free believing women to take on clothing that marked the difference between them and enslaved women.[102] It is common in contemporary Muslim ethical discourse to equate the covering of the female body with reduced sexual harassment. While al-Sarakhsi's argument here might sound similar, he is not claiming that bodily exposure reduces sexual harassment but instead that covering marks those women who are granted social and legal protection from male sexual attention and its lack—that is, those who must bear it as part of their social situation.[103] Prohibiting enslaved women from covering their bodies, particularly their heads and faces, meant not only greater vulnerability to inappropriate male behavior but also some level of exclusion from practices that marked the community of believers.

From among these early conflicting opinions about enslaved women's veiling, 'Umar's insistence on bodily covering as a means for differentiation between free and enslaved women won out. However, while early Hanafi jurists agreed that enslaved women could not dress like free women, they disagreed on the specific areas of the enslaved woman's body that could be exposed. Al-Shaybani held that a man can gaze upon the chest, breasts, hair, and legs (below the knee) of an enslaved woman if he is looking to purchase her.[104] He may also touch these parts of her body, even if such a touch is animated by desire. Outside the context of purchase, a man may still look on these parts of her body, but it is reprehensible to do so if it is animated by desire unless he is her enslaver. The tenth-century Hanafi jurist al-Jassas similarly mentions the opinion that an enslaved woman—regardless of whether she is *umm walad* or partially emancipated—prays without a head covering.[105] In discussing Qur'an 33:59, he argues that covering is only obligatory for free woman so as to distinguish between free and enslaved women.[106] While some jurists held that the entirety of the enslaved woman's body could be exposed (except the area from navel to knee), others held that she must also cover her back and torso, including the breasts.[107] Eventually, the dominant opinion of the Hanafi legal school held that men could look on and touch the entire body of an enslaved women except for her torso, upper thighs, and genitals.

While the early generation of Muslims was often concerned with marking social hierarchy and difference through clothing, for the early Hanafi jurists the justifications offered for modesty or exposure were more attuned to the dynamics of the slave market and the right of the enslaver to the labor of enslaved people. These are two most commonly appearing justifications in early Hanafi legal texts regarding the covering of enslaved women. Hanafi jurists commonly argued that, as a commodity bought and sold on the market, the enslaved person's body had to be available for inspection in order to ascertain its value.[108] In that vein, not just looking but also touching was necessary in order to verify the condition of the enslaved woman's body.[109] As sexual access to the enslaved woman was an enslaver's right of the enslaver, a man's ability to determine his sexual attraction to the woman was significant. So important was this consideration that, while the jurists generally allowed looking at or touching an enslaved woman's body only if doing so was not animated by desire, this was not the case at the slave market. Al-Sarakhsi states explicitly that if a man wishes to purchase a slave woman, he may look on her body even if he experiences desire just as one must look on a commodity in order to determine its appropriate value. Touching with desire, however, is not always necessary to ascertain the monetary value of the slave woman and is thus prohibited.[110]

The jurists' second concern pertained to the enslaved woman's need to go out in public spaces. Unlike free elite women, who had the privilege to stay within their homes, an enslaved woman must of necessity emerge into the world of men. To this end, Hanafi jurists often argued that requiring her to cover her body significantly would put an unnecessary burden on her. Al-Jassas argues that because the enslaved woman travels without close male kin, unrelated men have to be able to interact with her without too many restrictions.[111] This concern for creating ease for men when women emerge into the public space is expressed by other jurists as well. Al-Kasani also mentions that the law allows men to interact with enslaved woman as they do their female relatives, in order to prevent difficulties for men.[112] Otherwise, they would be inconvenienced in having to engage enslaved women in a very restrictive manner and might also experience an element of religious guilt for touching or looking at an unrelated woman. As the public space was the sphere that belonged to men, it was their need rather than the bodily dignity of the enslaved woman that was paramount.

The jurists were also concerned with maintaining the enslaver's property rights by not imposing restrictions that would hinder his ability to make use of an enslaved person's labor. For the law, the main responsibility and obligation of enslaved people is to fulfill the enslaver's demands on them. Al-Sarakhsi notes that an enslaved woman must emerge outside the home to fulfill the needs of her enslaver and does so in clothing that she wears within the home.[113] To require her to cover in the manner of a free woman would impose restrictions on her mobility and infringe on the rights of the enslavers to make use of the enslaved woman as they saw fit, an imposition that the jurists were clearly reticent to make. For the jurists, the rights of enslaved persons as human beings was in tension with the rights of enslavers over them. As we see in this discussion of an enslaved woman's body, the desire to ease men's interaction with enslaved women, as well as the right of the enslaver to make use of enslaved labor, took priority for the jurists over the bodily integrity of the enslaved woman.

The legal debates over the veiling of enslaved women gives us insight into the juristic process of determining individuals' legal rights and obligations. Despite the juristic statement about the need to cover the female body, we can see that enslaved women were not only exempted from veiling themselves; they were not even permitted to do so. Throughout these discussions, Hanafi jurists made clear distinctions between free and enslaved women. While both free and enslaved women were construed as passive legal subjects, their legal agency was vastly different. The discussion of bodily exposure and sexual autonomy demonstrates that enslaved women and free adult women were in fact differently constructed as female legal subjects. Idealized femininity intersected with freedom and enslavement to produce different legal persons despite their shared anatomical sex. Whereas freedom granted greater agency and autonomy to the free woman, the intersection of enslavement and femininity compounded the enslaved woman's subservience and subjection to dominion.

CONCLUSION

This chapter began with a statement by al-Sarakhsi about the fundamental difference between human males and females. This difference is supposedly so significant for al-Sarakhsi that it leads him to argue that males and females do not share the same genus. Based on that argument, we might assume that gender should cut across all other distinctions, such that enslaved men and free men are of the same genus despite the difference in their status as free and enslaved persons. Al-Sarakhsi's opinion matches other statements made by Hanafi jurists about an essential nature of gender that we considered in chapter 1. Such ideas would seem to indicate that Hanafi jurists held that men's and women's gendered natures were innate and transcended all other distinctions among humans. The case studies that we discussed throughout this chapter, however, indicate otherwise. In fact, we see that Hanafi jurists took seriously not only gender but other social identities (in this case enslavement) in determining individuals' legal capacity.

While Hanafi jurists certainly articulated essentializing statements about gender, the case studies on the marriage of enslaved people and the bodily exposure of enslaved women demonstrate that legal personhood was at the intersection of a number of different social identities. Rulings based on gender could be displaced when they conflicted with those based on enslavement. Free women had ownership over their own sexual commodity and surrendered their bodily autonomy of their own volition. Enslaved women, on the contrary, were bought and sold at the slave market and thus did not have the right to prevent men from touching or looking at them. They could be used sexually by their enslavers and could also be coerced into marriage. It is for this reason that after emancipation a freedwoman could choose whether to remain in a marriage that was contracted while she was enslaved. Moreover, just as the passivity and subservience that marked femininity did not mean that free and enslaved woman shared the same legal incapacities, so too the shared biological sex between enslaved and free men did not grant them the same legal personhood or degree of autonomy. While both the enslaved man and the enslaved woman shared enslavement as a legal impediment, the intersections of gender with enslavement were such that they produced different legal personhoods, and the enslaved man had greater legal agency than the enslaved woman.

Yet, despite the increased legal capacity of the enslaved man owing to masculinity, he did not have greater legal capacity than all other female legal subjects. The contrast between the legal personhood of the enslaved husband and the free adult woman is particularly illuminating. The free adult woman's legal personhood was constructed at the intersection of femininity, freedom, and legal majority. While idealized femininity was characterized by passivity and subservience, the intersection of gender, freedom, and legal majority granted the free adult woman greater sexual autonomy than enslaved men. If she had the financial means, as an enslaver she held power and dominion over enslaved people, both men and women. She could marry of her own will and could not be coerced into marriage. As a wife, however, she did not have the unilateral right of divorce that the enslaved husband held. Here it was the husband/wife relation that granted the enslaved husband greater right of divorce than the free wife. In contrast to these two legal persons, the enslaved woman had neither the sexual autonomy to make decisions regarding her sexuality nor the right of divorce. Thus, neither gender nor enslavement were the sole determiners of an individual's position in the social hierarchy. In determining the legal capacity of enslaved men and women, Hanafi jurists did not consider gender or enslavement as distinct categories, and neither had a fixed and predictable impact on the legal capacity of individuals. Instead, the two identities were coconstitutive. In the construction of the enslaved people's legal personhood, neither gender nor enslavement had a fixed and predictable impact on the legal capacity of individuals. The idealized gender norms articulated by Hanafi jurists that we discussed in chapter 1 were constantly in negotiation in relation to enslaved people.

3

Age and Gendered Legal Personhood

In recent years, the renowned religious scholar Habib 'Ali al-Jifri has been an outspoken opponent of child marriages and a pointed critic of religious justifications for the practice. Since al-Jifri lives in Yemen, where child marriage has been the subject of significant controversy, his position is of great consequence. Over the years there have been several attempts to establish a minimum age to marry in Yemen. In 2009, parliament passed a bill raising it to seventeen, but the Islamic Sharia Codification Committee ultimately rejected the law as un-Islamic.[1] When censured for marrying off their children, parents often provide religious and cultural justifications.[2] Opposing these practices are organizations promoting women's rights and human rights, organizations that have a different conception of marriage and childhood. "These early marriages rob the girl of the right to a normal childhood and education," argues Wafa Ahmad Ali of the Yemeni Women's Union.[3] "The girls are forced to have children before their bodies are fully grown instead of going to school and playing with other children."[4] The epistemological disconnect between these competing parties is evident in their comments. Whereas one side invokes the idea of childhood to oppose these marriages, the other appeals to the precedent of the sunnah and legal tradition. Since the Prophet Muhammad married his youngest wife when she was six and consummated the marriage when she was nine, to make moral or ethical claims against child marriage would run against this precedent and as Muhammad as an exemplar. These groups also argue that Islamic law has not laid down any minimum age for marriage.

It is within this landscape of competing norms that al-Jifri has been speaking out. In 2014, he posted a strong condemnation of child marriage on his English-language Facebook page, arguing that there is no religious sanction for the practice.[5] Labeling child marriage a crime, he chided those who support such a practice in the interest of upholding Islamic law as the arbiter of moral norms. Islamic law, he contends, is guided by legal maxims that prohibit practices that cause harm. Thus, he concludes, it is impermissible to marry a female child, who cannot endure the various demands of marriage.[6]

There are important discontinuities between al-Jifri's treatment of child marriage and similar discussions of the matter in premodern Islamic law. His interpretation is couched in modern conceptions of marriage, childhood, and harm. Moreover, much of the contemporary debate regarding child marriage, including al-Jifri's position, does not make a distinction between contracting a marriage and consummating it. Al-Jifri's statement collapses the distinction, arguing that minor marriages themselves are prohibited. Additionally, al-Jifri's assertions assume a modern conception of childhood that is based on age rather than biological developments such as puberty. Human rights organizations in Yemen consider an individual under the age of eighteen to be a child and thus deem any marriage with an individual under that age to be a violation of the child's rights. Their opponents argue that Islamic law establishes puberty as the distinguishing marker between children and adults. Thus, any girl who has entered puberty is no longer a child, and marriage to her is permissible under Islamic law. By deeming child marriages to be prohibited under Islamic law, al-Jifri redefines Islamic legal conceptions of childhood to conform to modern norms. Finally, what is perhaps most intriguing about al-Jifri's claims is his appeal to concerns for not just bodily harm but also mental and emotional anguish: "It is forbidden to marry off a young girl whose body and soul cannot tolerate the demands of marriage."[7]

As we will see in this chapter, al-Jifri largely seems to sidestep much of the basic conceptual parameters that constituted the premodern legal conversation on minor marriage, despite his claims to be speaking from the framework of legal precedent.[8] Instead, he largely focuses on broader legal maxims about the prevention of harm. While this concern with avoiding harm to minor children was certainly present in premodern legal discussions, the parameters of what constitutes such harm were understood quite differently. Many of these issues related to the rights of children stem from changing notions of childhood. While many premodern societies did not find marriage to children to be inherently immoral, this practice has become an increasingly controversial issue in the contemporary period. In these debates over the age of consent and child marriage, we see shifting constructions of childhood.

Childhood as a distinct stage of life separate from adulthood is a social construction that shifts based on temporal and geographical specificities. Historians of childhood have shown that the nineteenth and twentieth centuries saw both the extension of the period of childhood (largely the result of mandatory education) and the notion that childhood is a period of dependence.[9] The modern discomfort with recognizing childhood sexuality, and concerns with the autonomy and agency of children, have made these long-standing historical practices of child marriage increasingly unacceptable. This controversy over the legal age of consent and the minimum age of marriage centers on two main issues: the first, how to understand and define childhood; the second, whether sexual intercourse between an adult and a child can be consensual. To put it another way, these debates are largely concerned with whether children are discerning individuals capable of offering informed and meaningful consent.

This chapter explores the construction of childhood in Islamic legal discourse and particularly the law's construction of the child as a legal subject. Continuing my discussion of the intersections of different parts of an individual's identity with their legal personhood, here I show that age and life cycle also play a significant role in shaping an individual as a subject of the law. The first section of this chapter looks at how childhood was conceptualized in classical Hanafi legal discourse. The second section then explores the juristic debates around minor marriage in order to demonstrate how age functioned in constraining the subject's legal agency. I focus in particular on the case of minor marriage, as it reveals critical moments in legal texts where jurists reflected on the power dynamic that they were authorizing. Hanafis greatly valued the consent of both parties in contracting a marriage. Children, however, had no right to consent and could be married off by their fathers, paternal grandfathers, and legal guardians.[10] Focusing on this different valuing of consent indicates that Hanafi jurists saw consent as an important aspect of the autonomy and agency of a legal subject. In subjecting children to the will of adult guardians, they were well aware of the vulnerability they were imposing on the minor child. The disagreement among early jurists about the validity of minor marriage demonstrates that in the conflict between the legal agency of the child and the power of the family patriarch, it was the authority of the latter that was solidified in legal discourse.

WHAT IS CHILDHOOD IN ISLAMIC LAW?

Historians of childhood have long argued about whether childhood as a concept existed in the pre-modern world. In *Centuries of Childhood*, published in 1960, Philippe Aries made the compelling argument that childhood is a historically contingent concept.[11] Since then, his claim that the concept of childhood did not exist in the medieval world but instead developed in modernity has been widely challenged by historians of childhood.[12] Their disagreement with Aries provided the catalyst for a rich body of scholarship that gave varied accounts of the social construction of childhood. Most historians of childhood now agree that premodern societies did in fact understand childhood as a distinct part of the human life cycle. In addition to the literary and social analysis in favor of this conclusion, historians have argued that the legal definitions of the minor reflect society's recognition of childhood as constituting a special status.[13] Through these different accounts of childhood in the premodern world, it is apparent that the idea of childhood varied significantly from one place and time period to another.

As a historical tradition, Islam and Muslim societies have also had varied understandings of childhood. There have been few studies of childhood in Muslim thought and praxis overall, and even fewer of premodern Muslim thought and communities. Anver Giladi's work on early Muslim ideas give us a sense of the rich discussion across different genres (law, medicine, ethics, and literature) about childhood and practices of nursing and child-rearing.[14] He describes the ways in which premodern Muslim scholars concerned themselves with the welfare of children and counseled fathers on their care. Similarly, Afsaneh Najmabadi has argued that premodern texts on parenting assumed that it was the father and not the mother who was in charge of disciplining and educating children.[15] This is in distinct contrast with modern Muslim discourses on motherhood, which emphasize her role as the educator of children (future citizens of the nation) and the caretaker and manager of the household. Kathryn Kueny's work looks at the male scholarly and medical discourse that decentered the reproductive and child-rearing work of mothers by prioritizing the father's biological contribution to children's physiology and character.[16] Women's bodies were seen as receptive and passive, carrying the burden of bearing life, while fathers were seen as bringing forth children. Zahra Ayubi's latest work on the gendered aspects of child-rearing explores how it was understood in Islamic ethical discourse.[17] Child-rearing, she argues, was largely concerned with socializing children into particular gender roles. Boys were raised to become heads of the elite household, whereas girls were raised to take on a supportive role in the ethical transformation of those elite male heads of house.

The Qur'an describes children as both a blessing and a test from God. Numerous Qur'anic verses as well as hadith address the duties that are shared between parents and children. Parents are obligated to provide and care for their children, as well as to teach them about Islam and to focus on their moral development. The Qur'an defines the debt owed by the child to the parents by describing the pain in which the mother bore, delivered, and nursed the child. A fundamental aspect of righteousness in the Qur'an is to give parents their due respect and deference, even despite the senility that comes with age: "do good unto [thy] parents. Should one of them, or both, attain to old age in thy care, never say 'Ugh' to them or scold them, but [always] speak unto them with reverent speech."[18] One oft-cited hadith describes the multilayered hierarchical relationships of care: a ruler is a shepherd over his subjects, a man over his family, the wife over her husband's household and their children, and the servant over his master's property.[19] Another summarizes the mutual duties and obligations between parent and child: "One who does not show mercy to our young and does not respect the rights of our elders is not from us."[20]

While love and affection link parents and children, these emotional connections function within a hierarchical relationship. Children can claim certain rights over their parents, but parents are owed respect, deference, and obedience. The legal traditions of the Near East all emphasized the importance of parental obedience, particularly to the father. Sassanian law, for example, held that a child who disobeyed his father three times could be put to death.[21] Similarly, Jewish law and Roman law both held that a child who challenged the father's authority could be punished. While Islamic law restricted this paternal power to a considerable extent, it did grant the father significant authority and power over his children.[22] This paternal power was upheld by narratives about parental love, particularly that of the father. Al-Kasani argues that a father is profuse in his compassion (*al-shafaqa*) toward his children and looks out for their interest above that of his own.[23] If a father's or paternal grandfather's marital decision might seem to go against the interest of the child, it is probably because they elevated other interests of the child. Al-Kasani gives the example of the Prophet's trusted companion and later the first caliph, Abu Bakr al-Siddiq, who married his daughter 'Aisha to the Prophet while she was still a child and for a dower (*mahr*) of less than what a woman of her status and background would normally receive.[24] Al-Kasani argues that Abu Bakr's decision was based on considerations that were beyond the financial (such as the character of the Prophet and the possibility of a happy marriage with him). Thus, his decision centered 'Aisha's interests despite the reduced dower amount. The expansive power of guardians (particularly the father and paternal grandfather) over the minor makes clear not only the hierarchical nature of the adult-child relationship but also the impaired legal agency of children.

Childhood in Islamic law was understood as the period before puberty.[25] At puberty, children would enter into legal majority and acquire the rights that would be assigned based on their intersecting social identities. Childhood, however, was not understood to be a static period but rather a constantly evolving process toward adulthood. Premodern Muslim jurists saw childhood as a stage marked by the deficiency in one's not yet fully developed rational capacities.[26] The rational capacities of children, however, were constantly in flux. Jurists distinguished between the discerning (*mumayyiz*) and nondiscerning (*ghayr mumayyiz*) child. Discernment, for the legal jurists, was the rational capacity that allowed a child to comprehend the difference between benefit and harm. Stages of childhood were not distinguished based on age, but instead on what children could demonstrate regarding the development of their rational abilities.

Juristic discourse on the age of discretion (*sinn al-rushd*) is helpful for thinking about the priority given to rationality in the acquisition of legal agency. A great deal of juristic discussion focused on the restrictions that could be placed on an individual if that person reached legal majority but did not exhibit the requisite mental maturity necessary for acquiring legal agency.[27] These conversations also seem to indicate the possibility that a child might be able to demonstrate *rushd* before arriving at legal majority. For instance, one of the key means by which *rushd* could be established was through commercial transactions. Al-Kasani argued that a guardian could prevent a child from having access to his wealth until he demonstrated mental discretion. While other Sunni jurists disagreed on this matter, the Hanafis allowed a discerning child, with the consent of the guardian, to engage in commercial transactions so as to gain the experience necessary for acquiring mental maturity.[28] Acquiring full legal personhood was thus closely tied to an individual's ability to use their wealth sensibly and productively as a wealth-owning individual.

The last stage of childhood before an individual became an adult was prepubescence (*murahaqa*). At this point, the child entered into a liminal stage.[29] As children are not yet adults, they do not acquire all the rights and obligations of adulthood. However, certain aspects of the law become obligatory on them, and certain actions take on legal significance. Prepubescent children are thus required to perform prayer and cover their bodies in the ways required by Islamic law. However, prepubescent children could not, for example, conduct any commercial transactions without the consent of their guardians. The prepubescent male child also could not marry of his own accord or pronounce a divorce. There were, however, some significant differences between the legal schools on the legal status of prepubescent children. As will be discussed later in this chapter, Hanafi jurists differed from other Sunni legal schools on whether the penetrative act of a prepubescent male child carried legal weight.

In addition to lacking the ability to act independently, legal minors were also not held liable for things they were unable to understand. Thus, children were not required to perform certain obligatory ritual acts and were not prosecuted for criminal acts until they entered puberty. In legal discourse, intellectual abilities (*al-'aql*) and power of discernment were key to an individual's ability to acquire legal agency. While all individuals by virtue of their humanity had the capacity for this acquisition (*ahliyyat al-wujub*), the capacity to execute (*ahliyyat al-ada'*) belonged to individuals not only based on legal majority but also on their rational capacity.[30]

CHILDREN AS IMPAIRED LEGAL SUBJECTS

While Islamic law conceived of marriage as a contractual relationship between two parties, it did allow for one or both parties to be legal minors. Legal minors' marriages had to be arranged by the minors' guardian(s), however.[31] Muslim jurists differed on who could serve as a guardian in this capacity. At its most restrictive, the guardians who could marry off a minor were the father and paternal grandfather; this was the position held by the Malikis, the Shafi'is, and Hanbalis. At its most expansive, the guardians could be any agnate relative of the minor, as the Hanafis argued.[32] It is important to note, however, that the power granted to guardians in contracting the marriage of minors was not a matter of representing the minor's desire in a situation where the minor could not act. The jurists were very explicit that the guardian carried the power to compel the minor into marriage.

Marriage of and to children was a common practice in the premodern world, and particularly in the Near Eastern world, the cultural milieu that most immediately influenced the development of early Islamic law. Like Islamic law, Jewish law (halakhah) also values the consent of both parties in a marital contract. Thus, when children reached legal majority—thirteen for a male and twelve for a female—they could contract their own marriage.[33] Whereas some scholars of the Talmudic period (roughly 50–500 CE) were opposed to a father marrying off his minor daughter without her consent, this position was eventually not accepted as halakhic.[34] By the post-Talmudic period, fathers were permitted to marry off their minor daughters without their consent. Scholars understand this shift as primarily related to the concern over the licit fulfillment of sexual desire as well as the uncertainties of diasporic life for the Jewish community that made parents hesitant to delay the marriage of daughters. In practice, Jewish communities in the Near East and North Africa often married their daughters off at the age of twelve and their sons at an even older age.[35] However, halakhah did not allow a father to compel his male child into marriage. Such a marriage was considered to be illicit, akin to "prostitution" and thus prohibited.[36]

In the Roman context as well, child marriage was common, particularly in elite families. Roman law set a minimum age for marriage at twelve for girls and fourteen for boys, but violations of this law were not punished.[37] While some historians have argued that prepubescent marriage was quite common in Roman society, others have claimed that most Roman women were probably married in their late teens.[38] In the Byzantine context, marriage also required the consent of all parties, so girls could not marry before the age of thirteen—that is, the point at which they could give consent.[39] In the Sasanian context, the father was considered to be both the guardian and the owner of his children. Legal majority was set at the age of fifteen for both boys and girls; girls, however, were expected to be married while still minors. Middle Persian civil law allowed for a girl to be married at the age of nine, but consummation could not take place until she turned twelve. Some Sasanian jurists, however, argued that the marriage could be consummated at nine if the girl was physically mature.[40]

Islamic law thus developed in a world where the marriage of minor children (and girls in particular) was a common practice. As such, Islamic law reflects its location in this broader milieu in its permissiveness not only of minor marriage but also of the extensive rights of the father over his children. There were some significant shifts in this power granted to the father in Islamic law, however, as this paternal authority did not extend much beyond legal majority. Despite these differences, Islamic law authorized the father and paternal grandfather to compel a minor child (male or female) into marriage. In doing so, it established age as an impairment to legal agency.

While there are many case studies in legal discourse that would demonstrate the impaired legal agency of children, I focus on compulsion in marriage for two purposes: Firstly, because being compelled into marriage had implications that extended into the life of the child after puberty. This was in fact a subject of significant conversation between jurists, as they debated whether guardians other than the father or paternal grandfather had the right of compulsion and whether a child held the right to rescind a marriage contract at the onset of puberty. I see this discussion as a recognition on the part of jurists that granting a guardian the right to contract a minor's marriage meant they were potentially encroaching on the rights and autonomy of a (future) adult. Secondly, compulsion into minor marriage is an important case study because the implications of the compulsion are also gendered. Focusing on the compulsion to marry thus allows us to observe how the intersections of a gendered hierarchy within the adult-child hierarchical relationship produced different forms of legal impairments for male children and female children.

MINOR MARRIAGE AND THE GUARDIAN'S RIGHT OF COMPULSION

In her *Morality Tales*, a microhistory of the Ottoman court of Aintab in the sixteenth century, Leslie Peirce narrates the story of a minor girl who approached the court (with her mother), accusing her father-in-law of rape.[41] The girl had been married off by her father to another minor and had relocated to her husband's domicile. Because her husband was still a minor, the marriage had not been consummated. The girl's rape accusation, however, could not be proved, as she could not fulfill the prohibitive testimonial requirements of four male witnesses for proving coercive and illicit sexual intercourse. Peirce reports that while the case was dismissed, the judge ordered that the couple be moved into the husband's uncle's home, in a different city. Later, the girl returned to court to petition for a divorce, as she did not wish to remain with her husband.

Social and legal histories of the Ottoman period demonstrate that marriage of minors was quite common even as late as the seventeenth and eighteenth centuries.[42] In her book *In the House of Law*, Judith Tucker mentions a legal opinion issued by Khayr al-Din al-Ramli, a seventeenth-century Hanafi jurisconsult. He was presented with a question regarding a man who wished to consummate his marriage to a girl who was a legal minor. While the law permitted the marriage contract to be conducted at any age, consummation was usually delayed until the girl was able to bear penetration. In this case, the girl's father claimed that his daughter was not yet physically able to endure intercourse. Al-Ramli responded by stating that if the girl was "plump and buxom and ready for men" and the stipulated dower had been received, then consummation was the husband's right.[43] Minor brides' social position was a precarious one, and they often turned to courts to adjudicate situations in which their rights were violated. In the context of fourteenth-century Granada, young girls often came to court accusing their fathers of usurping their dowers and demanding that the judge intervene to help them reclaim their rights.[44]

Legal texts report several instances of child marriage in the Prophetic period as well as in the community of the early Muslims. The most prominent example, of course, is that of the Prophet himself. In justifying the right of guardians to marry off minor children, jurists often authorized the practice by citing the Prophet's marriage to Aisha.[45] Several other stories of the marriage practices of the early generation of Muslims are also evoked.[46] Al-Kasani mentions that the companion 'Abdullah b. 'Umar married off his minor daughter to 'Urwa b. al-Zubayr, and 'Ali b. al-Talib married off his minor daughter, Umm Kulthum, to 'Umar b. al-Khattab.[47] In his *Musannaf*, 'Abd al-Razzaq al-San'ani recounts that when 'Umar b. al-Khattab expressed his interest in marrying Umm Kulthum, 'Ali b. al-Talib responded hesitantly, stating, "she is young."[48] It seems that 'Ali's protest was read as an attempt to prevent the marriage, and when 'Umar asked for people to intervene on his behalf, 'Ali sent his daughter to 'Umar, saying that if he was still interested in marrying her after seeing her, then 'Ali would consent to the marriage.[49] The report explains that when Umm Kulthum came before 'Umar, he attempted to lift her dress to see her legs, at which she responded, "Stop! If you were not the Amir al-Mu'minin [leader of the believers], I would have slit your throat!"[50]

Given the prevalence of minor marriage in the Prophetic period, this practice was permitted by early jurists with little disagreement. Much of the early legal discussion centered instead on the question of who had the authority to compel a minor into marriage. In *al-Hujja 'ala Ahl al-Madina*, al-Shaybani discusses minor marriage within the larger chapter on marriage, focusing largely on the line of succession in guardianship and a minor's right to rescission.[51] Unlike other Sunni legal schools that only allowed the father to compel his minor child into marriage, the Hanafis granted the paternal grandfather and other legal guardians of orphaned minors this power as well.[52] Whereas the father and paternal grandfather could marry off the minor to whomever they considered suitable, setting any amount for the dower (*mahr*), non-immediate guardians were under greater scrutiny from the law. Thus, while a father could marry his daughter to an unsuitable match or agree to a dower amount that was not appropriate for a woman of her social status, other guardians were required by law to consider the fitness of the suitor and the appropriateness of the dower amount. However, with both immediate and non-immediate guardians, minors were subject to their decisions until they reached legal majority. Recounting the position of Abu Hanifa, al-Shaybani asserted that in a marriage contracted by the father or paternal grandfather, as opposed to marriages contracted by any other guardian, the child had no right of rescission (*khiyar al-bulugh*) when they reached legal majority.[53]

The expanded right of compulsion was granted to the father and paternal grandfather owing to the assumption that they had the best interests of the child in mind. Hanafi jurists often talked about the compassion and concern (*kamal al-shafaqa*) that a father or paternal grandfather holds for the child, a sentiment that would ensure they would not make decisions based simply on their own interest but on the child's.[54] The reality, of course, is far more complicated than these legal assumptions. While there are certainly court cases and legal opinions (*fatawa*) that demonstrate a father's concern for the safety or well-being of his minor daughter whom he has contracted in marriage, other cases show that fathers often usurped the dower of the minor bride.[55]

Since the Hanafis recognized a woman's legal capacity to contract her own marriage as well as that of other women, they allowed a mother to compel her minor child into marriage. In the section on the ability of a female enslaver to contract marriages for her enslaved men and women, al-Shaybani recounts an anecdote to support a woman's legal capacity to contract marriage.[56] One al-Musayyib ibn Najaba had a newborn daughter and visited his cousin Qari'a/Fari'a b. Habban to share the joyful news with her:[57]

> Fari'a, did you hear that a baby girl was born to me?
> She said: May she be blessed for you!
> He said: I offer to marry her to your son!
> She said: I accept!
> Then, after he had stayed for an hour or so, he said: I was not serious, I was just joking.
> She said: You made an offer of marriage, and I accepted.
> He said: 'Abd Allah b. Mas'ud will decide between us on this matter.
> Then 'Abd Allah entered, and they related the matter to him.
> He ['Abd Allah] said: Musayyib, did you mention marriage?
> He [al-Musayyib] said yes.
> He ['Abd Allah] then said that in marriage both seriousness and jest are the same, just as they are in divorce. He permitted Fari'a's statement: "I have accepted."[58]

As this story indicates, a mother had the legal capacity, at least in the early generation of Muslims, to not only contract marriage but to compel her child (in this case, her son) into marriage. The mother's right of compulsion, however, was not like that of the father or paternal grandfather. Her decision was subject to the same restrictions as that of other guardians, and her child could exercise the right of rescission on reaching puberty. As Carolyn Baugh notes, however, later Hanafi jurists did not discuss a mother's legal capacity to contract marriage for their minor sons. Baugh argues that this indicates such a practice was no longer common. Mothers continued to contract marriages of their minor daughters, however, as is evident in court cases from the Ottoman period.[59]

There was little challenge to the marital authority of the father over his minor children in early legal discourse. Two of the only such voices were those of Ibn Shubrama (d. 144/761), the eighth-century jurist and judge in Kufa, and the Mu'tazali jurist and judge, Abu Bakr al-Asamm (d. 220/843).[60] In *Mukhtasar Ikhtilaf al-'Ulama'*, al-Tahawi (d. 321/933) mentions briefly that Ibn Shubrumah is reported to have held that it was not permissible for a father to contract marriages of minor children.[61] A little over a century later, al-Sarakhsi mentions that both Ibn Shubrumah and Abu Bakr al-Asamm held that minor marriages were impermissible. He recounts their argument as threefold: (1) the Qur'an counsels the guardians of orphaned children to give the children control of their financial property once they reach a marriageable age.[62] If marriage were permissible before the children attained legal majority at puberty, then it would be meaningless for the verse to describe children's maturity through marriageability. (2) They argued that children are in need of guardianship only with respect to certain significant matters. In all other matters that do not carry such import; therefore, the guardian cannot make decisions on their behalf. Marriage, they argued, is an institution that allows for an individual to licitly fulfill sexual desire and the desire for progeny. Since a child is not in need of the former and cannot yet reproduce, contracting a marriage cannot be considered an issue of necessity that must be performed by the guardian while the child is in legal minority. (3) Lastly, they argued that marriage is a contract in which age plays a role in creating obligations between the couple after they reach legal majority. Given that the implications of the marriage contract would continue once the minor attained legal majority, it was not the guardian's prerogative to make a decision with such long-lasting effects.[63] Al-Sarakhsi's reasoning for Ibn Shubrumah's position had a long life. In *al-Badai' al-Sanai'*, al-Kasani provides an account that reiterates al-Sarakhsi's argument about the limits of guardianship. This time it was not Abu Bakr al-Asamm but instead 'Uthman al-Batti (d. 143/760–61) and Ibn Shubrumah who held this position.[64] According to al-Kasani, they reasoned that since granting the guardian the right to contract marriage would have effects that extended beyond minority, this would essentially be akin to granting the guardian the right to contract the marriage of a person of legal majority, which is not permissible.[65] The legal opinions of these three jurists, however, were overcome by the majority of jurists, who granted the right of compulsion over the marriage of minors to the father and paternal grandfather. These minority opinions became so unusual that future generations of jurists could hardly "make sense" of this position. Ridiculing Abu Bakr al-Asamm, al-Sarakhsi asserts: "Abu Bakr al-Asamm must have been deaf, for he seems to have not heard the hadith about the Prophet's marriage to 'Aisha when she was six and the consummation when she reached nine years of age, not to mention other narrations about the early marriage practices of the companions of the Prophet."[66]

Ibn Shubrumah's position, as reported by al-Sarakhsi and al-Kasani, expressed a concern that the guardian's decision would extend into the child's adulthood. He recognized that granting this authority to adult guardians in general, but fathers and paternal grandfathers in particular, had significant implications for a child. The right of the guardian to compel a minor into marriage meant that children had little autonomy and relatively no agency in the establishment of kinship connections that had significant impacts on their life. The right of compulsion also rendered children legally and socially voiceless individuals by depriving the children of the right to consent. Since marriage was conceived as a contract between two parties and established by bilateral agreement, juristic discussions often centered on the necessity (or lack thereof) of consent and the ability of the parties to enter into the contract. For the jurists, the right to consent and the ability to enter into a marriage contract were structured across a spectrum from full to no legal capacity and depended on several factors, the most important of which were gender, enslavement, and age. Free Muslim men were granted full legal agency to contract their own marriages; moreover, their consent was necessary for the validity of the marriage contract—they could not be compelled into marriage. Free women, children, and enslaved people, however, had varying levels of legal agency, and their consent and ability to contract their own marriage contracts depended on a series of factors. In Hanafi law, free women had the right to contract their own marriages with some restrictions based on ideas of suitability. Enslaved people, on the other hand, were given no legal capacity to enter into a marriage contract without the permission of their enslavers.[67] Similarly, children had no legal capacity to contract a marriage and could be compelled into one. Age was thus an important factor for a free individual's ability to exert agency and autonomy as a legal subject.

CONSUMMATION AND THE GENDERED IMPLICATIONS OF MINOR MARRIAGE

Hanafi jurists recognized the harm that was caused to children who had been compelled to marry, thus giving them no choice to annul the marriage after the advent of puberty, provided it had been contracted by a guardian other than the father and paternal grandfather.[68] Al-Marghinani explains that the right of rescission is granted to the child in recognition of the possible harm in being compelled into marriage—that is, the possibility of incompatibility.[69] The jurists' recognition of harm caused to an individual because of that individual's position in the social hierarchy was also coupled with their understanding that harm could also come from preventing the possibility of minor marriage. In a passage responding to the objections of Ibn Shubrama and Abu Bakr al-Asamm, al-Sarakhsi argues that finding a good match in marriage based on suitability is essential to the purpose of marriage.[70] Finding a compatible spouse is hard; and, if contracting the marriage for a girl were prohibited, the family might lose a good match.[71] Presumably, for al-Sarakhsi, this would cause harm not just to the family but also to the minor. Given the Hanafi assertion that marriage is a form of harm and humiliation for women, it would cause greater harm to a woman to be under the dominion of a man with whom she lacks compatibility; that is, she would find him unworthy of dominating over her.[72] Hanafi jurists seemed acutely aware of the different forms of harm that women and young girls could face with regard to marriage. It seemed, however, that in their conception of marriage, some or the other form of harm was inevitable for women. In such a hierarchical understanding of the world, jurists were unable to conceive of a marriage that was not premised on some form of harm to women, female children, and enslaved people.

Many aspects of minor marriage were gendered in ways that violated the autonomy of girls rather than boys. As the free boy reached legal majority, he acquired the rights of a free man, which entailed not only the financial responsibilities for the marriage but also the unilateral right of divorce (*talaq*), even if he could not exercise the right to rescission. A free woman could petition her husband to release her from the marriage contracted when she was a minor, but required his consent for the divorce to go through. The woman's request for divorce (*khul'*) also carried a financial penalty insofar as she had to return any dower given to her at marriage. In cases where the father or legal guardian usurped the dower (a possible financial incentive for contracting minor girls into marriage), this would have made leaving the marriage particularly difficult.

Gendered implications of minor marriage also appeared in the legal discussions on the consummation of the marriage. Islamic law allowed the possibility of consummation prior to puberty, given certain legal—and deeply gendered— considerations that reflect the gendered hierarchy explored in chapter 1. The sexual autonomy that is so fundamental to masculinity in Islamic law meant that juristic discussions focused exclusively on the consummation of marriage with a girl, with little attention paid to consummation of a marriage in which the husband was a minor.

In determining whether marriage with a minor girl could be consummated, the main legal considerations centered around her desirability. Hanafi jurists often employed the phrase, "one does have sex with those like her," to describe the desirable girl.[73] This phrase indicates that this legal determination was made based on cultural norms regarding the desirability of the female body. Yet there is little explicit discussion about what marks the distinction between desirability and the lack thereof.[74] In this section, I treat two legal discussions of illicit intercourse and "valid modes of privacy" to piece together the construction of a girl's desirability. We will see that her desirability to men (based on cultural norms) was coupled with her physical ability to serve as a locus of penetration.

We can begin to get a sense of what constitutes "desirability" by focusing on juristic discussions of "valid privacy," which, despite the sense of the words in English, actually centers on the circumstances necessary for consummation.[75] Obligations concerning financial maintenance and the wife's long-term sexual availability were both triggered by consummation and thus were of concern to the law. However, as sexual intercourse between the couple was seen as a private matter, legal discourse also took a newly married couple's time together in a private space as evidence of consummation of the marriage. There were, however, certain circumstances—including physical and legal impediments to intercourse—when privacy between the couple could not be taken as evidence of consummation.[76] Among the legal impediments were menstruation and lochia and a situation in which one person among the couple was fasting or preparing for pilgrimage. Physical impediments included conditions where the bride had a vaginal occlusion (*al-ratq* or *al-qarn*) or the groom was castrated (*al-majbub*), both of which would prevent vaginal penetration. Finally, one of the other physical impediments to consummation was if the bride was a minor. In his discussion of "valid privacy," al-Kasani stated that if the spouse was a minor who was not culturally understood to be the object of sexual intercourse, that is, "one does [not] have sex with those like her," then the possibility of penetration is hindered.[77] The phrase used here is ambiguous and seems to imply largely cultural norms about what is considered desirable in women. However, in making its lack an impediment to consummation, desirability is also tied to the possibility of penetration without physical harm to the girl.

The distinction between desirable and undesirable girls was crucial to determining whether marriage with a minor bride could be consummated by the adult groom. This juristic consideration was not limited to marriage alone but applied to other legal rulings that were brought into effect through sexual intercourse. For example, if an adult man were to have sex with an "undesirable" female child, he would not be prohibited from marrying the mother of the girl. Islamic law prohibits a man from marrying the mother of a woman with whom he has had sexual intercourse. In the case of sexual intercourse with an "undesirable" female child, however, such a prohibition did not go into effect.[78] Similarly, a man who performs an illicit penetrative act on a girl who is considered undesirable does not incur the *hadd* punishment. One could well argue that the man's sexual arousal and his act of penetration are an indication of his desire for the female child, and therefore that he should receive punishment. However, it is not just his sexual desire but rather legal discourse that determines "desirability" by reifying certain cultural norms. The man's action does not *legally* constitute sexual intercourse, and his experience of desire for the female child does not render her *legally* desirable. In fact, al-Sarakhsi condemns the man who has intercourse with a girl who is not yet "desirable" according to the law. Such individuals, he argues, act contrary to nature: "and the nature of sensible people does not incline towards sexual intercourse with a female child who is not desirable and is not able to endure penetration."[79]

Jurists recognized that allowing an adult man to penetrate a female child entailed the possibility of physical harm. Legal discourse thus addressed the possibility of perineal tearing (*ifda'*), tying it to a minor girl's "readiness" for sexual intercourse.[80] Al-Sarakhsi argued that if the man caused severe (third- or fourth-degree) perineal tearing, then he was required to pay an indemnity in addition to a dower.[81] In explaining the need for the dower, al-Sarakhsi clarified that sex is the insertion of one genital into another, an act that transpires even if the female child is not yet "desirable." While the man was not liable for the *hadd* punishment (i.e., flogging for fornication and stoning for adultery), owing to the deficiency in the legal definition of the sex act (the locus of penetration was not desirable as affirmed by the perineal tearing), he was still subject to discretionary punishments (*al-ta'zir*) because he acted in a manner that was not permitted to him legally.[82]

As sexual intercourse is legally defined as vaginal penetration, the only two considerations regarding consummation with a minor bride were her "desirability" and her ability to endure penetration.[83] The sexual desire of the female child herself becomes mostly inconsequential for the law. Hanafi jurists concerned themselves with ensuring that the female child was not physically harmed during sexual intercourse. However, in focusing on this alone, they centered male desire and rendered the child's own sexual desire invisible.

By contrast, the consummation of marriage with a boy receives little juristic attention. Al-Kasani's discussion of "valid privacy" uses the phrase, "one like him does not perform sex," to describe the minor groom.[84] With such a minor, if the couple were to be alone together, consummation would still not be legally established. What is interesting in the phrase used to describe the boy, however, is that *he* is the acting subject in sexual intercourse. While the undesirable girl is described as the one who would not conventionally have sex performed on her, the boy is described as one who would not normally perform the sex act.

Unlike the girl, the boy's coming into prepuberty (the liminal stage between childhood and adulthood) is marked by his physiological ability to achieve an erection. He enters into legal majority when he experiences a nocturnal emission.[85] Unlike the Shafi'is, the Hanafi legal school considers the penetrative act of a prepubescent minor boy to have legal effect. In a discussion of *zawaj al-tahlil*, a form of marriage that allows an irrevocably divorced couple to remarry, the question arises about whether sexual intercourse with a prepubescent groom would suffice to make remarriage permissible.[86] The Shafi'i position regarding this issue centers on the legal status of the minor. On the surface, the boy's penetrative act is not different from other sexual acts whereby legal rulings would go into effect: there is a valid marriage contract within which the act of penetration takes place. However, for the Shafi'is, the boy's legal minority renders this act lacking. The Hanafis respond to the Shafi' argument by shifting focus away from the legal status of the boy and turning instead to female sexual desire as the determining factor of the legal validity of such a marriage. In a discussion of this issue, al-Sarakhsi turns to a hadith according to which the Prophet stipulated that remarriage to the previous husband was contingent on the woman "tasting the honey" of the second husband, who must, in turn, also "taste of her honey."[87] The vagueness of the hadith lends itself to multiple interpretations. The word "honey" was read by some jurists as a metonymy for ejaculation, thus disqualifying sexual intercourse with a prepubescent boy. Al-Sarakhsi defended the Hanafi position by arguing that "honey" refers instead to the sexual pleasure that the woman attains through intercourse. While the prepubescent boy is not be an adult male, the woman is able to derive enjoyment from his penetrative act.[88] The concern here is not the boy's "desirability"—he remains the subject, the penetrator, who acts on the adult woman and in so doing fulfills her sexual desire. Similarly to al-Kasani, al-Sarakhsi described the prepubescent boy, using the phrase, "a boy, the like of which engages in sexual intercourse."[89] This phrase is descriptive not of the pubescent boy's desirability but instead of his own desire and ability to engage in sexual intercourse. Regardless of the acknowledgement of the female subject as desiring, such language indicates a continued conception of the penetrability of the female body and the impenetrability of the male body.[90] The consummation of this marriage with a minor groom is thus predicated on his ability to penetrate and the awakening of his sexual desire. His desirability was, at best, peripheral to the legal discussions.

It is always hard to ascertain where legal texts engage with social practices on the ground as opposed to hypothetical situations set up to work out particular legal issues. Regardless of whether the scenario reflected reality or not, if we continue with the legal scenario here, we can assume this: given the boy's legal minority, the marriage was likely contracted by his guardians and without his consent. As I mentioned in chapter 2, Hanafi jurists were only willing to consider the possibility of a man being coerced into sex if he was compelled by a public authority. Given these assumptions about men's sexual desire, it is quite possible that al-Sarakhsi and al-Kasani assumed that the boy would willfully engage in sexual intercourse. We should not, however, simply accept the juristic assertion that the boy not only willfully participated in this consummation but was the one acting on the adult woman. It is quite possible that, like the enslaved man, Hanafi jurists assumed the prepubescent boy's nascent desire meant he would not refuse the opportunity to engage in licit sexual intercourse, even if the marriage was not consensual.[91] The sexual autonomy of the prepubescent male child, therefore, was, like that of the female child, also compromised by male guardians.[92]

AGE, SEXUAL STATUS, AND THE LEGAL AGENCY OF WOMEN

Within the social hierarchies that determined the legal rights that an individual could claim, legal minority meant not only that children had no ability to consent but that their consent was rendered legally insignificant. This allowed the law to grant adult guardians, particularly the household patriarchs (father and paternal grandfather), the power to impose their will on the children of the household. However, this kind of impaired legal agency had different implications for male and female children. The power of compulsion granted to guardians might have tied male children to kinship relationships (and their concomitant financial obligations) to which they did not consent; for female children, the power of compulsion entailed the possible violation of their sexual autonomy. This gendered discrepancy also manifested itself in the social practice of minor marriage. As

Carolyn Baugh has noted, early jurists discussed the minor marriage of both male and female children; in subsequent generations of jurists, however, the conversation about minor grooms was diminished significantly.[93] By the Ottoman period, the marriage of minor boys, though still practiced, was far less prevalent than the marriage of minor girls.[94]

The gendered implications of legal agency continued even into adulthood. An examination of the juristic discussions of suitability (*kafa'*) in marriage demonstrates that for free female subjects, it was not only age but also sexual status that impacted their legal agency. Whereas the male child would, on attaining legal majority, acquire the capacity to marry without any familial intervention or interference,[95] for the female child, *kafa'a* ensured that she remained subject to the approval of the marriage by her male kin.

The Hanafi legal school required that a free woman, whether a virgin or not, must consent to the marriage. She could, however, also contract her own marriage.[96] Abu Hanifa purportedly held that a free woman could contract her own marriage, regardless of whether she was a virgin or nonvirgin (*thayyib*). He believed that guardianship over a girl was only legitimate because of her inability to make sound decisions regarding herself. Once she reached legal majority, she was no longer in need of guardianship. Puberty thus marked not only legal majority but also a threshold that carried an individual from immaturity to maturity, granting her the right above her guardians to make decisions regarding her life.[97] The Maliki, Shafi'i, and Hanbali legal schools, however, required that a female—whether adult, child, or enslaved—be married off by a guardian. They also allowed for the father and paternal grandfather to compel a woman of legal majority into marriage if she was a virgin. Only a free adult *thayyib* could not be compelled into marriage.

In contrast to the other Sunni legal schools, the Hanafis granted age greater importance than sexual status in the expansion of a free woman's legal rights. This is most evident in the difference between the legal schools with regard to the *thayyib*—that is, a prepubescent—girl who was divorced after a consummated marriage. As a nonvirgin, she gained the right of consent and could not be compelled into marriage. However, because she had yet to reach legal majority, her legal agency was still constrained by age. This confluence of age and sexual status posed a conundrum for the Sunni jurists. If they prioritized age over sexual status, then her guardians could compel the child into marriage again. If they prioritized sexual status, then her *thayyib* status would protect her from the imposition of her guardians' will over her own. The Shafi'is prioritized sexual status and argued that she could no longer be compelled into marriage by her guardians. By contrast, the Hanafis held that a nonvirgin child was still subject to the decisions of her guardians because of her age.[98]

The free woman's legal agency to contract her own marriage was not unrestricted, however. While she did not need permission, her guardians could challenge the marriage contract if they deemed her spouse unsuitable.[99] Early Hanafi jurists disagreed on the parameters within which guardians could challenge a free woman's agency over her marital decisions. Abu Hanifa held that a marriage contracted by a woman without her guardian was valid regardless of the spouse's suitability; indeed, it only came under scrutiny *if* her guardians challenged the woman's decision. In contrast, his student al-Hasan b. Ziyad al-Lu'lu'i believed that the marriage of a woman without a guardian was valid only if the groom was suitable. Abu Yusuf vacillated between different opinions—from stating that a marriage without a guardian was not valid, to declaring that the marriage was valid if the groom was suitable, to determining that the marriage was valid regardless of suitability. Al-Shaybani, however, held that a marriage without a guardian should be held in suspension until the guardians were consulted. If they validated the marriage, it would be accepted; however, if they challenged the woman's decision, the marriage was determined to be invalid unless she married a suitable spouse.[100] The Hanafi opinion eventually solidified around recognizing the free woman's legal agency to contract her own marriage. However, this right was constrained according to familial interests, since the woman's marital decision could not be separated from kinship structures and the family's stake in her marriage.[101]

Despite the free woman's ability to contract her own marriage, the presence of the guardian who contracted the marriage on her behalf was still assumed by Hanafi legal texts to be the norm in marriage.[102] Proper femininity for a young virgin woman was connected with shyness and timidity; given this, the guardian's contracting of the marriage was seen as her right rather than as a curtailment of her legal agency. Both al-Sarakhsi and al-Kasani argued that having to contract her own marriage would force her to attend a gathering of men and openly express her desire for the marriage, making her engage in a kind of public statement that she might feel shy about expressing. The matter was also one of social censure, as she might be seen as impudent and brazen for such an act.[103]

This juristic conception of virgin femininity also carried over to the way in which the free virgin woman could consent to a marriage. Following a hadith, Hanafi jurists held that a free virgin woman's consent could be intimated through her silence.[104] Virginity was not a matter of concern for male subjects, whose expression of consent had to be openly verbalized and affirmed. Masculinity was characterized by boldness and its proponents did not shy away from expressing sexual desire for women.[105] What was praised and appreciated in the young virgin woman (her shyness and timidity) was blameworthy in a young man.[106]

Silence was not only the way that consent could be established for virgin women. Hanafi jurists had extended discussions of whether other responses would constitute consent. Among the different signs considered were laughter, crying, and other reactions that could not be clearly interpreted as a form of refusal. From these extended discussions, it becomes clear that only an articulate and explicit refusal on the part of the virgin woman could be thought of as the absence of consent to marriage. Thus, while legal majority granted a free woman autonomy and the right to consent, her sexual status as a virgin compromised the expression of that consent. What jurists refused to accept as consent from free men or free nonvirgin women was readily accepted as consent from a free virgin woman and justified through arguments about virginal femininity.[107] The intersection of age, life cycle, and gender was key in the legal right of consent granted to adult-free-women.

In *Women in the Mosque*, Marion Katz argues that the life cycle was central to early Islamic legal distinctions made about women's mosque attendance. Prepubescent female children were not yet fully subject to laws regarding mobility and veiling. Younger women's mobility restrictions were largely based on their sexual maturity, reproductive capacity, and eligibility for marriage. Elderly women—namely, those considered to be postmenopausal—were seen as neither desirable for marriage nor capable of reproduction; they therefore had increased public mobility.[108] Similarly, as a free woman's sexual status shifted from virgin to *thayyib*, she acquired greater rights to speak and express her will in public. The legal marker for this shift is the consummation of marriage. For all Sunni legal schools, the free *thayyib* woman's femininity no longer needed to be constrained by silence, shyness, and timidity. In marriage, a woman must express her consent verbally and unambiguously, an act that makes clear her will and desire. For the jurists, the difference between the virgin and nonvirgin represented a movement from the natal to the marital household. This shift in status also allowed women to emerge from the constraints of their natal kinship network. Al-Sarakhsi argued that marriage exposed a woman to men and gave her greater experience with them, allowing her to gauge them well and become familiar with their wiles and deceit. It is for this reason that a free nonvirgin woman could exist independently of male protection or guardianship, even if she was no longer married.

The different femininities inhabited by the virgin and *thayyib* were also interlinked with age in a complex configuration. As I mentioned previously, for the Hanafi jurists, the minor female nonvirgin did not acquire the legal agency of an adult *thayyib* because of her youth.[109] Interestingly, the never-married free woman of advanced age could also acquire the legal status of the nonvirgin. Al-Sarakhsi stated, for example, that if a free virgin woman were to grow older and gain the life experience to hold well-reasoned positions,[110] then she could also acquire the legal status of *thayyib*. The main reason for placing the virgin under male protection, he claimed, was out of fear of social discord, something that would no longer remain a concern if a woman were to acquire a seasoned sense of discernment.

Although shifting constructions of femininity certainly allowed free women to negotiate and expand their position as legal subjects, these women never acquired the full legal agency and autonomy granted to free male subjects. We see this perhaps most clearly in the legal discussions of the custody of children in case of divorce. Hanafi law gave a mother priority in custodial care over boys until the age of seven and girls until the age of twelve, since both boys and girls were considered to be in need of their mothers' greater compassion and unique ability for their physical care. The father, on the other hand, had legal rights over the children even when they were in their mother's custody—owing not only to his compassion for them but to the soundness of his opinions.[111]

In justifying why the father was best suited for this role, al-Sarakhsi argued that only the father had the necessary vigilance and sense of jealousy (*ghirah*) for the protection of the children, especially the daughter, who would become an enticement for men perhaps even before she reached legal majority.[112] Since women were ostensibly more easily deceived and not as intelligent as men, it was in the girl's best interest to return to her father's care for marriage.[113] The mother remained deficient in relation to the patriarch of the household despite the fact that she carried multiple social advantages of freedom, adulthood, and nonvirginity. Indeed, as was indicated in a previous chapter, the mother could acquire power and dominion as an enslaver. Moreover, as a property owner, she had the legal right to manage and dispose of her wealth as she saw fit. The particular disadvantages that accrued to her, however, were in her status as a wife, mother, and daughter. Where she stood as a free woman, her legal rights largely mirrored those of free men.

CONCLUSION

Ishita Pande, in writing about the figure of the child wife in Indian historiography, argues for the importance of the feminist critique of patriarchy to thinking about the intersections of age and gender hierarchies.[114] Such an approach is critical to developing a richer account of the history of gender and sexuality. By thinking about the categories of gender and childhood together, we can see how legal personhood was varied and multifarious in Islamic law.

In this chapter, I have focused on minor marriage as an illuminating case study to think about childhood through the impaired legal agency of individuals based on age and gender. Legal minority entailed that children had little autonomy as legal subjects and that they lacked the legal capacity to act in social and commercial transactions. Legal discourse did not see children as subjects who had the rational capacity to offer consent. This understanding of childhood meant that children not only lacked the right to consent but could also be compelled into marriage by their guardians. This right of compulsion granted to guardians (particularly the father and paternal grandfather) was fairly unanimous, with few dissenting voices. Early jurists who objected to this were largely concerned with the imposition of one individual's will over another; an imposition that would extend into the latter individual's life as an adult. These voices, however, did not win out as legal discourse solidified, and as guardians of children were granted the right to compel those children into marriage.

The legal inability to consent represents a different mode of vulnerability from being compelled. Jurists could have maintained that children could not marry of their own accord because they do not have the right to consent. This is different, however, from allowing guardians to enter those children into marriage relationships (and, in the case of minor girls, even possibly permitting consummation of the marriage). In describing a nineteenth-century case in the British colonial courts in India, the historian Gauri Viswanathan tells us this about a thirteen-year-old child, Huchi, who came to court seeking to end an arranged marriage: She denied that the marriage had been consummated with her eighteen-year-old husband. In the conclusion of the case, the colonial judge held that, owing to Huchi's age, she was incapable of making decisions regarding marriage.[115] By linking age with autonomy, Viswanathan argues, the judge framed the child as an object in need of patriarchal protection who *"ought not to be heard."*[116] We see a similar construction of the child in Islamic legal discourse. While Hanafi jurists recognized the importance of an individual's agency in their marriage decisions, by granting guardians the power to compel minors into marriage, they not only failed to grant children autonomy but also used the construction of childhood as a period of rational deficiency to justify subjecting them to the will of their father and grandfather.

While the concept of legal minority functioned to impair the legal agency of both male and female children, the implications of being compelled into marriage were far greater for girls than for boys. For the boy, being compelled into such a marriage carried a financial burden to which he did not consent. However, as he came of age, he would acquire the rights and authority of a husband, including the ability to divorce his wife. The girl, however, was compelled into a marriage that compromised her sexual autonomy, that rendered her subject to the authority and dominion of the husband, and that left her with limited options for exiting an undesirable marriage. A person's consent to entering into a marriage relationship was important to the jurists. However, the right to consent was determined on the basis of one's standing in the social hierarchy. Children, like enslaved people, had no right to consent; free nonvirgin women had a greater right of refusal than did free virgin women. Yet, in this social hierarchy, it was the free adult male who held the fullest possibilities of self-determination and autonomy. As Kecia Ali puts it, "Any free male in his majority and of sound mind had free rein over his marital affairs."[117] The ability to exercise agency and autonomy over oneself, as well as over others, was thus dependent on the intersections of gender, age, and life cycle in Islamic legal discourse.

4

Gender and Legal Personhood
in Hanafi Law

In 1995, Jamal Badawi published *Gender Equity in Islam: Basic Principles*.[1] Badawi, an Egyptian-Canadian professor, preacher, and popular speaker, is professor emeritus at the Sobey School of Business at Saint Mary's University in Halifax, Nova Scotia. He is a member of the Fiqh Council of North America and a highly sought-after speaker. *Gender Equity in Islam* was one of the most widely read English-language texts on women's rights in Islam, there having been five reprints in the twenty-five years since its publication. Badawi continues to be invited to speak on this topic in Muslim communities around North America.[2] The book attempted to clarify misconceptions among Muslims and non-Muslims about spiritual, social, and economic relationships between men and women in Islam through an examination of the Qur'an and the Sunnah. Most importantly, Badawi's book insists on equity rather than equality in thinking about gender relations in Islam. He argues that "equality" is often used to refer to absolute equality—that is, equality in every aspect of comparison. He instead prefers the term "equity" because it connotes "justice and overall equality in the totality of rights and responsibilities of both genders and allows for the possibility of variations in specific items within the *overall balance and equality*."[3] That is, while there might be particular aspects of the law that differentiate based on gender, Badawi claims that in the overall balance, the genders are equal in God's eyes. How, then, might we understand the need for gender-differentiated laws? For Badawi, this can be understood if we keep in mind that the roles played by men and women in society are "*complementary and cooperative* rather than competitive."[4]

While Badawi's book is an innovative and intriguing attempt to grapple with Qur'anic passages, Prophetic traditions, and legal rulings that gender privileges, its silences are just as compelling. There is next to no mention of legal rulings regarding enslaved people or children. For example, in a discussion of property rights, Badawi is at pains to insist that Islamic law granted women property rights just as it did for men. He further argues that women were granted financial security through the dower at marriage as well as through their continued status as independent property owners even as a married woman. In this entire discussion, no mention is made of enslaved people, who had no property rights, whether men or women. Nor is any mention made of the enslaved wife, whose dower was considered the property of her enslaver.[5] One might argue that legal rulings regarding enslavement are not mentioned because this is no longer a relevant social category. Consider, however, that differences in women's legal rights based on their status (female child, virgin, mother, postmenopausal) also do not receive any attention in *Gender Equity in Islam*. Badawi does not recognize that gender was not the only element that determined an individual's legal rights in Islamic law. The only ethical conundrum that the author feels compelled to contend with is the one that exists between men (assumedly all men) and women (assumedly all women). The entire conversation about gendered rights and obligations is framed within the gender binary.

Badawi's assumption about the gender binary is not unique. Many scholars writing on gender in Islam make similar assumptions. Seyyed Hossein Nasr, a scholar of Sufism, makes a similar argument about the complementary roles of men and women. God, he contends, has created humans in pairs (i.e., men and women) and there must therefore be some level of difference between the two parties of the pair.[6] These differences are not just anatomical and biological but also psychological and spiritual.[7] Islam has legislated these differences between the genders in a complementary orientation so as to maintain social harmony and equilibrium that facilitate an individual's ability to live a virtuous life, which is the ultimate goal of human existence from an Islamic perspective. Both Badawi's and Nasr's accounts of Islamic gender relations exhibit what Ayesha Chaudhry has described as traditionalists and neotraditionalists among postcolonial Muslims upholding a patriarchal, idealized cosmology.[8] In this cosmology, God sits at the top of the hierarchy, with the rest of creation ontologically ranked: humans sit above all other creation, with men ranked above women.

While I agree with Chaudhry that premodern Muslim discourse functioned within a patriarchal idealized cosmology, the hierarchical ranking was not established through gender alone. As I have demonstrated throughout this book, multiple social identities determined the position of different collectives within the social hierarchy. In the social order imagined by both Badawi and Nasr, there is no mention of freedom, enslavement, or age as social factors that mediate whether an individual can occupy those reified constructions of masculinity and femininity.

This understanding of men and women as singular categories is a post-Enlightenment idea. As Omaima Abou-Bakr has argued, in the early twentieth century, modernist Muslims adopted an idea of strict gender roles based on biological essentialism.[9] This essentialist understanding of gender came to be seen as a fundamental aspect of the Islamic worldview that was then read back into the premodern Islamic tradition. The gender binary looms large in modern Muslim discourse, where power relations are largely thought through two figures alone: men and women. While they may play different roles throughout their lives as husband/wife, mother/father, and so on, their essential and static gendered natures mean that they must occupy the same roles despite their changing relations or life situations. This is not a social world in which you will find enslaved men who cannot inhabit the activity and power that characterizes masculinity. In such a narrative, how might we account for the female enslaver who was given control over an enslaved man? Despite her femininity, as an enslaver she held dominance, power, and authority over a man who, owing to his enslavement, was configured as passive.

In this chapter, I provide an overview of legal personhood in early Hanafi jurists' discourse. I argue that legal personhood was constructed at the intersection of different social identities rather than gender alone. This book has focused on three key social identities (gender, age, and enslavement) in order to demonstrate the intersectional and relational nature of legal personhood. These three identities, however, were not the only ones considered by Hanafi jurists, who also took lineage, religion, class, and so on into account. Along with gender, these categories formed a complex matrix that saw many different iterations throughout legal discourse. While Hanafi jurists often articulated hegemonic masculinity as active and emphasized femininity as passive, this idealized gender construction spoke to a hierarchical understanding of social existence rather than an essential and unchanging nature of gender. Although Hanafi jurists held anatomical sex to be male, female, and intersex, the juristic imagination was populated by a multitude of gendered legal persons.

Thus, in this chapter, I make three central arguments about legal personhood in early Hanafi law:

1. Gender was not the only social identity Hanafi jurists considered in constructing legal personhood. Rather, a variety of social identities functioned alongside gender in the construction of legal personhood, key among them being age and freedom/enslavement. Gender, then, is not *the* category by which Hanafi jurists ordered society. In this complex legal terrain, the most advantaged position in the social hierarchy could not be determined through a singular social identity or in abstraction. While we might say that the fullest legal personhood was granted to the free adult Muslim man, class, lineage, and race were also given legal consideration.

2. Legal personhood was, therefore, constructed intersectionally—that is, at the intersection of different social identities. These different social identities cannot be parsed from each other and do not simply compound their effects but instead must be understood as interconnected entities.

3.   In addition to its intersectional nature, legal personhood in early Hanafi law was also shifting and relational. While Islamic legal discourse fixed a set of social identities through which it recognized legal persons, these social identities were not fixed to an individual. The legal personhood of an individual shifted with changes in their life circumstances, as well as in their relations to other legal persons. Whether a child grew to adulthood or an enslaved person was emancipated, the change in an individual's life cycle or life circumstances shifted their legal personhood. Similarly, as a free, adult woman became a wife, or an enslaved man became a husband, or an enslaved woman became an *umm walad* (mother of a child), their shifting relations to other legal persons also caused a change in their legal personhood. This relational aspect of legal personhood gives us a sense that legal persons were not imagined by Hanafi jurists as autonomous and independent subjects. Legal persons were mutually constituted and interdependent.

This chapter sketches out these arguments by bringing in supporting evidence from the case studies analyzed throughout the earlier chapters of the book. In bringing these arguments together, I aim to demonstrate that the category of "gender" did not exist as a group that had shared interests or a shared social position that led to a shared legal personhood as men or women. In questioning gender as a useful category for studying power relations in Islamic law, I seek to show how the focus on gender as a category of analysis in the study of Islamic law presents legal discourse as a "straightened tradition."[10] As Fatima Seedat has argued, such a reading of the legal tradition excludes any discussion of the fluidity and ambiguity that premodern Islamic law was able to accommodate. Reading against this tendency allows us to trace the process by which modern Muslims have imposed their own gendered assumptions onto premodern Islamic law.

THEORIZING LEGAL PERSONHOOD IN HANAFI LAW

In a discussion of the marriage of enslaved women, the tenth-century Hanafi jurist Abu Bakr al-Razi al-Jassas said:

> And God named enslaved women "maidens" [*fatayat*] through the verse: "from among the believing maidens."[11] *Al-fatah* is the word used for a young girl [*al-shabbah*] whereas the free elderly woman is not called *fatah*. The young and elderly enslaved woman, however, are both called *fatah*. It is said that she [the elderly enslaved woman] is called a young girl, even if she is elderly, because an enslaved woman is not dignified with the respect and reverence given to an elderly [free] woman.[12]

Al-Jassas's statement here distinguishes between several different types of women. A young woman, usually also assumed to be a virgin and never previously married, is distinguished from the older woman. The difference between them is not simply one of age but also of social status. As women age, they receive more respect and reverence and are allowed greater mobility. Jurists were far more comfortable with the public presence of matronly women who were considered to be undesirable to men.[13]

Age was not the only marker of social status here, however. As al-Jassas goes on to explain, an enslaved woman could never attain the status of a matron. Regardless of her age, she had to remain in a subordinate position in the social hierarchy. While age and life cycle were means by which women could climb the social hierarchy, this was true for free women alone.[14] Here, enslaved women (both young and old) sat at the bottom of the hierarchy.

How might we understand the nature of legal personhood based on al-Jassas's statement? How did age, enslavement, and gender come together in determining the legal capacities and legal agency of these different categories of women?

Intersectional Personhood

In her 1989 article, "Demarginalizing the Intersection of Race and Sex: A Black Feminist Critique of Antidiscrimination Doctrine, Feminist Theory, and Antiracist Politics," the Black feminist and critical race theorist Kimberlé Crenshaw provides a framework for analyzing the specificities of the intersectional subordination and discrimination faced by Black women.[15] The existing dominant feminist and antiracist frameworks, she argues, have taken a single-axis approach, looking at sexism and racism as distinct categories of oppression. Such a framework builds an understanding of discrimination from the experiences of those who are most privileged within the singular category—that is, those who would not face discrimination *but for* their racial or sexual identities. Our understanding of sexism, Crenshaw argued, is based on the experiences of White women, those who are privileged by their Whiteness and would not face discrimination if it were not for their sexual identity. Similarly, the understanding of racism is based on the experiences of Black men who are discriminated against on account of to their racial, but not their sexual, identity.

To clarify her critique, Crenshaw discusses several cases in which the court's framing and interpretation of the experiences of Black women failed to understand the intersectional discrimination they faced. In a lawsuit filed by five Black women against General Motors (GM), the court rejected the plaintiff's claim, arguing that Black women workers were not considered a special class in antidiscrimination laws. The court reasoned further that since GM had hired women (albeit White women) prior to 1964, there was no sex-based discrimination in the seniority system. For Crenshaw, this and other cases demonstrate that single-issue analysis, one that can only see sex and race discrimination as distinct categories, fails to recognize that Black women sit at the intersection of these different categories and thus experience discrimination in a number of ways.[16] Crenshaw gives us the metaphor of traffic at a four-way intersection: if an accident takes place at the intersection, it will likely be because of cars traveling from many different directions. Similarly, we can understand that an incident of discrimination can be the result of multiple intersecting factors rather than one alone.

While Crenshaw developed intersectionality as a critical lens for thinking about the discrimination faced by Black women, the concept has become a useful lens for analyzing the intersecting nature of social structural arrangements of power more generally.[17] In my reading of Islamic law, it opens up rich analytical possibilities for thinking about the power relations that were at play in the construction of legal personhood. Furthermore, examining the intersections of different categories that were at play gives us a more holistic understanding of the systems of power authorized by the law.

If we return to al-Jassas and read his statement through Crenshaw's metaphor, we can see how gender, age, and enslavement intersect to create at least *three* distinct categories of women: free young women, free elderly women, and enslaved young and old women. As Marion Katz has argued, "gender and its attendant legal implications are deeply modulated by reference to other markers of personal and social status."[18] Seedat has gone even further and argued that the category "woman" does not exist in the law. By comparatively examining women's legal capacity in modern and premodern legal discourses, she demonstrates that women's legal subjectivity in premodern legal discourse was situational and varied, insisting that jurists did not have a concept of "woman."[19] There is no assumption about shared interests or social position that would construct them as a single preexisting group prior to the categories of enslavement and age. Subsequently, legal rulings were also not based on "woman" as an abstract category. Furthermore, gender, age, and enslavement also cannot individually account for the complicated nature of the social hierarchy that was authorized and naturalized by Hanafi legal discourse. Early jurists did not assume that gendered legal rulings would apply consistently to all women. Instead, they developed different legal rulings for different categories of women based on their age and social statuses. Free women, enslaved women, free female children, enslaved female children, married women, and unmarried women were all different categories of women subject to different legal rulings.

If the different categories of women did not share legal personhood as "women," how did the law differentiate between them based on the particular configurations of their social identities? How did those identities interact with one another and how did they impact individuals' legal capacities? In order to better understand the nature of intersectional legal personhood, I propose that we read the relation between these social identities as co-formative rather than additive. An additive framework, Patricia Hill Collins argues, addresses the absence of certain identities in analysis by calling attention to their absence.[20] In such an approach, we might consider enriching our analysis by adding those other identities to those already under examination. The additive approach, however, runs the risk of centering one identity as a "master category of analysis" while making others peripheral.[21]

That is, it would largely center gender as the primary social identity and then bring in age and enslavement as additional but less important identities that shape legal personhood. Such an approach would assume that free women, enslaved women, adult women, and female children are all members of the single category "woman." Conversely, free men, enslaved men, male children, and so on are also all assumed to share in their masculinity as a privileged status. Age and enslavement would be brought in to demonstrate the particularities of gendered vulnerabilities without decentering the assumption that the fundamental vehicle of their oppression is gender. Analyzing the relation of these identities through coformation, by contrast, "posits holistic analysis of a seamless process of mutual construction."[22] Such an approach recognizes that these social identities are interdependent and mutually constructed and thus cannot be disassembled and analyzed as separate entities. Regarding legal personhood in early Hanafi law, a coformative approach allows us to recognized that the intersection of different social identities create an entirely *new self*—that is, a new legal person who must be analyzed and understood as a separate entity. To analyze each intersection of social identities as creating a unique legal person would require us to abandon the idea that gender had a greater role in shaping the legal personhood of an individual than the other identities.

To make clearer my point about the creation of a new personhood, let us consider the figure of the enslaved woman whom we have encountered throughout this book. In an additive approach, her legal personhood would be understood as the convergence of three distinct sets of legal incapacities: gender, age, and enslavement. If she were an enslaved girl, then her legal minority would be assumed to add another layer of legal incapacity and vulnerability. An additive approach would see "woman" as a singular legal person and assume that "femininity" imparts a shared set of legal impediments to all individuals sexed female. Gender would stand as a social identity with a defined set of legal incapacities that exist prior to the legal person. Enslavement would be understood similarly. As we saw in chapter 1, the jurists articulated a conception of masculinity and femininity that was understood through the active/passive binary. Masculinity was characterized by activity, read as self-determination, bodily and sexual autonomy, and the ability to hold authority over others. The foil of masculinity was femininity, defined by its passivity, a lack of self-determination, inhibited bodily and sexual autonomy, and subordination to authority. In reading the enslaved woman's legal personhood through an additive approach, we might assume that both the enslaved woman and the free woman shared in femininity. The difference between the two would be understood as the further disadvantage of enslavement that affected the enslaved woman.

An additive framework for analyzing legal personhood, however, would be unable to account for the many discrepancies in the legal personhood of free and enslaved women and the different ways that gender and enslavement impact them. The enslaved woman certainly shares with the free woman certain constraints to legal agency. For example, both these legal categories of women would be unable to lead men in ritual prayer owing to their gendering as women. They would also be unable to hold political authority. There are, however, also significant differences in their legal capacities for which an additive framework would be unable to account. The free woman had to consent to her marriage, had to the right to demand a dower from her husband, and had the right of property ownership, which opened up for her the possibility of acquiring both wealth and authority over other individuals, particularly as an enslaver. The enslaved woman as a sexual commodity was seen as the property of her enslaver, who could compel her into marriage or make sexual use of her if the enslaver were male. The enslaved woman also had no right over her dower in marriage, as this was seen as the rightful property of the enslaver. Finally, jurists put fewer restrictions on the enslaved woman's mobility, arguing that such restrictions would infringe on the enslaver's right to her labor. In permitting the male gaze on and the physical touching of the enslaved woman's body, Hanafi jurists differentiated between enslaved and free women through the mechanisms of bodily autonomy and integrity. While we might see restrictions on mobility and required modesty as legal and social disadvantages today, in the early modern Islamic social world, increased restrictions marked an elevated social status. Thus, we can see how gender did not entail a fixed legal personhood.

Enslavement also did not extend a shared legal personhood to all enslaved people. We see this particularly in the legal discussions of marriage and sexual use of enslaved people. While Hanafi law permitted the enslaver to compel both the enslaved man and woman into marriage, the enslaved husband held the right of divorce and thus held greater avenues for exiting a marriage into which he was compelled. This difference in enslaved-gendered agency was even more pronounced in the other Sunni legal schools, which did not allow for an enslaved man to be compelled into marriage. Similarly, the sexual accessibility granted to the enslaver by Hanafi law differed according to the gender of the enslaved person. Enslaved women could be used sexually by their enslavers. The enslaved man, on the other hand, was not conceptualized by the law as a sexual commodity in the same manner and thus retained a greater level of sexual autonomy. In the figure of the enslaved man we can see that maleness also did not entail a fixed set of legal advantages that extended to all individuals sexed male. The enslaved adult man was not characterized by any of the qualities of self-determination, autonomy, or authority that characterized maleness. While the enslaved man could not be made use of sexually, he could be compelled into marriage, his sexual and reproductive capacities considered the property of the enslaver.

To understand the vulnerabilities of the enslaved woman, then, we must think of the intersection of gender, age, and enslavement particular to her as a space where a new legal person was created. Yet the enslaved adult woman's legal personhood cannot be understood simply as the compounded vulnerabilities of femininity plus enslavement. I propose instead that these different social identities come together in a seamless manner, mutually constructing one another. The nexus of these different identities then acquires particular meaning in each articulation of legal personhood. They cannot be disaggregated from one another in order to see how each individual part works outside its interaction with the whole.[23]

The coformative approach thus helps us understand the discrepancies in legal agency between the free and enslaved men and women that I have discussed in the first three chapters of the book. Each social identity does not carry meaning that exists prior to its intersection with others; instead, the synthesis of a unique configuration of social identities creates a particular set of legal in/capacities. If we look at things this way, we can see that the intersection of freedom, adulthood, and femininity rendered the free adult woman subordinate as a sexual subject but also granted her a degree of sexual autonomy and ownership over herself as a sexual commodity. In the enslaved man, we note that he was protected from sexual use but deprived of self-determination. Looking at matters through the issue of sexual autonomy, we see there is little distance between the free woman and enslaved man, despite the fact that one is sexed female and the other male. We cannot uncouple gender from enslavement, freedom, or age. Neither gender nor enslavement as social identities were characterized by a particular legal capacity or a particular set of constraints on legal agency that were shared across all people sexed female or designated as enslaved. Rather, each of these social identities are interdependent and take on particular meaning as they conform.

Legal Personhood as Relational

The feminist legal theorist Ngaire Naffine argues that modern legal systems, particularly those emerging from liberal traditions, present themselves as impartial, treating all individuals equally regardless of their particularities. This legal person is thought of as sovereign, self-legislating, and autonomous, unencumbered by relations of dependence, deriving their rights and duties from personally chosen contracts. This frees them from customs and traditions, as well as familial relations and community obligations that are not of their choosing. Naffine describes this imagined legal person in modern systems as one who, "only ventured into society when he chose to do so, when he needed something done; when other people served a clear instrumental purpose. Otherwise, he was largely content with his own company and could manage well on his own."[24] This idea of the modern legal person is also understood to be universal, an abstraction that can be applied equally to all individuals, allowing for the assigning of liberal rights and duties to all individuals irrespective of human variation and difference.[25] Feminist legal theorists have, of course, critiqued this triumphalist account, arguing that women have never been allowed to be sovereign, autonomous, and rational subjects. What is important about their critique is the argument that this abstracted notion of the modern legal person is in fact based on a conception of the social order in which only particular types of individuals can flourish. The legal person imagined by the law, Naffine contends, is a middle-class man who is able-bodied, autonomous, rational, educated, monied, competitive, and self-interested.[26]

Legal historians contrast this modern legal person with the socially stratified medieval worlds in which a person's legal status depended on custom, law, and one's location within the family. Legal personhood in early Hanafi law was neither abstracted nor did it center the individual outside of their social, familial, and communal ties. In this legal world, personhood was constructed as both relational and situational, by which I mean that: (a) legal personhood was established based on the social relations in question and was mutually constructed/constituted by those relations; and (b) legal personhood was dependent on the situation. As situations and relations changed, so did the individual's legal personhood. Legal personhood was therefore not fixed but dynamic and constantly shifting. Autonomy existed instead on a spectrum, with individuals acquiring greater or lesser autonomy depending on the relation in question. No individual, however, was seen as fully autonomous in the sense of being free from their social relations or from the obligation to exist in relations except through their own personal choice. Social relations were understood to be a fundamental aspect of human existence. The relational and situational nature of legal personhood meant that the authority and privilege, or, conversely, the legal incapacities and subordination, ascribed to an individual were not seen as essential to them but instead pertained to that particular combination of relation and situation alone.

To understand the relational and situational nature of legal personhood, let us consider the power to compel children into marriage granted to the father and paternal grandfather that I discussed in chapter 2. While the other Sunni legal schools held that only the father and paternal grandfather had this authority of compulsion, the Hanafis allowed other individuals who were designated as legal guardians of a minor child to also compel the child into marriage. The difference between the marriage contracted by the father and paternal grandfather versus other legal guardians was manifested in the child's ability to exit the marriage after reaching puberty (legal majority). The marriage contracted by agnate relatives could be broken at that point, whereas the marriage contracted by the father and paternal grandfather was not subject to rescission. Instead, the minor child would have to wait until legal majority to exercise their right of divorce (in the case of the minor groom) or petition for divorce (in the case of the minor bride). The extensive powers given to the father and paternal grandfather were embedded in the juristic assumption that these two individuals were of sound opinion and had the child's best interests in mind. Despite the fact that historical records show that mothers routinely arranged the marriages of their minor daughters (less so minor sons), Hanafi jurists presumed that the mother could not be relied on to make sound judgements in establishing new kinship connections.

If we look at the juristic determination to grant the paternal grandfather greater authority than the mother in contracting these marriages, it would seem that it is the shared masculinity of the father and paternal grandfather that confers this authority; however, it was in fact an effect of the father/child relationship. Certainly, if we look at the juristic determination to grant the paternal grandfather greater authority than the mother in contracting these marriages, we might think that it is the shared maleness between the father and paternal grandfather that confers this authority. I point to the relational aspect of this authority, however, not to downplay the gendered nature of authority but to urge us to consider that this authority is neither essential to individuals who were sexed male by the law nor is it acquired by all men. If we analyze this authority as one granted to legal persons sexed male, then there are several discrepancies that we would have to account for. The most obvious of these is the fact that the minor son, also sexed male, was subject to compulsion in marriage. While the marriage of minor sons was perhaps less prevalent as a social practice than the marriage of minor daughters,[27] as a matter of legal principle the son's masculinity did not grant him the self-determination that would protect him from compulsion. Similarly, the law did not recognize all fathers as patriarchs. Islamic law generally did not recognize kinship ties of enslaved people, who could not exercise authority over others in society and thus could not serve as guardians. As an enslaved person, the enslaved father was neither a patriarch of a family nor did he carry the legal capacity to exercise authority over his children. The law recognized only free fathers as carrying the power and authority of a patriarch.

The free father was believed to have a vested interest in the family and in controlling the kinship relations that were established through marriage. As the father of a son, the paternal grandfather also held the position of patriarch and was equally invested in these decisions. The paternalistic ethic of care that governed the father-child relationship assumed that paternal instincts would prevent the father/paternal grandfather from making decisions that would harm the child's welfare. Furthermore, since the child was also a member of the family, marital decisions that were of benefit to the family were also seen to be in the best interest of the child. It is for this this reason that Hanafi jurists did not allow rescission for the marital decisions of the father/paternal grandfather. The father and paternal grandfather's authority and power were thus only acquired when a particular relation was established—that is, once a man was married and became a father (and subsequently when his own children had children). Yet this paternal authority did not extend to all the relations that that individual was embedded in. That is, while the father/paternal grandfather also held authority as a husband and enslaver, those relations differed significantly. While we might be tempted to see children, wives, and enslaved people all as dependents, each one of these represented a unique form of dependency that constructed unique legal personhoods, creating different modes of legal agency and power relations. The legal personhood of father and minor child, then, are relational and mutually constructed.

Thus, a change from a father/minor child relation to a father/adult child relation shifted the legal agency ascribed to both.

As a free child approached puberty, they entered into a liminal stage defined by Hanafi jurists as prepubescence (*murahaqa*). In this stage, the free child began to acquire rights to self-determination. Thus, they could contract their own marriage, with the marriage being suspended until the guardian consented to it.[28] Hanafi jurists also allowed a free prepubescent child to begin engaging in commercial transactions under the supervision of their guardian, so that they might acquire experience in handling financial matters.[29] In this liminal stage, the free child was being socialized to enter the world of free adults.

As free children came into legal majority, they attained greater legal agency. In a world where the ability to procreate and fatherhood were markers of increased social status, puberty (marked by nocturnal emission) marked a free boy's entrance into society as a potential patriarch. As al-Kasani argued, nocturnal emission marks the boy's ability to procreate, which allows him to move from the domain of children into that of fathers.[30] For a free girl as well, puberty marked the possibility of marriage and procreation. If she was already married, consummation and moving into the marital home marked a shift in her legal personhood, granting her greater social status and autonomy. We can see this most clearly in the juristic discussions of virginity and matronhood, where the former is marked by shyness, timidity, and naiveté, and the latter by emotional and intellectual maturity and a greater say over her own matters.[31] The free adult, then, whether male or female, could no longer be compelled into marriage. Unlike the other Sunni legal schools, Hanafi jurists did not permit a free woman to be married off by her father without her consent. She could also contract her own marriage, although it could be challenged by her male kin if they held that her choice of spouse was not suitable.

The relational nature of legal personhood meant that individuals occupied multiple legal personhoods at the same time, depending on the different relations in which they were embedded. For an individual to occupy multiple legal personhoods meant that the intersectional configuration of social identities that shaped an individual's legal personhood was not an essential aspect of an individual but instead dynamic and constantly shifting. Theories of identity as performative might be helpful in grasping legal personhood's relational nature in early Hanafi law. In writing about the complex creation of identity between personal and social structures, Stuart Hall writes that "identity is not a set of fixed attributes, the unchanging essence of the inner self, but a constantly shifting process of *positioning* . . . In fact, identity is always a never-completed *process* of becoming—a process of shifting *identifications*, rather than a singular, complete, finished state of being."[32] Hall's account points to the fact that identity is not simply a personal matter but is shaped by social structures (in our case, a legal system). These social structures not only create identities as a vehicle through which power relations are exercised but they also provide the conditions that result in the internalization of these identities by the individual. This allows us to see that identity is not a reflection of an individual's essence but instead something that is acquired and differentially performed based on shifting contexts and social relations.[33]

To demonstrate this point, let us turn to the free adult wife. As a free woman, she had ownership over her own sexual commodity and the self-determination that allowed her to contract her own marriage. Neither the free minor girl nor the enslaved adult woman had the legal capacity to exercise such self-determination. Both the free minor girl and the enslaved adult woman could be compelled into marriage and neither could exit that marriage until emancipation (in the case of the enslaved wife) or legal majority (in the case of the minor bride). The free adult woman, on the other hand, acquired self-determination both through freedom and legal majority. Once she married, however, the free woman acquired the legal personhood of a wife, a relation that required her to take on a subordinate position to her husband and to relinquish her sexual autonomy and mobility.[34] Her legal agency was only constrained in relation to her husband, however. She still maintained ownership rights and, as such, could be an enslaver, thereby exercising power and authority over the people she enslaved. As Kecia Ali has mentioned, femininity certainly constrained the position of the female enslaver.[35] She could not, for example, make sexual use of enslaved men. Where early sources mention instances of female enslavers interpreting scripture to claim such a right, there was no hesitance in intervening in a manner that violated her ownership rights.[36]

Femininity was certainly at play in the position given to the female enslaver; we should be hesitant, however, to read this femininity as a shared identity across the female enslaver and enslaved women. The role that femininity played in the construction of the legal status of an individual was "relational and not absolute."[37] Like male enslavers, female enslavers were oriented toward slavery as a relation of property that gave them both an economic advantage as well as a means for acquiring authority and social status.[38] She still held ownership over the sexual capacities of both enslaved men and women. She could compel them into marriage, and any children born to the women she enslaved were her property. Additionally, as Islamic law did not have coverture laws, a wife retained her property rights—her husband could not exercise control over the people she enslaved. As both a wife and a female enslaver, then, a free adult woman could occupy different legal personhoods at the same time. This allowed her to have different positions in the power structure that shaped the social order, moving between a position of power and submission depending on the relation and situation.[39]

The relational and situational nature of legal personhood can also help us understand the socially stratified mode of enslavement in the Islamicate context.

While enslaved people were deprived of property ownership and were subject to the authority of their enslavers, those enslaved by the elites in society could acquire a significant amount of wealth and also take up positions of public authority. Even those enslaved in urban households, particularly enslaved men, might find themselves managing a business or engaging in commercial transactions on behalf of the enslaver. Hanafi jurists often discuss what manner of financial and commercial transactions were permissible for an enslaved person and which ones would be invalid or suspended until the enslaver's consent could be ascertained.[40] In early Hanafi law, no single legal capacity or legal agency defined an individual at all times or in all relations.

The social world imagined by early Hanafi jurists was made up of a complex web of social hierarchies, and an individual's place in this world was not defined by one identity but a multitude of intersecting identities. While I have focused in this book on gender, age, and enslavement, social identities relating to religion (Muslim versus non-Muslim), class, and race were also at play in determining an individual's social location and their resultant legal status.[41] Understanding the intersectional nature of legal personhood allows us to recognize, as Marion Katz has argued, that neither "man" nor "woman" were legal persons. Gender was only one of the social identities that shaped a person's legal status. What mattered was not that you were a man or woman but instead what *kind* of man or woman you were, free/enslaved, adult/child, and so on. I have also argued that each one of these intersecting social identities created an entirely new legal person. While we might be tempted to privilege the shared gender of the free adult man and the enslaved adult man, they were in fact very different legal persons. The enslaved adult man, despite the fact that he is sexed male, did not occupy any of the characteristics of activity, self-determination, and autonomy that marked maleness. Centering the gender of these two figures would prevent us from recognizing the social marginalization and vulnerabilities of the different categories of people sexed male who did not enjoy the power and privilege occupied by the free adult male. Even among free men, status and lineage (*nasab*) made a significant difference in one's social status.

In addition to its intersectional nature, legal personhood in early Hanafi law was also relationally constructed; that is, individuals acquired a particular legal personhood as they came into a particular social relation. This is evident in Hanafi jurists' imagination of the individual as one who was embedded in a network of complex social relations. Recognizing the relational nature of legal personhood helps us understand how the enslaved man could be compelled into marriage by his enslaver and yet, once oriented as an enslaved adult husband, retain a husband's right of divorce (albeit in two pronouncements rather than three). As I have argued, individuals inhabited multiple legal personhoods at the same time, allowing them to exercise different legal capacities depending on the particular relation in question.

WHAT CAN WE SAY ABOUT GENDER IN EARLY HANAFI LAW?

If, as I claimed above, neither "man" nor "woman" was a legal person in early Hanafi law, what can we say about the role of gender in constructing legal personhood in legal discourse? In this section, I will demonstrate that while early Hanafi jurists certainly articulated idealized gender norms, these conceptions of gender along the active/passive binary were used to justify legal precedents and were not a functioning logic of the law. As we saw in chapter 1, there are many instances where early Hanafi jurists both articulated and reasoned with assumptions about hegemonic masculinity as active, agential, and dominant, and emphasized femininity as passive and subordinate. However, we have also observed that individuals sexed male and female by the law could occupy both activity and passivity. Masculinity and femininity in early Hanafi law were, therefore, not the primary logic through which jurists determined individuals' legal agency and capacity.

Gender was in fact not the primary mode of ordering social relations in early Hanafi law. In fact, the intersectional and relational nature of legal personhood helps us see that early Hanafi law did not function on the assumption of a gender binary. While jurists assumed that humans exist as two sexes and also recognized intersexuality and gender ambiguity, this did not translate into two gendered subjects.[42] Hanafi legal discourse was populated by a multitude of gendered subjects. Following decolonial feminist scholars who have argued that gender as a mode of organizing relations is a colonial construct, I propose that these observations about legal personhood force us to question whether gender as a salient category of analysis can seamlessly map on to premodern Islamic law. In the sections that follow, I begin with an overview of the critiques made by gender historians and decolonial feminists about gender as a category of analysis. Employing this scholarship as my theoretical framework, I then argue for decentering gender in the study of Islamic law in order to fully grasp the complex web of relations through which power was exercised in legal discourse.

Is Gender a Useful Category of Analysis?

There are perhaps few pieces that have had such tremendous impact as Joan Wallach Scott's 1986 article, "Gender: A Useful Category of Historical Analysis."[43] Published around the time that women's history as a field felt the urgency for a clearly articulated theory about the concept of gender, Scott's article was an attempt to offer a more "usable theoretical formulation" of gender as a category of analysis.[44] She critiqued feminist historians who tended to analyze gender as a distinct category from other relations of oppression and also for their reliance on physical difference as fixed and universal across historical time. Such an assumption, Scott argued, gave gender an ahistorical character and saw history as "epiphenomenal, providing endless variations on the unchanging theme of a fixed gender inequality."[45] In Scott's assessment, the field needed a concept of gender that could stand as a category of analysis while at the same time rejecting that the gender binary must necessarily exist in an antagonistic relationship that is both inevitable and universal.[46] She thus proposed a theory of gender as a category of analysis that rested on two propositions: "gender is a constitutive element of social relationships based on perceived differences between the sexes, and gender is a primary way of signifying relationships of power."[47] These two propositions draw on four interrelated elements: (1) culturally available symbols that can have multiple and at times contradictory meanings; (2) normative concepts that give meanings (and constrain meaning) of these symbols; (3) politics and social organizations that structure these normative concepts; and (4) gender's subjective identity.[48]

Scott's article and analytical framework have had a tremendous impact in the fields of gender history, as well as women's studies more broadly, with the *American Historical Review* describing it as "canonical."[49] The idea of gender as an category of analysis, however, has not been without its own set of critiques. Gender historian Jeanne Boydston argues that while Scott criticizes the assumed fixity and universality of the oppositional gender relation, her theory still falls back on the gender binary. Scott's proposal that "gender is a constitutive element of social relationships based on perceived differences between the sexes" only deflects the assumption about sexual difference away from a naturalized body to a perceived body.[50] While the four interrelated elements make room for changing and culturally distinct gender systems, it only offers variations to—but does not challenge—the assumed universality of the gender binary.[51] Boydston argues that Scott's second proposition not only further entrenches the gender binary but also renders difficult the possibility of imagining "distinctions between males and females that are not invidious to one or the other group, and thus correspondingly difficult to conceive of distinctions that do not register as primary axes for allocating authority."[52] Boydston cautions that gender as a named category now functions as a set of universalized premises, flattening complex historical processes and meanings;[53] she further contends that certain feminist historical accounts disregard the very local character of the concept, instead universalizing the *local* that is particular to the United States and Western Europe.

Many non-Western historians have argued that not all societies were organized around gender. Boydston offers as an example historical and anthropological studies that abandon questions focused on sexual opposition (such as gendered division of labor or authority) and center instead on the character and status of the sexual binary. Historians of Native American cultures have pointed out, for example, that while the male/female binary was present historically in Native American cultures, it always intersected with other binaries such as war/peace, young/old, or plant/animal.[54] These studies challenge our assumption that the male/female binary was the primary signifier of differential relations of power. Anthropological accounts of the two-spirit people in Native American cultures also push us to complicate the gender binary by recognizing that for many cultures, the sexed body was not tied to gender.[55] Fundamentally, then, these studies give us different possibilities for defining gender, "from social relations in which a male/female binary may be present and important, but not necessarily primary, to a system of gender in which multiple other axes of identity frequently modify and sometimes entirely overwhelm the binary and in which the binary, even when present, cannot be reduced to oppositionally sexed bodies."[56]

Decolonial feminists have posed similar questions about both the universality of gender and the gender binary as a colonial construct. The decolonial African feminist Oyèrónkẹ Oyèwùmí has argued that feminist scholars treat both gender as a category as well as women's oppression as a universal, assuming also that gender is the explanatory factor to understand the subordination of a group called "women."[57] The modern Western system, Oyèwùmí argues, is animated by a bio-logic, a mode of thinking that centers biology as the rationale according to which society is ordered and hierarchies are established. In this bio-logic, an individual's biology determines their social status. The social category of woman is then based on a particular body type, understood always in relation to the other body type that is categorized as man. In the Western system, "physical bodies are *always* social bodies . . . [;] there is really no distinction between sex and gender."[58] Oyèwùmí contrasts this system to precolonial Yorùbán society, which, she argues, did not know the category "woman" until its introduction by colonizers. That is, "women" were not assumed to be a preexisting group based on a shared body type that coalesced around shared interests or social status.[59] In the traditional Yorùbán family, kinship roles and categories were not based on gender, and thus power centers within the family were also diffused and not gender-specific. This is in sharp contrast to the modern Western construct of the nuclear family in which gender is both the fundamental organizing principle as well as the primary source of gendered oppression. As the nuclear family is defined by two parents and children, this leaves little room for other kinship relations and essentially traps a woman in the role of "wife," which she carries with her throughout her other social locations.[60] In Yorùbán society, it was instead seniority that formed the fundamental organizing principle.

> Yorùbá society was hierarchically organized, from slaves to rulers. The ranking of individuals depended first and foremost on seniority, which was usually defined by relative age. Another fundamental difference between Yorùbá and Western social categories involves the highly situational nature of Yorùbá social identity. In Yorùbá society before the sustained infusion of Western categories, social position of people shifted constantly in relation to those with whom they were interacting; consequently, social identity was relational and was not essentialized.[61]

Through her analysis of precolonial Yorùbán society, Oyèwùmí presents a critique of the universality of gender assumed by feminist scholars. She argues that if we take the idea of gender as a social construction seriously, then we must also understand the possibility that it does not look the same in every place and every time period. If we can recognize this, Oyèwùmí argues, then we must also accept the possibility that there were both social and temporal contexts in which gender did not exist.[62] Gender, then, cannot always serve as the appropriate map for studying non-Western and precolonial societies.[63]

The challenges of using gender as a category of analysis in the study of the Islamicate context more specifically has been raised by the feminist historian and gender theorist Afsaneh Najmabadi. Describing her study of gender's role in the formation of Iranian modernity, she explains that her initial reading of gender in Qajar Iran (1785–1925) could not contend with some of the materials she was finding in her research. It was only after she interrogated the narrative implicit in the category of gender that she realized the binary construction of man/woman was a production of early modern Iran and not the cultural logic of gender for premodern Iran. This realization led her to question whether gender as a category of analysis can travel transhistorically without an investigation into our assumptions about the category. In speaking of Qajar Iran, Najmabadi argues that this was not a world of a gender binary where men and women were considered complimentary, but instead one where men and women were thought to be of the same essence, with woman being an imperfect man. In such a world, all genders were defined in relation to adult manhood.[64] She proposes instead that we study both masculinity and femininity as concepts that are "internally fractured."[65] In a binary understanding of gender, both masculinity and femininity are fixed and stable, leading us to read any fractures of masculinity as effeminization. An understanding of these concepts as internally fractured would then lead us to abandon the idea that these categories are coherent or exist in a simplistic binary relation.

These critiques about the Eurocentricity of the category of gender provide a useful theoretical framework for thinking about gender and premodern Islamic law. Analyzing legal personhood through a decolonial framework allows us to recognize that gender was neither a binary in legal discourse nor the primary identity for ordering social relations. It is only through a decentering of the category of gender in our analysis that we can grasp the nature of the complex social hierarchy through which individuals acquired legal personhood in Islamic law. Decentering gender also allows us to recognize and name the power relations that existed among different categories of people, a recognition that challenges the universal assumption of women's subordination.

Beyond Gender in the Study of Islam

The issue of women's legal personhood in Islamic law is a vexed question, and women's disadvantaged status in Islamic law has been a contested subject of critique since the nineteenth century. Focusing primarily on positive law, Orientalist scholars painted a picture of Islamic law as rigidly patriarchal and unchanging.[66] Gender scholars have intervened in this debate to complicate such narratives of gender oppression by looking at legal practice. Social historians like Judith Tucker and Leslie Peirce have argued that while legal courts upheld social hierarchies, they often intervened to mediate the excesses of male power and authority. Rather than presenting women as disadvantaged objects of the law, these scholars demonstrate that women often expected the judge to intervene on their behalf and employed gendered strategies to influence court decisions in their favor.[67] Scholars have also turned to substantive law as a means to further explore and investigate women's legal status and its implications in how jurists developed legal rulings and institutions. Scholars like Leila Ahmed have argued that women's autonomy and legal status was greatly reduced through Islamic law.[68] Alternatively, Muslim women scholars like Azizah al-Hibri and Asifa Quraishi-Landes approached Islamic law with an eye to extract gender egalitarian legal rulings while critiquing the patriarchal elements as the resultant effect of juristic bias.[69]

The early 2000s saw a shift away from a reclamation of legal rulings and broad historical narratives to a more focused study of the historical context within which Islamic law and its resulting gendered assumptions developed. These scholars also explored legal personhood, offering different arguments about the status of women as legal subjects. In interrogating the legal construction of marriage and divorce, Kecia Ali has noted the relation between gender and slavery as categories of legal disability in Islamic law.[70] These two categories, she argues, were not independent of one another; both enslaved people and women "were overlapping categories of legally inferior persons constructed against one another and in relation to one another—sometimes identified, sometimes distinguished."[71] However, despite their interconnectedness, only gender is a permanent and enduring impairment to legal subjecthood in Islamic law, while conditions such as enslavement and legal insanity are temporary in nature. Gender, she argues, is the most crucial distinction between individuals in Islamic law.[72]

Judith Tucker sees woman as a legal subject as a matter of "doctrinal tension."[73] She notes that while women's agency in economic matters was largely similar to that of men, in other aspects of the law women were more constrained. Thus, while women were recognized by law as independent property owners, their agency, insofar as they were members of families, was hampered by the interests of the family and the patriarchal society to which they belonged. This is particularly evident in women's mediated right to contract a marriage and their lack of the unilateral right to divorce.[74] Depending on the legal arena, Tucker claims, the tension between women's full and impaired legal agency was resolved by allowing the interests of a patriarchal society to supersede: "Woman as family member (whose marriage will affect her male relatives and therefore must be vetted by them) and Woman as part of patriarchal society (whose behavior must be policed and restricted, thereby limiting her knowledge of and activity in the public sphere) trump the Woman as equal legal subject."[75]

Echoing Tucker's observation about women's inconsistent legal agency, Marion Katz argues that while gender has a central role in juristic thought, "gender and its attendant legal implications are deeply modulated by reference to other markers of personal and social status."[76] That is, in early Islamic legal discourse, "woman" was not a homogeneous category but was mediated by other factors such as age and enslavement.[77] Similarly, Baber Johansen recognizes the multiple social hierarchies that functioned in shaping an individual's agency in social exchange (i.e., the exchange of noncommodities for goods or monetary values, typified by marriage).[78] Speaking of the distinction between commercial (commodity for commodity) and social exchange, Johansen argues that while commercial exchange was accessible to all who were deemed to have rational capacity, an individual's admission into social exchange depended on their (or their family's) location within five social hierarchies: religion, gender, kinship, generation, and freedom as opposed to enslavement.[79] Johansen also remarks that for the Hanafis, "the importance of the gender criterion outweighs that of the difference between free male persons and male slaves."[80]

These observations raise critical questions about how Islamic law determined individuals' legal capacity and, subsequently, their legal agency. All four of the scholars I mentioned above recognize the important role played by gender in legal discourse while also noting a tension in its centrality in relation to other social identities. My interrogation of gendered legal personhood in early Hanafi law builds on this scholarly conversation, exploring the ambiguities and tensions outlined above, although I argue that neither man nor woman exists as legal persons in early Hanafi law. The question about women's legal status is one that scholars bring to Islamic law rather than one that animates Islamic law from within. As Fatima Seedat has claimed, "while femaleness functions as a distinguishing characteristic of the legal subject, what characterizes femaleness is inconsistent; it is a mobile concept that seldom coincides in all respects with any singular physical woman."[81] The impulse to search for women's legal status or speak of men's legal advantage and privilege assumes the naturalness and universality of the gender binary. It also assumes that gender was the primary category that structured power relations. This assumption, however, fails to grasp the complex web of intersecting social identities that constructed an individual's agency and personhood in legal discourse. As I have demonstrated in this book, the intersectional nature of legal personhood in early Hanafi law meant that an individual inhabited not just gender but a multitude of other identities that ordered social relations. The different social identities were also mutually constitutive, meaning that neither man nor woman (nor free nor enslaved) carried meaning as a legal category outside their particular formulation in a particular legal person. The relational nature of legal personhood also alerts us to the fact that power was exercised not through individual identities but through their relations to other legal persons. As scholars who are motivated by a desire to critique the exercise of power in securing inequitable relations, we must question the universality of the gender binary and the utility of gender as a category of analysis in order for us to grasp the power relations that were authorized by Islamic law.

I recognize that posing this argument about decentering gender as a category of analysis can come across as an attempt to question and thus further marginalize gender in the study of the Islamic intellectual tradition. It is not unusual for those of us who do this work to get asked whether the concern with patriarchy and gender inequality is a distinctly modern one that we are projecting back onto the premodern Islamicate context. In order to distinguish myself from those whose critique is intended to marginalize such questions that scholars bring to the Islamic tradition, I wish to clarify the intent and import of my questioning of gender as a useful analytical category in the study of premodern Islamic law. Over the past several decades, there has been a tremendous amount of work done on the study of gender in the premodern Islamicate context. This body of scholarship is sophisticated in its historical approach and analytical engagement. However, as I have argued, studying Islamic law with gender as an analytical category has given us a rich and complex picture of the law's intricacies. Over the past several decades, a tremendous amount of sophisticated work has been done on gender in the premodern Islamicate context more generally, without which my argument here would not be possible. This body of scholarship has posed critical questions about the relationship between positive law and legal practice, the dialectical relationship between legal practitioners and those subjected to the law, as well as the gendered assumptions that have shaped legal hermeneutics.[82] My purpose in decentering gender, then, is not to argue that questions pertaining to gender are irrelevant to premodern Islamic law. Rather, my intent in posing this argument is twofold: (1) to consider that the concept of gender changes as it moves transhistorically and (2) to reckon with the Eurocentricity of gender as a category, both in its assumed meaning as well as the methodological purposes to which it is deployed. If we are to take decolonial feminist scholars' proposals seriously, then we must critically interrogate our assumptions regarding the category of gender and its content, abandoning both any assumption of its coherence as well as the role it might play in social relations.[83]

Recent scholarship on gender and Islam more broadly has noted the inadequacy of thinking about the premodern Islamicate context through a simple male/female binary, moving toward both the study of masculinities as well as a complication of the gender binary. Analyzing genres like exegesis, Islamic ethics, Islamic medicine, and Sufism, scholars have argued that only a particular category of elite men was able to occupy the privileged status of men. In her analysis of Islamic ethical discourse, Zahra Ayubi has noted that ethicists constructed the ethical male subject not just in relation to men but also in relation to men who were seen as unrefined owing to their lower-class status.[84] Sara Abdel-Latif has also noted the binary of elite man/women and other non-elite actors in Sufi hagiographies. She argues that focusing on the ways in which gender, skin color, class, age, non-Arab origin, and so on intersect allows us to see how elite free men secured their position in the social hierarchy by effeminizing these other figures and rendering them inferior.[85] In their study of hadith and exegesis, Ash Geissinger proposes that in the hierarchical understanding of gender, it was the sane, able-bodied, freeborn Muslim adult man who inhabited the masculinity that acquired power and authority. In the context of Islamic law, "all other categories of persons are positions at various removes below."[86] Elsewhere, Geissinger argues that gender in Islamic discourses was "internally fractured" by social distinctions such as enslavement, lineage, religion, age, and so on.[87] Serena Tolino's piece on the gender binary in premodern Islamicate societies also supports complicating the gender binary. Through an analysis of Arabic lexicography, Islamic medicine, and Islamic law, Tolino demonstrates that Islamicate societies and discourses were based on a binary of man and "other," where "man" was adult, urban, male, sane, and able to procreate, and all "others" were understood in opposition to this privileged subject:

> we should imagine the two genders as a continuum on a scale of perfection, on top of which we find the free adult Muslim man. It is difficult to make a proper classification on who we find below him on the ladder, but certainly we do not only find women, as a proper gender binary would suppose.[88]

The turn toward a more complex analysis of the gender binary, as well as the study of varied constructions of masculinities is a critical development in the study of Islam and gender. The scholarship of Geissinger, Ayubi, Tolino, and Abdel-Latif complicates a universalizing assumption of women as an oppressed category in the premodern Islamicate context. They present us instead with a complex picture of the different ways in which the social hierarchy was modeled. The most advantageous individuals were not all males but a particular category of elite men whose power and privilege was maintained through the subordination and instrumentalization of a multitude of other collectives in society, including nonelite men, enslaved people, children, non-Muslims, non-Arabs, and so on. Despite these complications, the hierarchy is still governed by the logic of a binary—that is, one group of subjects (elite men, instead of all men) are ranked above the oppressed (i.e., all others, instead of just women). Such a logic "translates any fractures of masculinity into effeminization,"[89] which is most evident in the lumping together of all subordinated people into one category, in binary opposition to elite men. While this binary is helpful for understanding how certain masculinities are constructed in relation to hegemonic masculinity, it is not helpful for mapping the power relations that existed between individuals in the subordinated category. It is also unable to account for the fact that power and authority were not fixed in one particular gender or identity but were instead fluid and shifting in nature.

That is, one individual—who might be disadvantaged in relation to elite men— could occupy a position of power and authority in relation to another individual who was also in a subordinated class. Thus, rather than studying gender in Islamicate societies and discourses, I propose that we study the *relations* through which power was exercised. This approach would allow us to move away from questions about what counted as man, effeminizing other men as a way of recognizing their social subordination, or placing free women and enslaved women in a shared category of the oppressed. I suggest instead that we think about the relations between the different legal persons and how power functioned in each relation to establish a particular place in the social hierarchy for different legal persons.

To make my point clearer, let us consider the free/enslaved relations that I have discussed in this book. We would not be able to understand the power and authority granted to enslavers over the enslaved if we approached this relation through gender as a category of analysis. An enslaver acquired their status not through their gender but through their status as both an adult and a free person. Given this, both men and women were able exercise power and authority through the enslaver/enslaved relation, provided they were propertied people. To approach Islamic law through gender as an analytical category, with the assumption of the universality of gender oppression as well as the legal incapacity of women, would not allow us to see the ways in which free adult women exercised power over enslaved men. In fact, it was through their relation to the people they enslaved that they acquired a certain power and authority in society. As the historian Stephanie Jones-Rogers has argued regarding White women enslavers in the American South, they were invested in the institution of slavery because their status as enslavers gave them an ability to negotiate their position in society through their economic power.[90] We see this in the Islamicate context as well. Free adult women were not only enslavers but also participated in the slave trade, particularly in the training and selling of both *qiyan* (enslaved singing girls) and *jawari* (enslaved women). Free adult women also utilized enslaved women as sexual commodities to negotiate their own power and agency, as when the free wife might gift her husband an enslaved woman (particularly one that he might desire) as a way of pleasing him.[91]

An analytical approach that centers gender would also prevent us from understanding the ways in which the free woman's legal agency and capacity were negotiated through the vulnerabilities of the enslaved woman. The form of sexual autonomy granted to the free adult woman, as well as her status as property owner, or her social and legal status as free wife and mother, can only be understood as a privilege through the presence of enslaved women, who was not granted similar rights or legal status. To place free and enslaved women in a singular category of gender oppression would fail to recognize the power differentials between them and the ways in which free adult women might actively participate in the vulnerabilities and oppression of enslaved women. We see this, for example, in the juristic discussion of the impermissibility of bringing in an enslaved woman as a co-wife if a man is married to a free woman. Jurists prohibited such a marriage because it would harm the free woman to bring in a co-wife of lower status. The opposite scenario—in which a man took on a free woman as a wife when he was already married to an enslaved woman—was met with no such objection.[92] We can see this hierarchy between free and enslaved women maintained even in social practices of physical violence. In writing about the enslaved courtesan (*jariya*) in early Abbasid Baghdad, Pernilla Myrne has noted that while the practice of whipping an enslaved person might have been common practice, this was not acceptable with regard to the free wife.[93] She tells, for example, that when Inan, a well-known and celebrated enslaved courtesan, was flogged by her enslaver, she cried out that she was a free woman and thus should not be treated in this way.[94] While both the free wife and the enslaved woman endured violence, the form it took reflected their different positions in the social hierarchy. They both occupied status as dependents of the husband and enslaver, but their dependency did not impart a shared position in the social hierarchy. Similarly to Oyèwùmí's observation regarding Yorùbán society as a context where biology did not determine social roles, we see in early Hanafi law as well a distinction between the legally assigned sex and assigned gender roles. While different subjects might all be legally assigned female, this did not mean that they shared a single legal personhood.

In the world of early Hanafi law, gender was not the primary mode for ordering social relations and the complex terrain of legal personhood cannot be mapped by relying on gender. As Seedat has argued, a woman's legal agency and ability to act were determined through the social facts that jurists attached to the female-sexed body.[95] Where jurists articulated conceptions of hegemonic masculinity as active and emphasized femininity as passive, we must be attuned not just to that articulation but also what function it served for the jurists. As we have seen in case studies throughout this book, this idealized gender norm was constantly disrupted or displaced where it intersected with other social identities. They appeared when they were useful in justifying legal precedence and were set aside where they contravened the complex social hierarchy imagined by the jurists.

In making this point, I am not arguing that jurists did not hold this idealized conception of gender. The gendered narrative would serve no use in justifying legal precedence if it did not reflect commonly held beliefs around gender. Certainly, the appearance of this idea in other genres of the Islamic intellectual tradition also points to its pervasiveness. What I am saying, however, is that this idealized conception of gender was not an overarching logic of the law or the guiding framework for determining individuals' legal agency. Hanafi jurists routinely constructed a varied and complex understanding of gender at its intersection with other social identities. To read these gendered norms as a reflection of a gendered ontology is perhaps more reflective of a modern conception of gender than one that reflects the worldview of the jurists. Sa'diyya Shaikh has made a similar argument with regard to gender in the work of the Sufi luminary Muhyi al-Din ibn al-'Arabi, critiquing contemporary scholars who have read Ibn al-'Arabi's use of masculine and feminine states to correspond with biological gender. Shaikh argues instead for reading this as a "gendered symbolic," i.e. a gendered language for describing the nature of reality.[96] Contrary to other scholars who have read the masculine/feminine binary as an authorization of traditional gender roles and naturalized it as an Islamic metaphysics,[97] Shaikh argues that reading it in a different way opens up the possibility for using this binary as a means to subvert patriarchal gender constructs.

I find Shaikh's reading of Ibn al-'Arabi useful as a framework for thinking about the juristic articulation of masculinity and femininity. As I mentioned in chapter 1, while jurists both articulated and at times reasoned with the stated principle of masculinity as active and femininity as passive or receptive, there are other aspects of the law where Hanafi jurists argued for the active role of women as a means for defending an earlier ruling by the Hanafi legal school. Gender, then, carried no fixed meaning in legal discourse but acquired meaning as it intersected with other social identities and through particular social relations. Gender was neither primary in ordering social relations, nor was it a binary. Rather than being informed by a gender binary that dictated gender roles, early Hanafi legal discourse was populated by sexed subjects who took on many gendered roles leading to a multiplicity of gendered subjects. Gender was both unstable, multiple, and varied.

CONCLUSION

Throughout the different chapters of this book, I have asked what role gender plays in the construction of legal personhood in early Hanafi law and, specifically, how gender interacted with other social identities. As we saw in chapter 1, Hanafi jurist often articulated gendered norms around masculinity and femininity that point toward an essentialized understanding of gender. If we step away from these idealized gender norms and engage in a close reading of case studies, however, we can see that the juristic process for determining the legal rights and obligations of individuals was informed by a lot more than just the individual's gender. Gender instead intersected with several other social identities in the construction of legal personhood. Not only did gender intersect with other social identities, but gender was also more complex than a simple binary. Idealized conceptions of masculinity and femininity did not always map on to legally assigned sex; that is, a male-identified legal subject did not necessarily inhabit the characteristic features of masculinity. The intersectional nature of legal personhood does not mean gender was not relevant as a juristic category. As we have seen through the many case studies discussed in this book, an individual's assumed gender continued to play a significant role in determining their legal agency. Gender had certain ramifications that at times cut across the other social identities, cutting off some possibilities entirely for people who shared anatomical sex. We saw this, for example, in the legal determination of the impermissibility of all women holding positions of political authority. Despite these particular legal rulings, throughout the different aspects of the law, gender did not operate as a distinct category but instead intersected with a number of other identities that collectively shaped the legal personhood of an individual and determined their place in the social hierarchy.

Studies of gender in Islamic law often conceptualize it as a separate category of analysis, distinct from enslavement, age, religion, class, and so on. Studies of slavery or religious difference in Islamic history have similarly considered their analytical categories as distinct from gender. The effect of such an approach is the flattening of otherwise complex hierarchies in the social world imagined by jurists. An intersectional approach reveals instead a far more complicated social hierarchy, one in which social identities were not an essential aspect of an individual but shifted depending on their social positions and relations. As their relations and positions shifted, so did their legal personhood. The free man who was both Muslim and propertied held perhaps the most privileged position in this social hierarchy. However, even the power and privilege of this free propertied man were complicated by particularities of race and lineage. Whether one was of Arab descent or from the tribes related to the Prophet, all impacted an individual's agency in different aspects of the law.

The intersectional and relational nature of legal personhood is a productive theoretical space for Muslim feminists. The hierarchical social order imagined and authorized by Islamic law meant that jurists insisted on the inherent differences between humans rather than their similarities. This insistence on difference led to a construction of legal personhood that recognized the complexity of human subjectivity by constructing a multiplicity of legal persons based on their positions and situations in society. This mutability of legal personhood viewed the human as always in the process of becoming rather than a fixed and static self. The relational aspect of legal personhood also recognized that humans grow and change through their relations to others. The focus on the relational self rather than the autonomous self of liberal thought not only recognizes that ethics is situational but also centers mutuality in ethics. Such a conception of the self is powerful in its recognition that our humanity is realized only through our relations to others. While the notion of legal personhood in early Hanafi law was certainly hierarchical, its intersectional and relational nature provides space for Muslim feminists to move beyond a mode of critique to think with and through the Islamic legal tradition.

NOTES

INTRODUCTION

1. Akhtar Hamid Khan, *Komila se Aurangi Tak: Mushahidat-o-Tasurat* (Karachi: City Press Book Shop, 1998).

2. Khan, 49.

3. As Barbara Metcalf has argued, this text became a classic gift for Muslim brides in the early twentieth century in India. See Barbara Metcalf, *Perfecting Women: Maulana Ashraf ʿAli Thanawi's* Bihishti Zewar (Berkeley: University of California Press, 1992), 3.

4. Khan, *Komila se Aurangi Tak*, 72.

5. Khan, 72.

6. Khan, 73. See also Metcalf, *Perfecting Women*, 25, for her translation of these terms.

7. For more on this approach, see Fatima Seedat, "Gender and the Study of Islamic Law: From Polemics to Feminist Ethics," in *The Routledge Handbook of Islam and Gender*, ed. Justine Howe (London: Routledge, 2020), 86.

8. Leila Ahmed, *Women and Gender in Islam: Historical Roots of a Modern Debate* (New Haven, CT: Yale University Press, 1993).

9. Ahmed, 88.

10. Scholars like Azizah al-Hibri and Asifa Quraishi-Landes approached Islamic law with an eye to extracting gender-egalitarian legal rulings while critiquing patriarchal elements as the results of the jurists' bias. See Saadia Yacoob, "Islamic Law and Gender," in *The Oxford Handbook of Islamic Law*, ed. Anver M. Emon and Rumee Ahmed (Oxford: Oxford University Press, 2018), 6–10.

11. Kecia Ali, *Marriage and Slavery in Early Islam* (Cambridge, MA: Harvard University Press, 2010).

12. Ali, 8.

13. Ali, 47.

14. Baber Johansen, "The Valorization of the Human Body in Muslim Sunni Law," in *Law and Society in Islam*, ed. Devin J. Stewart, Baber Johansen, and Amy Singer (Princeton, NJ: Markus Wiener Publishers, 1996), 71.

15. Johansen, 72.

16. Johansen, 82.

17. Judith Tucker, *Women, Family, and Gender in Islamic Law* (Cambridge: Cambridge University Press, 2008), 149.

18. Of the four Sunni legal schools, only the Hanafis allow a free adult virgin woman to contract her own marriage. However, the father retains the right to contest the marriage if he finds the match objectionable on grounds of incompatibility. See Mona Siddiqui, "Law and Desire or Social Control: An Insight into the Hanafi Concept of *Kafa'a* with Reference to the Fatawa 'Alamgiri," in *Feminism and Islam: Legal and Literary Perspectives*, ed. Mai Yamani (New York: New York University Press, 1996), 49–68.

19. Tucker, *Women, Family, and Gender*, 173.

20. Marion Katz, "Gender and Law," in *Encyclopedia of Islam*, ed. Kate Fleet et al., 3rd ed., https://referenceworks.brillonline.com/entries/encyclopaedia-of-islam-3/gender-and-law -COM_27397?s.num=0&s.f.s2_parent=s.f.book.encyclopaedia-of-islam-3&s.q=gender +and+law.

21. Katz, 3.

22. For a recent study of gender and legal subjecthood, see Fatima Seedat, "Sex and the Legal Subject: Women and Legal Capacity in Hanafi Law" (PhD diss., McGill University, 2014).

23. [Ash] Geissinger, *Gender and Muslim Constructions of Exegetical Authority: A Rereading of the Classical Genre of Qur'ān Commentary* (Leiden: Brill, 2015), 33.

24. Seedat, "Sex and the Legal Subject," 262.

25. For a more detailed account of this scholarly work, see chapter 4.

26. Everett Rowson, "The Categorization of Gender and Sexual Irregularity in Medieval Arabic Vice Lists," in *Body Guards: The Cultural Politics of Gender Ambiguity*, ed. Julia Epstein and Kristina Straub (New York: Routledge, 1991), 50–79.

27. See also Everett Rowson, "Homoerotic Liaisons among the Mamluk Elite in Late Medieval Egypt and Syria," in *Islamicate Sexualities: Translations across Temporal Geographies of Desire*, ed. Kathryn Babayan and Afsaneh Najmabadi (Cambridge, MA: Harvard University Press, 2008), 204–38 and "The Traffic in Boys: Slavery and Homoerotic Liaisons in Elite 'Abbāsid Society," *Middle Eastern Literatures* 11 (2008): 193–204. For studies of the eunuch in Islamic history, see Shaun Marmon, *Eunuchs and Sacred Boundaries in Islamic Society* (New York: Oxford University Press, 1995); David Ayalon, *Eunuchs, Caliphs, and Sultans: A Study in Power Relationships* (Jerusalem: Magnes Press, 1999); and, more recently, Jane Hathaway, *The Chief Eunuch of the Ottoman Harem: From African Slave to Power-Broker* (Cambridge: Cambridge University Press, 2020).

28. See Dror Ze'evi, *Producing Desire: Changing Sexual Discourse in the Ottoman Middle East, 1500–1900* (Berkeley: University of California Press, 2006).

29. See Ze'evi, *Producing Desire* and Khaled el-Rouayheb, *Before Homosexuality in the Arab-Islamic World, 1500–1800* (Chicago: University of Chicago Press, 2009).

30. See Indira Gesink, "Intersex Bodies in Premodern Islamic Discourse: Complicating the Binary," *Journal of Middle East Women's Studies* 14 (2018): 152–73 and "Intersex in

Islamic Medicine, Law, and Activism," in *The Routledge Handbook of Islam and Gender*, ed. Justine Howe (London: Routledge, 2020), 116–29. Gesink's work on intersexuality challenges the argument made by Paula Sanders in her article, "Gendering the Ungendered Body: Hermaphrodites in Medieval Islamic Law," in *Women in Middle Eastern History: Shifting Boundaries in Sex and Gender*, ed. Nikki R. Keddi and Beth Baron (New Haven, CT: Yale University Press, 1992), 74–95, which argued that Islamic law relied so heavily on the gender binary that it could not tolerate intersex individuals. When confronted with sexual ambiguity, Sanders argued, Muslim jurists assigned a male or female gender to the individual in order to protect the social order and maintain male dominance.

31. Geissinger, *Gender and Muslim Constructions*, 16.

32. Manuela Marin, "Women, Gender and Sexuality," in *The New Cambridge History of Islam*, vol. 4, *Islamic Cultures and Societies to the End of the Eighteenth Century*, ed. Robert Irwin (Cambridge: Cambridge University Press, 2010), 356.

33. Marion Katz, *Women in the Mosque: A History of Legal Thought and Social Practice* (New York: Columbia University Press, 2014) and "Textual Study of Gender," in *Islamic Studies in the Twenty-First Century: Transformations and Continuities*, ed. Leon Buskens and Annemarie van Sandwjik (Amsterdam: Amsterdam University Press, 2016), 87–107.

34. Tucker, *Women, Family, and Gender*. For a more detailed account of the arguments made by Katz, Marin, and Tucker, see chapter 4.

35. Charlotte Fonrobert makes a similar argument regarding gender in early Halakhic discourse. See Charlotte Fonrobert, "The Semiotics of the Sexed Body in Early Halakhic Discourse," in *How Should Rabbinic Literature Be Read in the Modern World*, ed. Matthew A. Kraus (Piscataway, NJ: Gorgias Press, 2006), 79–104.

36. For a detailed account of feminist scholarship on the idea of sex and gender and the relation between the two, see Gayle Rubin, "The Traffic in Women: Notes on the 'Political Economy' of Sex," in *Toward an Anthropology of Women*, ed. Rayna R. Reiter (New York: Monthly Review Press, 1975), 157–210; Judith Butler, *Gender Trouble: Feminism and the Subversion of Identity* (1989; repr. New York: Routledge, 2007); and Anne Fausto-Sterling, *Sex/Gender: Biology in a Social World* (London: Routledge, 2012).

37. For a similar argument regarding Jewish law, see Max Strassfeld, *Trans Talmud: Androgynes and Eunuchs in Rabbinic Literature* (Berkeley: University of California Press, 2022).

38. For an account of how *jins* has come to mean "sex" and "sexual desire" in contemporary Persian, see Afsaneh Najmabadi, "Genus of Sex or the Sexing of *Jins*," *International Journal of Middle East Studies* 45 (2013): 211–31.

39. Butler, *Gender Trouble*, 3.

40. Ngaire Naffine, *Law and the Sexes: Explorations in Feminist Jurisprudence* (Sydney: Allen & Unwin, 1990), 54.

41. Yacoob, "Islamic Law and Gender," 9.

42. See Mahdi Zahraa, "Legal Personality in Islamic Law," *Arab Law Quarterly* 10 (1995): 193–206 and "The Legal Capacity of Women in Islamic Law," *Arab Law Quarterly* 11 (1996): 245–63.

43. Seedat, "Sex and the Legal Subject."

44. Al-Zuhayli further divides the legal capacity of acquisition into complete (*kamilah*) or diminished (*naqisah*). He ascribes diminished legal capacity only to the fetus, which

carries certain rights, such as the right to inherit or to receive a bequest once it is born alive. The potentiality of the fetus's life is also protected by the law, as an individual who causes a miscarriage is obligated to pay blood money. See Wahbah al-Zuhayli, *Usul al-fiqh al-Islami* (Damascus: Dar al-Fikr, 2008), 1:166. For more on legal capacity see Salah Muhammad Abu al-Hajj, *Sabil al-Wusul ila 'ilm al-usul* (Amman: Dar al-Faruq, 2007), 243–44.

45. Qur'an 7:172–73. This verse is also mentioned by al-Sarakhsi in his discussion of *ahliyya* in his legal theoretical text: see Muhammad b. Ahmad al-Sarakhsi, *Usul al-Sarakhsi* (Beirut: Dar al-Ma'rifah, 1997), 2:332. Wadad Kadi argues that while Muslim scholars disagreed about whether these verses describe an event that actually took place or was instead metaphorical, they all agreed that these verses indicate that God has extracted a promise from humanity to worship him alone and live life in obedience to him. See Wadad Kadi, "The Primordial Covenant and Human History in the Qur'ān," *Proceedings of the American Philosophical Society* 147, no. 4 (2003): 333–34.

46. al-Zuhayli, *Usul al-Fiqh al-Islami*, vol. 1.

47. Rudolph Peters describes this as the age when a minor is able to understand the basic aspects of financial matters. See Rudolph Peters, "Capacity (*Ahliyya*)," in *The Oxford International Encyclopedia of Legal History*, ed. Stanley N. Katz (Oxford: Oxford University Press, 2009).

48. Al-Zuhayli, *Usul al-Fiqh al-Islami*, 1:167–68. Peters argues that the full capacity to act in financial matters is not acquired at puberty but when the individual demonstrates sound judgement (*rushd*) ("Ahliyya").

49. Al-Zuhayli, *Usul al-Fiqh al-Islami*, 1:169–92.

50. Seedat, "Sex and the Legal Subject."

51. Marion Katz, "The Neglected History of Furū' and the Premodern/Modern Binary," *Islamic Law Blog*, January 14, 2021, https://islamiclaw.blog/author/marion-katz/.

52. Kimberlé Crenshaw, "Demarginalizing the Intersection of Race and Sex: A Black Feminist Critique of Antidiscrimination Doctrine, Feminist Theory, and Antiracist Politics," *University of Chicago Legal Forum* 140, no. 1 (1989): 314–43; Patricia Hill Collins and Sirma Bilge, *Intersectionality*, 2nd ed (Cambridge: Polity Press, 2021); Jennifer Nash, "Intersectionality and Its Discontents," *American Quarterly* 69 (2017): 117–29.

53. Crenshaw, "Demarginalizing the Intersection," 314.

54. For a thorough summary of these critiques, see Nash, "Intersectionality and Its Discontents."

55. Collins and Bilge, *Intersectionality*, 2.

56. Collins and Bilge argue that intersectionality has six core constructs: relationality, power, social inequality, social context, complexity, and social justice (*Intersectionality*, 31–36).

57. Collins and Bilge, 23.

58. Patricia Hill Collins, *Intersectionality as critical social theory*, (Durham: Duke University Press, 2019), 28.

59. Michel Foucault, *The History of Sexuality*, vol. 1, *The Will of Knowledge* (New York: Pantheon Books, 1978). See also see David Halperin, "Forgetting Foucault," in *How to Do the History of Homosexuality* (Chicago: University of Chicago Press, 2002); Daniel Boyarin, "Are There any Jews in 'The History of Sexuality'?" *Journal of the History of Sexuality* 5, no. 3 (1995): 333–55; Ruth Mazo Karras, "Prostitution and the Question of Sexual Identity in Medieval Europe," *Journal of Women's History* 11, no. 2 (1999): 159–77.

60. Stuart Hall, *Familiar Stranger: A Life Between Two Islands*, ed. Bill Schwarz (Durham, NC: Duke University Press, 2017), 16.

61. Collins and Bilge, *Intersectionality*, 167.

62. Ali, *Marriage and Slavery*.

63. Carolyn Baugh, *Minor Marriage in Early Islamic Law* (Leiden: Brill, 2017).

64. Katz, *Women in the Mosque*.

65. Tucker, *Women, Family, and Gender*.

66. Ya'akov Meron gives three periods of the development of Hanafi law: ancient, classical, and postclassical. For Meron, the ancient period (or what others have referred to as the formative period) lasted until the end of the tenth century and was a period in which the developing law was characterized by chaos and a lack of systemization. Meron marks the beginning of the classical period with the works of the Baghdadi jurist Muhammad al-Quduri (d. 428/1037) in the eleventh century and ends it with Abu Bakr b. Mas'ud al-Kasani at the close of the twelfth century. He argues that the classical period was characterized by a greater systemization of the legal material and more sophisticated argumentation and explanations of the legal rulings. While Joseph Schacht (*An Introduction to Islamic Law* [New York: Clarendon Press, 1964]) claims that the classical period was characterized by lack of legal creativity (*taqlid*), Meron insists that it was in the postclassical period that jurists stayed close to the precedent of their particular legal schools and primarily produced commentaries to explicate and defend those legal rulings. The postclassical period, according to Meron, starts in the early thirteenth century, with the famous text *al-Hidayah* by Burhan al-Din al-Marghinani (d. 593/1197). See Ya'akov Meron, "The Development of Legal Thought in Hanafi Texts," *Studia Islamica* 30 (1969): 73–118. Christopher Melchert, on the other hand, places the beginning of the classical period almost a century earlier. He argues that it begins with Abu Ja'far al-Tahawi (d. 321/933), when we see the development of a self-conscious affiliation with the Hanafi school. See Christopher Melchert, *The Formation of the Sunni Schools of Law, 9th–10th centuries C.E.* (New York: Brill, 1997), 116. See also the periodization schemes of Wael Hallaq, *The Origins and Evolution of Islamic Law* (Cambridge: Cambridge University Press, 2005), 2–3, and David Vishanoff, *The Formation of Islamic Hermeneutics: How Sunni Legal Theorists Imagined a Revealed Law* (New Haven, CT: American Oriental Society, 2011), xv.

67. Hallaq argues that it was in the formative period (ending in the middle of the tenth century) that the distinguishing and constitutive features of Islamic law were developed. Any subsequent developments after this period were "'accidental attributes' that—despite their importance for legal, social and other historians—did not affect the constitution of the phenomenon we call Islamic law. With or without these changes, Islamic law, for our present purposes, would have remained Islamic law, but without the legal schools or the science of legal theory, Islamic law cannot be deemed, in hindsight, complete" (Hallaq, *Origins and Evolution*, 3).

68. Ali, *Marriage and Slavery*, 15. For more information on the development of the legal schools, see Melchert, *Formation of Sunni Schools*, xxii–xviii; Noel Coulson, *A History of Islamic Law* (Piscataway, NJ: Transaction Publishers, 2011), 62–73; Ahmed El Shamsy, *The Canonization of Islamic Law: A Social and Intellectual History* (New York: Cambridge University Press, 2013), 167–93; Brannon Wheeler, *Applying the Canon in Islam: The Authorization and Maintenance of Interpretive Reasoning in Ḥanafi Scholarship* (Albany: State University of New York Press, 1996), 1–113; and Hallaq, *Origins and Evolution*.

69. For a detailed discussion on *tarjih* and the scholarly debates around it, see Talal al-Azem, introduction to *Rule-Formulation and Binding Precedent in the Madhhab-Law Tradition: Ibn Quṭlubghā's Commentary on The Compendium of Qudūrī* (Leiden: Brill, 2017). I am grateful to Sohaira Siddiqui for introducing me to al-Azem's work.

70. al-Azem, 16.

71. Muhammad b. Ahmad al-Sarakhsi, *Kitab al-Mabsut*, 31 vols. (Beirut: Dar al-Ma'rifa, 1989), and 'Ala al-Din Abu Bakr b. Mas'ud al-Kasani, *Badai' al-Sana'i' fi tartib al-Shara'i'*, 10 vols. (Lubnan: Dar al-Kutub al-'Ilmiyah: 2010).

72. Norman Calder, "al-SaraKhsī," in *Encyclopedia of Islam*, ed. P. Bearman et al., 2nd ed., https://referenceworks.brillonline.com/entries/encyclopaedia-of-islam-2/al-sarakhsi-SIM _6620?s.num=0&s.f.s2_parent=s.f.book.encyclopaedia-of-islam-2&s.q=al-Sarakh%CC %B2s%C4%AB.

73. Al-Azem, *Rule-Formulation*, 67.

1. GENDERING THE LEGAL SUBJECT: MASCULINITY AND FEMININITY IN LEGAL DISCOURSE

1. Seyed Abu'l a'la Maududi, *Purdah shar'i aur ijtima'i nuqta-e-nigah se* (Punjab: Maktaba Jamat-e-Islami, 1959).

2. "Islami nizam-e-mu'ashrat" (Maududi, 143).

3. "Is jahan-e-khalq main jitni karigari tum deikhtay ho wa sab inhi joron ki tazwij ka karishma hai" (Maududi, 143). To support his assertion, Maududi cites the Qur'anic verse: "All things We made in pairs" (51:49).

4. Maududi, *Purdah*, 143. This is the translation into English that Maududi himself provides in the text. In my discussion of Maududi's work, I use the term "sexual principle" rather than "law of sex," as I believe it more accurately captures what Maududi describes as principles that govern the cosmos.

5. Maududi, 143.

6. Maududi, 145. I am grateful to Shabana Mir for pointing me to Maududi's book and his use of the active/passive binary. For a critique of this argument about Islam's conception of gender and for a gender fluid reading of the active/passive binary, see Sa'diyya Shaikh, *Sufi Narratives of Intimacy: Ibn 'Arabī, Gender, and Sexuality* (Chapel Hill: University of North Carolina Press, 2012), chapter 4.

7. "Qanun-e-fitrat" (Maududi, *Purdah*, 156).

8. Maududi, 156.

9. Maududi, 158.

10. Maududi, 159. This idea of the woman as a manager of the household was common language in early modern Muslim discourse. For more on the housewife in early modernity, see Afsaneh Najmabadi, "Crafting an Educated Housewife in Iran," in *Remaking Women: Feminism and Modernity in the Middle East*, ed. Lila Abu-Lughod (Princeton, NJ: Princeton University Press, 1998), 91–125; Omnia Shakry, "Schooled Mothers and Structured Play: Child Rearing in Turn-of-the-Century Egypt," in *Remaking Women: Feminism and Modernity in the Middle East*, ed. Lila Abu-Lughod (Princeton, NJ: Princeton University Press, 1998), 126–70.

11. Cynthia Freeland, "Nourishing Speculation: A Feminist Reading of Aristotelian Science," in *Engendering Origins: Critical Feminist Readings of Plato and Aristotle*, ed. Bat-Ami Bar On (Albany: State University of New York Press, 1994), 155.

12. Charlotte Witt, "Form, Normativity and Gender in Aristotle: A Feminist Perspective," in *Feminist Reflections on the History of Philosophy*, ed. Lilli Alanen and Charlotte Witt (Dordrecht: Kluwer Academic, 2004), 117–36. "Hylomorphism" is a term used to describe Aristotle's theory that everything in nature has two principles: matter and form. Witt argues that the gendered notion of hylomorphism is not intrinsic to Aristotelian metaphysics. In an attempt to reclaim Aristotle's theory that nature contains norms and values, she argues that these gendered notions were extrinsic to his theory of hylomorphism and reflected the gender norms of Aristotle's cultural context.

13. Susan Moller Okin, *Women in Western Political Thought* (Princeton, NJ: Princeton University Press, 1979), chapter 4.

14. Elizabeth Spellman argues that for Aristotle the rational element in enslaved people can hear and obey orders but not deliberate. For Aristotle, enslaved people are likened to animals, the key difference between the two being that enslaved people have enough reason to understand the orders of their enslavers. A father is also permitted to rule over children as the rational element of their soul needs further maturation. Elizabeth Spellman, "Aristotle and the Politicization of the Soul," in *Discovering Reality: Feminist Perspectives on Epistemology*, ed. Sandra Harding and Merrill B. Hintikka (Dordrecht: Kluwer Academic, 1983), 18–19.

15. R. W. Connell, *Masculinities* (1993; repr. Berkeley: University of California Press, 2005).

16. Connell, 68.

17. Connell, 71. See also R. W. Connell and James W. Messerschmidt, "Hegemonic Masculinity: Rethinking the Concept," *Gender and Society* 19, no. 6 (2005): 848.

18. IConnell and Messerschmidt, 838.

19. Al-Sarakhsi, *Al-Mabsut*, 9:54.

20. For more on doubt in Islamic Law, see Intisar Rabb, *Doubt in Islamic Law: A History of Legal Maxims, Interpretation, and Islamic Criminal Law* (Cambridge: Cambridge University Press, 2014).

21. See Rudolph Peters, *Crime and Punishment in Islamic Law* (Cambridge: Cambridge University Press, 2006), 62.

22. Rabb, *Doubt in Islamic Law*, chapter 3.

23. Al-Sarakhsi, *Al-Mabsut*, 9:55. The terms *fa'il* and *maf'ul biha* are used grammatically to denote subject and object positions in a sentence. Between their linguistic meaning and their grammatical usage, I interpret the two terms as designating the male as an active subject and the female as a passive object, respectively.

24. While the term *asl al-fi'l* literally means the "source of the act," I am translating it here as the "effective cause." The idea of the effective cause mirrors the Aristotelian conception of the male sperm as the effective cause or generator of reproduction. In referring to the male as the source of the sex act, al-Sarakhsi is using a similar notion of the penetrative act as the generator of the sex act. Without this penetrative act of the male subject, there is no sexual intercourse that is recognizable under the law.

25. Sara Omar has made a similar observation on Islamic legal definitions and conceptions of sexual intercourse in her article "From Semantics to Normative Law: Perceptions of *Liwāṭ* (Sodomy) and *Siḥāq* (Tribadism) in Islamic Jurisprudence (8th to 15th Century CE)," *Islamic Law and Society* 19 (2012): 222–56.

26. Al-Sarakhsi, *Al-Mabsut*, 9:55.

27. Al-Sarakhsi, 9:55.

28. Al-Sarakhsi, 9:55

29. Al-Sarakhsi, 9:53.

30. Muhammad b. al-Hasan al-Shaybani, *al-Jami' al-Saghir* (Karachi: Idarat al-Quran wa al-Ulum al-Islamiyah, 1990), 281. I have not found any account of al-Shaybani articulating his reasoning on this position.

31. "As for the adulteress and the adulterer flog each of them with a hundred stripes, and let not compassion with them keep you from [carrying out] this law of God, if you [truly] believe in God and the Last Day; and let a group of the believers witness their chastisement" (Qur'an, 24:2).

32. Al-Sarakhsi, *Al-Mabsut*, 9:55.

33. See n. 38.

34. Omar, "From Semantics to Normative Law," 237.

35. Ash Geissinger makes a similar argument in "'Are Men the Majority in Paradise, or Women?' Constructing Gender and Communal Boundaries in Muslim B. Al-Ḥajjāj's (D. 261/875) *Kitāb Al-Janna*," in *Roads to Paradise: Eschatology and Concepts of the Hereafter in Islam*, ed. Sebastian Günther and Todd Lawson (Leiden: Brill, 2017), 323.

36. Al-Kasani, *Badai' al-Sana'i'*, 9:184.

37. Burhan al-Din al-Marghinani, *Al-Hidaya fi Sharh Bidayat al-Mubtadi'* (Beirut: Dar al-Ihya' al-Turath al-'Arabi: 1995), 2:348.

38. Muḥammad b. Idris al-Shafi'i, *Al-Umm*, 7 vols. (al-Qahirah: al-Dar al-Miṣriyah lil Ta'lif wa al-Tarjamah, 1966), 5:156. The words *nakih* and *mankuha* can vary in meaning, depending on context. They can be construed to mean penetrator and penetrated but also "one who marries" and "one who is married." Al-Shafi'i's statement could thus also be translated as "man is the one who marries" and "woman is the one who is married." Regardless of the polyvalence of the terms, what remains constant is the attribution of activity to the male and passivity to the female.

39. See Kecia Ali, "'The best of you will not strike': Al-Shafi'i on Qur'an, Sunnah, and Wife-Beating," *Comparative Islamic Studies* 2, no. 2 (2006): 143–55, and Katz, *Women in the Mosque*.

40. Ali, *Marriage and Slavery*, 25.

41. Ali, 189.

42. "Wa fi asl al-milk 'ala al-mar'ah naw' dhillah" (al-Sarakhsi, *Al-Mabsut*, 5:23).

43. "Fa qala al-nikaḥ riqq" (al-Sarakhsi, 5:23). It is important to recognize that while marriage and slavery are analogized by the jurists, wives are not their husbands' slaves. Scholars have also disagreed on continuities and discontinuities that exist between the conceptual parallels of marriage, ownership, sale, and slavery in Islamic law. For more about this scholarly conversation, see Ali, *Marriage and Slavery*, 51.

44. The word al-Sarakhsi uses here is *al-mu'min* (a believer). This statement is instructive not only as a commentary on the gender hierarchy in his text but also his religious cosmology. Muslims should not be under the control and dominion of non-Muslims and were deserving of a respect and dignity that non-Muslims did not necessarily have a right to. For example, a Muslim woman could not be married to a non-Muslim man, as she would have to enter into his dominion, allowing a non-Muslim to have dominion over a Muslim. What is perhaps most interesting here is that, in theory, Muslim women should also receive the

same dignity and respect as Muslim men; the gender hierarchy *should* be disrupted by the religious hierarchy. However, as we will see later, social order necessitates that the gender hierarchy prevail.

45. For al-Sarakhsi, it is not the law's construction of marriage that produces this dilemma. As I discuss later, al-Sarakhsi considers the gendered imbalance in the marriage relationship to be a social necessity ordained by God.

46. While Islamic law conceives of licit sex both within marriage as well as through concubinage, there is a clear distinction for al-Sarakhsi between sexual intercourse between a married couple and an enslaver and his female slave.

47. "Fi al-taghalub fasadan wa fi al-iqdam bighayri milk ishtibah al-ansab wa huwa sabab li-diya' al-nasl" (al-Sarakhsi, *Al-Mabsut*, 4:191).

48. Al-Sarakhsi, 5:185.

49. "Hifẓ al-nisa' wa al-qiyam 'alayhinna wa al-infaq" (al-Sarakhsi, 4:193 and 5:185).

50. Al-Kasani, *Badai' al-Sana'i'*, 3:374.

51. See Judith P. Hallet and Marilyn B. Skinner, eds., *Roman Sexualities* (Princeton, NJ: Princeton University Press, 1998); Marilyn B. Skinner, *Sexuality in Greek and Roman Culture* (Oxford: Blackwell, 2005); Maryanne Cline Horowitz, "Aristotle and Woman," *Journal of the History of Biology* 9 (1976): 183–213; and Ruth Mazo Karras, "Active/Passive, Acts/Passions: Greek and Roman Sexualities," *American Historical Review* 105, no. 4 (2000): 1250.

52. Horowitz, "Aristotle and Woman," 192. For a study of how the ancient medical tradition relied more on humors of the body than anatomy in determining an individual's sex, see Tyson Sukava, "Blending Bodies in Classical Greek Medicine," in *Exploring Gender Diversity in the Ancient World*, ed. Jennifer Surtees and Jennifer Dyer (Edinburgh: Edinburgh University Press, 2020), 43–53.

53. Horowitz, "Aristotle and Woman," 196–97.

54. Craig Williams, *Roman Homosexuality: Ideologies of Masculinity in Classical Antiquity* (Oxford: Oxford University Press, 1999), 14.

55. Williams, 31–32.

56. Jonathan Walters, "Invading the Roman Body: Manliness and Impenetrability in Roman Thought," in *Roman Sexualities*, ed. Judith P. Hallett and Marilyn B. Skinner (Princeton: Princeton University Press, 1997), 32.

57. Walters, 8.

58. Even the sex of the child was determined based on this relationship of domination between the male and female. If the male sperm dominated in quantity and quality, then the child was born male; if the female sperm dominated, then the child was sexed female. Intersexuality was understood as the absence of either sperm's prevalence over the other (Ze'evi, *Producing Desire*, 37–38). For a more detailed account of Medieval Muslim discourse on conception and the two-seed theory, see Kathryn Kueny, *Conceiving Identities: Maternity in Medieval Muslim Discourse and Practice* (Albany: State University of New York Press, 2013), 53–58.

Ibn Sina's theory synthesized Aristotelian and Galenic theories of conception. Aristotle held that women contributed the material cause or matter in the form of menstrual blood. The male, on the other hand, contributed sperm, the efficient cause that acted on the menstrual blood. Galen admitted both male and female sperm, believing that both sperms contributed to form and matter but that female sperm was less powerful than male sperm. Ibn Sina argued that there was female sperm, but that it was the same species as menstrual blood. However, he held that male sperm was characterized by a greater degree of fermenting power and female sperm by a greater degree of receptivity to fermentation. For more information about Aristotelian and Galenic accounts of conception, see Thomas W. Laqueur, *Making Sex: Body and Gender from the Greeks to Freud* (Cambridge, MA: Harvard University Press, 1990), 39–42. For Ibn Sina's theory, see Ahmad Dallal, "Sexualities: Scientific Discourses, Premodern," in *Encyclopedia of Women and Islamic Cultures*, ed. Joseph Suad Joseph (Leiden: Brill, 2006), 3:401–7.

59. Louise Marlow, *Hierarchy and Egalitarianism in Islamic Thought* (Princeton, NJ: Princeton University Press, 1997), 25.

60. Marlow, 28.

61. Marlow, 64.

62. Elizabeth Urban, *Conquered Populations in Early Islam: Non-Arabs, Slaves and the Sons of Slave Mothers* (Edinburgh: Edinburgh University Press, 2020).

63. Ahmed, *Women and Gender in Islam*, 88.

64. Ahmed, 33. As Fatima Seedat points out, the normative narrative about the advent of Islam characterizes the situation of women in pre-Islamic Arabia as particularly dire. Islam, these narratives argued, radically shifted the position of women, granting them spiritual equality with men and curbing male authority and dominance. Ahmed's argument that I mention above seems to be an implicit response to these prevailing narratives. See Fatima Seedat, "When Islam and Feminism Converge," *Muslim World* 103 (2013): 405.

65. Geissinger, *Gender and Muslim Constructions*, 63–64.

66. Geissinger, 64.

67. Ayesha Chaudhry, *Domestic Violence and the Islamic Tradition* (Oxford: Oxford University Press, 2014), 11.

68. Chaudhry, 12.

69. Chaudhry, 12.

70. Zahra Ayubi, *Gendered Morality: Classical Islamic Ethics of the Self, Family, and Society* (New York: Columbia University Press, 2019), 10.

71. Ayubi, 113.

72. Ayubi., 115.

73. Ayubi, 120.

74. Ayubi, 240.

75. Omar, "From Semantics to Normative Law," 223.

76. For more information on the legal position on sodomy, see Omar, "Semantics," 223, and El-Rouayheb, *Before Homosexuality*, 118–23.

77. In keeping with his manner throughout his legal text, al-Sarakhsi provides an account of Abu Hanifa's justification for his legal opinion. This account, however, is more reflective of al-Sarakhsi's defense of legal precedent than a transmission of the legal arguments articulated by the early generation of jurists.

78. The precise phrase used by al-Sarakhsi is "ilaj al-farj fi al-farj 'ala wajh maḥzur la shubhah fihi li qasd safh al-ma" (*Al-Mabsut*, 9:77).

79. "Mushtaha ṭab'an" (al-Sarakhsi, 9:77).

80. Al-Sarakhsi, 5:148 and 9:76.

81. Their position here does not extend to any and all bodily orifices of all individuals. Bestiality and pedophilia were not considered to be acts of illicit sexual intercourse because both children and animals were not legally considered objects of desire.

82. Al-Kasani, *Badai' al-Sana'i'*, 9:186. As mentioned earlier in this chapter, Omar describes al-Razi making a similar argument regarding the repugnance of anal intercourse ("From Semantics to Normative Law," 237). What is interesting in al-Kasani's statement here is that the unnaturalness concerns a man's desire to be penetrated rather than a man's desire to penetrate. We could perhaps read his statement to mean that he could still consider it natural for a man to take on the penetrative role in anal intercourse, with only the man who is being penetrated acting in an "unnatural" manner.

83. Al-Sarakhsi, *Usul al-Sarakhsi*, 1:243.

84. The question of the relation between premodern and modern conceptions of sexual identity has been the subject of significant debate among historians of sexuality. On the one hand is Michel Foucault's famous provocation that sexual identity as we understand it today is a modern construction. While some scholars have argued for discontinuity between premodern and modern constructions of sexuality as an identity, others have argued that historical inquiry produces a more nuanced perspective. For critical engagements with Foucault's work on sexuality, see Halperin, *How to Do the History*, and Karras, "Prostitution." For a more recent engagement with this debate, see Joseph Marchal, *Appalling Bodies: Queer Figures before and after Paul's Letters* (Oxford: Oxford University Press, 2019), chapter 1.

85. Halperin, *How to Do the History*, 38.

86. See el-Rouayheb, *Before Homosexuality*; Ze'evi, *Producing Desire*; and Rowson, "The Categorization of Gender."

87. Al-Sarakhsi, *Al-Mabsut*, 9:78; al-Kasani, *Badai'*, 9:186.

88. Boyarin, "Are There Any Jews," 341.

89. Boyarin, 344.

90. In her book, *Virgin Territory: Configuring Female Virginity in Early Christianity* (Oakland: University of California Press, 2022), Julia Kelto-Lillis makes a distinction between physiology (the function of the body) and anatomy (the structure and shape of the body). They argue that reading early Christian texts about bleeding and pain in sexual intercourse reflect the body's physiology and cannot be read as evidence that these texts had a conception of the hymen (what Kelto-Lillis argues is anatomy). I use Kelto-Lillis's distinction here to argue that the juristic discussion of the desirability of the anus for penetration was concerned with the physiology (its suppleness and warmth) that makes it akin to the vagina rather than thinking of it anatomically and thus as a part of the body distinct from the vagina.

91. For more on the legal discussions of anal intercourse, see El-Rouayheb, *Before Homosexuality*, chapter 3.

92. "Al-mar'a min qarniha ila qadamiha 'awrah" (Al-Sarakhsi, *Al-Mabsut*, 10:145). Al-Sarakhsi supports his claim by citing a hadith to the effect that a woman's very being is to be concealed ("al-mar'a 'awratun masturatun" [10:145]).

93. Men's *'awra* is between the navel and the knee. They must cover this part of their body in front of all individuals, male and female, and are only allowed to reveal their entire body to their wives and concubines.

94. Al-Sarakhsi's emphatic statement does not mean that he actually holds that women's bodies must always be concealed in all circumstances. Rather, this is a categorical statement about the fundamental nature of women, a statement that nonetheless recognizes the practical exceptions that allow women to expose their bodies to varying degrees in certain relationships.

95. Despite this permission to look at the naked body of one's spouse or concubine, al-Sarakhsi continues to argue that it is more appropriate for the two not to look at each other's fully naked bodies. This discomfort with nudity is partly based on hadith and the cultural norms of the early generations that al-Sarakhsi provides as proof texts. He mentions, for example, a hadith according to which 'Aisha never saw the full nakedness of the Prophet's body. The legal discussion of gazing is guided not only by concerns about desire but also by a broader ethic about the rights and dignity of the human body that is independent of the individual who inhabits it. Even in situations where individuals are legally permitted to look on the naked body, they are discouraged from doing so. In fact, the dignity of the body extends so far that an individual is discouraged from looking at their own body. See Al-Sarakhsi, *Al-Mabsut*, 10:149.

96. Al-Sarakhsi lays out four categories of women that a man may look on: (1) his wife or concubine, (2) his female relatives, (3) the female slave of another, (4) unrelated free women. The male gaze on a wife or concubine is perhaps the least complex for al-Sarakhsi. With female relatives, a man may look on the parts of her body that the law considers places of beautification, which normally include the hair, head, face, chest, arms, and legs. The unrelated free woman carries the greatest restrictions in covering. The free woman is required to cover the most in public, and men may not look on most of her body with the exception of the face or even simply the eyes, depending on the legal school. Enslaved women were not allowed to cover in ways that resembled free women. They were thus prohibited from covering their head and face. There was significant disagreement over what parts of the enslaved woman's body a man was allowed to look on. For the early Hanafis, men were allowed to touch and look on all parts of the enslaved woman's body except between the navel and knee and her torso and back.

97. Katz, *Women in the Mosque*.

98. Enslaved women were also allowed greater mobility and were not permitted the level of bodily covering that was imposed on free women. This was largely justified owing to their condition of enslavement and putting the needs and demands of the slave owner as paramount. See more on this in chapter 2.

99. Katz, *Women in the Mosque*, 3.

100. Al-Sarakhsi is adamant that bodily exposure of a man's female relatives is only permissible if he is certain that both he and the female relative do not feel any desire (*Al-Mabsut*, 10:149).

101. Al-Sarakhsi argues that to require women to be concealed from all men would create undue hardship. This notion of hardship is not so much out of concern for women's comfort but for the fulfillment of social roles. With regard to female relatives, for example, he says that to require them to cover their entire bodies in front of male family members would create undue hardship, as women at home often dress in a manner that allows them to do household work (*Al-Mabsut*, 10:149). The most direct legal conclusion is thus

abandoned for the sake of ease through the principle of *istihsan*. This is a legal method employed when jurists, owing to certain considerations, diverge from the conclusions of analogical reasoning. For more information on *istihsan*, see R. Paret, "Istiḥsān and Istiṣlaḥ," in *Encyclopedia of Islam*, ed. P. Bearman et al., 2nd ed., https://referenceworks.brillonline .com/entries/encyclopaedia-of-islam-2/istihsan-and-istislah-COM_0395?s.num=0&s.f.s2 _parent=s.f.book.encyclopaedia-of-islam-2&s.q=Isti%E1%B8%A5s%C4%81n+and+Isti%E1 %B9%A3la%E1%B8%A5.

102. He considers four possible forms of the gaze: (1) male gaze on the male body, (2) female gaze on the female body, (3) female gaze on the male body, and lastly (4) male gaze on the female body. Al-Sarakhsi acknowledges female desire but does not engage it substantively or in any significant detail. Furthermore, when he does consider female desire, it is peripheral to the legal determination.

103. Generally, al-Sarakhsi does not consider the possibility of homoerotic desire. Katz argues that the figure of the beardless youth as an object of male desire only emerges in legal texts after the eleventh century (*Women in the Mosque*, 105). This argument seems to be confirmed by my reading of al-Sarakhsi. Same-sex desire only arises as a concern in his text in the context of sodomy.

104. These gendered prayer postures were not unique to the Hanafi legal school and were maintained in some form or another by other legal schools as well. For more information, see Marion Katz, *Prayer in Islamic Thought and Practice* (Cambridge: Cambridge University Press, 2013), chapter 5.

105. Al-Kasani, *Badai' al-Sana'i'*, 2:24.

106. [Ash] Geissinger, "'Umm al-Dardā' Sat in *Tashahhud* like a Man': Towards the Historical Contextualization of a Portrayal of Female Religious Authority," *Muslim World* 103 (2003): 319.

107. See for example, Andrew Buncombe, "New York Metro's Campaign to Stop 'Man-Spreading'," *Independent*, December 20, 2014, https://www.independent.co.uk/news/world /americas/overcrowded-new-york-metros-campaign-to-stop-man-spreading-9938025 .html. See also #manspreading, X, accessed October 12, 2023, https://twitter.com/hashtag /manspreading?f=live.

108. Emma Jane, "'Dude . . . Stop the Spread': Antagonism, Agonism, and #manspreading on Social Media," *International Journal of Cultural Studies* 20, no. 5 (2017): 462.

109. Connell, *Masculinities*, 71.

110. Al-Sarakhsi, *Al-Mabsut*, 5:208.

111. Muhammad b. Ismail al-Bukhari, *Sahih al-Bukhari*, trans. Muhammad Muhsin Khan, 9 vols. (Riyadh: Dar-us-Salaam Publications, 1997), 1: book 6, hadith 301.

112. Al-Kasani, *Badai' al-Sana'i'*, 3:375.

113. According to the Hanafi legal school, women could not serve as witnesses in cases of *hadd* and retaliation (*qisas*).

114. The Hanafis did, however, allow the woman's father and paternal grandfather to contest the marriage if the man was considered incompatible with the woman's social standing. For more on spousal suitability as a form of exercising social control, see Siddiqui, "Law and Desire."

115. Geissinger, "Umm al-Dardā' Sat," 313.

116. Geissinger, 313.

117. Geissinger makes a similar argument in "Are Men the Majority."

118. See Katz, *Prayer in Islamic Thought*, chapter 5.

2. GENDER AND THE CONSTRUCTION OF ENSLAVED SUBJECTS

1. Hanafi jurists distinguish between two types of nullity related to acts and sales: *fasid* nullity and *batil* nullity. In *batil* acts or sales, an essential element of the legal act is missing. In such a case, *batil* means that the act or sale is deemed nonexistent and therefore has no legal effect. If an act or sale fulfills its necessary elements but not its conditions of validity, then it is *fasid*, or null. In Hanafi law, many *fasid* acts or sales are classified as such because they contain conditions that contradict the nature of the act or sale. The legal existence of the *fasid* sale allows for the possibility that if the nullifying condition is removed or mitigated, the sale will be validated. For more on *fasid* and *batil* as legal designations, see Y. Linant de Bellefonds, "Fāsid wa Bāṭil," in *Encyclopedia of Islam*, ed. P. Bearman et al., 2nd ed., https://referenceworks.brillonline.com/entries/encyclopaedia-of-islam-2/fasid-wa-batil-COM_0215?s.num=0&s.f.s2_parent=s.f.book.encyclopaedia-of-islam-2&s.q=%E2%80%9CF%C4%81sid+wa+B%C4%81%E1%B9%ADil%2C%E2%80%9D.

2. Al-Sarakhsi, *Al-Mabsut*, 13:13.

3. Johansen, "Valorization," 82.

4. Johansen, 81.

5. Ali, *Marriage and Slavery*, 13–16.

6. Johansen, "Valorization," 84.

7. I am grateful to Stephanie Jones-Rogers's work for pushing me to broaden my understanding of sexual violence endured by enslaved people. See Stephanie Jones-Rogers, *They Were Her Property: White Women as Slave Owners in the American South* (New Haven, CT: Yale University Press, 2019).

8. See, for example, al-Kasani, *Badai' al-Sana'i'*, 14:65; and al-Marghinani, *Al-Hidayah*, 2:31.

9. For more on impediments to legal capacity, see the section on legal personhood in the introduction.

10. Al-Sarakhsi, *Al-Mabsut*, 5:83–84.

11. Bernard K. Freamon, *Possessed by the Right Hand: The Problem of Slavery in Islamic Law and Muslim Cultures* (Leiden: Brill, 2019), 32.

12. Freamon, 85.

13. Like Roman law, Sunni law conceptualized enslavement as traveling through the mother's womb. Thus, a child assumed the enslaved status of its mother, regardless of whether the father was free or enslaved. The only time the children of an enslaved woman were considered free was if she was a concubine of the enslaver. It is not clear why Sunni jurists adopted this position from Roman law. Jonathan Brown mentions that Ibn Taymiyya (d. 728/1328) made a brief note that because ownership of animals is determined through the mother, jurists made a similar determination in relation to freedom and enslavement of humans. See Jonathan Brown, *Slavery and Islam* (London: Oneworld Academic, 2019), 77–78. For a detailed discussion on enslavement in different legal systems in the Near East, see also Freamon, *Possessed by the Right Hand*, chapter 1.

14. While it was not permitted for Muslims to be enslaved, if a person converted to Islam while enslaved, they would remain enslaved.

15. Freamon, *Possessed by the Right Hand*, 176.

16. This prohibition was perhaps more a rule on the books than a reflection of social practice. As Chase Robinson demonstrates, Arabs continued to be enslaved, though perhaps in lesser numbers than people of other races and ethnicities. See Chase Robinson, "Slavery in the Conquest Period," *International Journal of Middle East Studies* 49 (2017): 158.

17. Freamon, *Possessed by the Right Hand*, 181.

18. Freamon, 181.

19. Freamon, 199.

20. Hugh Kennedy, *When Baghdad Ruled the Muslim World: The Rise and Fall of Islam's Greatest Dynasty* (Cambridge, MA: Da Capo Press, 2006), 214.

21. Marek Jankowiak, "What Does the Slave Trade in the Saqaliba Tell Us about Early Islamic Slavery?" *International Journal of Middle East Studies* 49 (2017): 171.

22. Jankowiak, 171.

23. I have borrowed this term from Freamon, *Possessed by the Right Hand*, 97.

24. Qur'an 24:33 reads: "And as for those who are unable to marry, let them live in continence until God grants them sufficiency out of His bounty, And if any of those whom you rightfully possess desire [to obtain] a deed of freedom, write it out for them if you are aware of any good in them: and give them [their share of] the wealth of God which He has given you. And do not, in order to gain some of the fleeting pleasures of this worldly life, coerce your [slave] maidens into whoredom if they happen to be desirous of marriage; and if anyone should coerce them, then, verily, after they have been compelled [to submit in their helplessness], God will be much-forgiving, a dispenser of grace!" The translation of this sura is from Muhammad Asad, *The Message of the Qur'an: The Full Account of the Revealed Arabic Text Accompanied by Parallel Transliteration* (London: Book Foundation, 2003); all further English translations of the Qur'an are from this edition.

25. The Hanbalis were the only legal school that allowed for a *mukatab* or *mukataba* to be sold but required that the purchaser honor the contractual enfranchisement; Robert Brunschvig, "Abd," in *Encyclopedia of Islam*, ed. P. Bearman et al., 2nd ed., https:// referenceworks.brillonline.com/entries/encyclopaedia-of-islam-2/abd-COM_0003?s .num=0&s.f.s2_parent=s.f.book.encyclopaedia-of-islam-2&s.q=abd.

26. Brunschvig, "Abd."

27. Brunschvig, "Abd."

28. Madeline C. Zilfi, *Women and Slavery in the Late Ottoman Empire: The Design of Difference* (New York: Cambridge University Press, 2010), 179–80.

29. See Qur'an 2:177, 4:92, 24:33, 58:3.

30. Al-Bukhari, *Sahih al-Bukhari*, book 2, hadith 23, trans. M. Muhsin Khan, Sunnah .com, accessed October 15, 2023, https://sunnah.com/bukhari.

31. Brunschvig, "Abd."

32. Freamon, *Possessed by the Right Hand*, 97.

33. For more on the rights of enslaved people in Islamic law, see Brown, *Slavery and Islam*, chapter 2.

34. Brunschvig, "Abd."

35. Brown mentions that Ibn Qudama claimed an enslaved person was granted the right to own property, provided the enslaver permitted this. Ibn Quadama's rationale was that by virtue of their humanity, the enslaved person held the capacity of ownership (*Slavery and Islam*, 91).

36. Brunschvig, "Abd."

37. Individuals with *ihsan* status are referred to as *muhsan/muhsana*. The term in legal discourse as well as hadith largely denotes a person who is liable to be put to death by stoning if convicted of illicit sexual intercourse. To acquire the status of *muhsan/muhsana*, the person must be Muslim, free, and have had sexual intercourse in marriage. Unlike the Hanafis, who require that the person conferring the status themselves be a *muhsan*, the Maliki and Shafi'i legal schools allowed enslaved spouses and *kitabi* wives to confer the status of *ihsan*. For more information, see J. Burton, "Muḥṣan," in *Encyclopedia of Islam*, ed. P. Bearman et al., 2nd ed., https://referenceworks.brillonline.com/entries/encyclopaedia-of-islam-2/muhsan-SIM_5435?s.num=0&s.f.s2_parent=s.f.book.encyclopaedia-of-islam-2&s.q=Mu%E1%B8%A5%E1%B9%A3an.

38. Johansen, "Valorization," 74.

39. Al-Sarakhsi, *Al-Mabsut*, 5:129.

40. "Wa hadha lianna al-'abd mamluk malan fala yajuz an yakun malikan lil mal" (al-Sarakhsi, *Al-Mabsut*, 5:129).

41. Al-Sarakhsi, 28:115. The term redhibitory vice (*'aib*) in Islamic law refer to defects in a commodity that is significant to a level that allows the buyer to return the commodity back to the seller. Since Islamic law recognizes the enslaved person as both human and a commodity, greater restrictions were place on returning an enslaved person back to the seller based on these vices.

42. Brunschvig, "Abd."

43. Moses Finley, *Ancient Slavery and Modern Ideology* (London: Chatto and Windus, 1980).

44. Ruth Mazo Karras, *Slavery and Society in Medieval Scandinavia* (New Haven, CT: Yale University Press, 1988), 5.

45. Franz Rosenthal, *The Muslim Concept of Freedom Prior to the Nineteenth Century* (Leiden: Brill, 1960), 41.

46. Bernard K. Freamon, "Definitions and Conceptions of Slave Ownership in Islamic law," in *The Legal Understanding of Slavery: From the Historical to the Contemporary*, ed. Jean Allain (Oxford: Oxford University Press, 2012), 41; id., *Possessed by the Right Hand*, 153.

47. Freamon, *Possessed by the Right Hand*, 23–24.

48. Brown, *Slavery and Islam*, 98.

49. Brown, 36–37.

50. Karras, *Slavery and Society*, 6.

51. Karras, 6.

52. Urban, *Conquered Populations in Early Islam*, 8.

53. Ali, *Marriage and Slavery*, 44.

54. Al-Sarakhsi, *Al-Mabsut*, 5:129.

55. Muhammad b. al-Hasan al-Shaybani, *Kitab al-Hujja 'ala ahl al-Madina*, 4 vols. (Beirut: 'Alam al-Kutub, n.d.), 3:360.

56. Hanafi jurists supported their reasoning by citing a report according to which Ibn 'Umar stated that the sexual use of an enslaved woman is only permitted to the person who

has the legal agency to manumit her or gift her. Al-Shaybani also cites reports that early figures such as Ibrahim al-Nakha'i and Hassan al-Basri held that it was reprehensible for an enslaved man to take on a concubine or for an enslaver to marry his enslaved man and woman to one another without good reason (al-Shaybani, *Kitab al-Hujja* 3:360). See also Al-Sarakhsi, *Al-Mabsut*, 5:129.

57. Brunschvig, "Abd."

58. Brunschvig, "Abd."

59. Al-Sarkahsi, *Al-Mabsut*, 5:129.

60. Al-Sarakhsi argues that believers and disbelievers are oriented differently toward sexual desire. The believer, he claims, engages in the act of intercourse for the sake of fulfilling this divine command (i.e., procreation) and not for the sake of fulfilling their desire for sexual intercourse. However, for those individuals who do not seek divine pleasure, the fulfillment of sexual desire becomes the motivating factor for engaging in sexual intercourse. Eventually, however, both parties fulfill God's plan by procreating.

61. Despite this emphasis given to the desire for progeny, it is important to recognize which legal subjects were recognized as having both the right to fulfill this desire and to hold guardianship over their children. Whereas the wife's (whether free or enslaved) desire for children was recognized by the law, the concubine's presumed desire was given no such priority. Consequently, a man could practice coitus interruptus with his concubine regardless of her wishes. Similarly, the right of guardianship over one's children was only recognized for a free man of free children. Neither free mothers of free children nor enslaved mothers and fathers could serve as full guardians over their own children.

62. "Li darurat hajatihi ila qada' al-shahwa wa baqa' al-nasal" (al-Sarakhsi, *Al-Mabsut*, 5:129).

63. I use the term "coercion" here rather than "compulsion" as Hanafi jurists often used the term *ikrah* (coercion) instead of *ijbar* (compulsion) to describe the power of the enslaver over the enslaved person regarding marriage.

64. Ali, *Marriage and Slavery*, 40.

65. Al-Kasani, *Badai' al-Sana'i'*, 3:341.

66. "Wa liana al-'abd milkuhu bi jami' ajza'ihi mutlaqan" (al-Kasani, *Badai' al-Sana'i'*, 3:342).

67. al-Kasani, 3:341–42.

68. They were, however, aware of the possible abuses of this power, especially in the hands of legal guardians who were not the father or paternal grandfather. For more on this, see chapter 3.

69. Urban, *Conquered Populations in Early Islam*, 9.

70. Patricia Crone, *Roman, Provincial, and Islamic Law: The Origins of the Islamic Patronate* (Cambridge: Cambridge University Press, 1987), 36–38.

71. Interestingly, Ali notes that she is not aware of any discussion in which Shafi'i considers the case of a female enslaver marrying off an enslaved man (*Marriage and Slavery*, 45).

72. Ali, *Marriage and Slavery*, 45–47.

73. Ali, 48. Some early sources, such as the *Musannafs* of 'Abd al-Razzaq al-San'ani and Ibn Abi Shayba, seem to indicate that the earliest generations of Muslims debated about the enslaver having authority over the enslaved husband's divorce rights. The companion Ibn Abbas, for example, is said to have held that the enslaver can pronounce divorce on an enslaved husband's wife. Others maintained that the enslaved husband's divorce would not go into effect except with the enslaver's permission. By the time of the early generation of

the legal schools, however, the jurists were largely agreed on the opinion that the enslaved husband had control over divorce (Ali, 154–55).

74. Al-Kasani, *Badai' al-Sana'i'*, 3:341.

75. "Wa kadha al-zahir min hal al-'abd al-imtina' min ba'd tasarruf al-mawla ihtiraman lahu fa yabqa al-nikah fa yufidu fa'idatan tamah" (al-Kasani, 3:343).

76. For more information on this, see the section "Women, Sexual Intercourse, and Dominion" in chapter 1.

77. Although there is plenty of literary and historical evidence that sexual use was made of enslaved men. See the discussion in the previous section.

78. As I discussed in chapter 1, the free woman's ability to marry of her own will was still constrained by familial interests through compatibility (*kafa'a*) laws.

79. Ali, *Marriage and Slavery*, 40.

80. For more on this, see Julia Bray, "Men, women and slaves in Abbasid Society," in *Gender in the Early Medieval World: East and West, 300–900*, ed. Leslie Brubaker and Julia M. H. Smith (Cambridge: Cambridge University Press, 2004), 133.

81. Pernilla Myrne, "A Jariya's Prospects in Abbasid Baghdad," in *Concubines and Courtesans: Women and Slavery in Islamic History*, ed. Matthew Gordon and Kathryn A. Hain (New York: Oxford University Press, 2017), 64.

82. Myrne, 64.

83. Rabb, *Doubt in Islamic Law*; Asifa Quraishi-Landes, "A Meditation on *Mahr*, Modernity and Muslim Marriage Contract Law," in *Feminism, Law and Religion*, ed. Marie A. Failinger, Elizabeth R. Schlitz, and Susan J. Stabile (Farnham: Ashgate, 2013), 173–95.

84. See Kecia Ali, "Concubinage and Consent," *International Journal of Middle East Studies* 49 (2017): 148–52.

85. "Malakti bud'aki fa-khtari" (Al-Sarakhsi, *Al-Mabsut*, 5:98–99).

86. Al-Kasani, *Badai' al-Sanai'*, 3:601.

87. "Wa huwa milkuha amru nafsiha" (al-Sarakhsi, *Al-Mabsut*, 5:99), and "wa laha wilayah raf' al-darar 'an nafsiha" (al-Kasani, *Badai' al-Sanai'*, 3:600–01).

88. Hanafi jurists did discuss extensively the possibility of men being coerced by other men to commit illicit sexual intercourse. They were conflicted, however, on whether it was physiologically and affectively possible for a man to penetrate a woman without sexually desiring to do so. They concluded that men could make a claim of coercive sex only if the man was a person in public authority. For more on the sexual coercion of men see Hina Azam, *Sexual Violation in Islamic Law: Substance, Evidence, and Procedure* (New York: Cambridge University Press, 2015).

89. For more on this, see the section "Satr and 'Awra: Masculinity and Femininity as Gendered Dispositions" in chapter 1.

90. "ilqi 'anki al-khimar ya dafar" (al-Sarakhsi, *Al-Mabsut*, 10:151). Al-Kasani (*Badai' al-Sana'i'*, 10:483 and al-Marghinani (*Al-Hidaya* 1:53) both mention this report but they also add at the end 'Umar's rebuke for presenting herself as a free woman ("atatashabbahina bil-harair"). E. W. Lane defines the term *dafar* as a reviling statement used mostly for enslaved women. See E. W. Lane, *Arabic-English Lexicon* (Lahore: Islamic Book Centre, 1978), 1:890, https://babel .hathitrust.org/cgi/pt?id=coo.31924005505189&seq=60&q1=%D8%AF%D9%81%D8%B1.

91. Abu Bakr 'Abd al-Razzaq b. Hammam al-San'ani, *Al-Musannaf* (Beirut: Al-Maktab al-Islami, 1983), 3:133–34, no. 5053.

92. Al-San'ani, 3:134, nos. 5054 and 5055.

93. Al-San'ani, nos. 5052–65.

94. An enslaved woman who has borne her enslaver a child.

95. Abu Bakr Ahmad b. 'Ali al-Razi Al-Jassas, *Mukhtasar Iktilaf al-Ulama* (Beirut: Dar al-Basha'ir al-Islamiyah, 1995), 1:230.

96. I am grateful to Omar Anchassi for his help with translating this word.

97. Abu Bakr 'Abdallah b. Muhammad b. Ibrahim Ibn Abi Shayba, *Al-Kitab al-Musannaf fi Ahadith wa al-Athar* (Riyadh: Maktaba al-Rushd, 1988), 2:41, no. 6240.

98. Al-San'ani, Abu Bakr 'Abd al-Razzaq b. Hammam, *Al-Musannaf* (Beirut: Al-Maktab al-Islami, 1983). 1:136, no. 5062.

99. Zilfi, *Women and Slavery*, 46.

100. Ahmed, *Women and Gender in Islam*, 14.

101. Ahmad b. al-Hussain b. 'Ali Al-Bayhaqi, *Sunan al-Bayhaqi al-Kubra* (Mecca: Maktaba Dar al-Baz, 1994), 2:226, no. 3037.

102. Al-Sarakhsi, *Al-Mabsut*, 10:151. Qur'an 33:59 reads: "O Prophet! Tell thy wives and thy daughters, as well as all [other] believing women, that they should draw over themselves some of their outer garments [when in public]: this will be more conducive to their being recognized [as decent women] and not annoyed. But [withal,] God is indeed much- forgiving, a dispenser of grace!" Al-Sarakhsi gives no indication why he interprets the term "believing women" in this verse to only include free women and not enslaved women.

103. The well-known sixteenth-century Egyptian Hanafi jurist Ibn Nujaym grappled with this problem. In discussing Qur'an 33:59, he makes the interesting claim that while harassing any woman is prohibited, harassing free women is a greater threat to the social order than harassment of enslaved women. It is for this reason, he argues, that the Qur'anic verse requires free believing women and not enslaved believing women to cover themselves in public. See Zayn al-Din b. Ibrahim b. Muhammad Ibn Nujaym, *Al-Bahr al-Ra'iq: Sharh Kanz al-Daqa'iq* (Beirut: Dar al-Kutub al-'Ilmiyyah, 1997), 8:357.

104. Muhammad b. al-Hasan al-Shaybani, *Kitab al-Asl* (Lahore: Dar al-Ma'arif al-Nu'maniyah, 1981), 3:71.

105. Al-Jassas, *Mukhtasar Ikhtilaf al-Ulama*, 1:230.

106. Abu Bakr Ahmad b. 'Ali al-Razi Al-Jassas, *Sharh Mukhtasar al-Tahawi* (Medina: Dar al-Siraj, 1983), 1:702.

107. Al-Sarkahsi, *Al-Mabsut*, 10:151–53.

108. Al-Sarkahsi, 10:151.

109. "Basharatiha min al-lin wa al-khushuna" (al-Kasani, *Badai' al-Sana'i'*, 10:483).

110. Al-Sarakhsi, *Al-Mabsut*, 10:160.

111. Al-Jassas, *Mukhtasar Ikhtilaf al-Ulama*, 1:702.

112. "Daf'an lil haraj 'an al-nas" (al-Kasani, *Badai' al-Sana'i'*, 10:483).

113. Al-Sarakhsī refers to these as "work clothes" in relation to both the enslaved woman and the man's female relatives: "Wa innama takhruj fi thiyab mihnatiha" (*Al-Mabsut*, 10:151).

3. AGE AND GENDERED LEGAL PERSONHOOD

1. IRIN, "Yemen: No Law Protecting Children against Early Marriages," *Women Living under Muslim Laws*, February 21, 2010, https://wrrc.wluml.org/node/6000.

2. IRIN, "Yemen."

3. IRIN, "Yemen."

4. IRIN, "Yemen."

5. The post appeared in April 2014, a couple of weeks before another bill stipulating a minimum age for marriage was submitted to the prime minister. The post's appearance on his English-language page, rather than on his Arabic-language page, however, raises some questions about who the intended audience might be.

6. Habib 'Ali al-Jifri, "The Crime of Child Marriages," Facebook, April 6, 2014, https://www .facebook.com/habibalieng/posts/pfbid0M3Z6GGJ8NX3UL6Y68rtfZqPC50fWELzcxm LjcvpnLngmKp3nGXdhhnqEgvsRSDpDl.

7. Al-Jifri, "Crime." The English-language post uses the phrase "body and soul." In an Arabic interview on this topic, al-Jifri uses the language of "darar nafsi." The word *nafsi* can be understood to refer to harm that is both physical as well as psychological. See: "Munaz-arat al-Islam," interview by Usama al-Azhari, April 18, 2015, CBC Egypt, YouTube video, 4:56:55, https://www.youtube.com/watch?v=ufswELr220g.

8. It is important to note here a differentiation between the term "minor," which I use in this chapter, and the concept of the "child" in what we today refer to as child marriages. Childhood and adulthood are configured along different parameters in premodern Islamic law. Legal majority was defined as the onset of puberty for men and women (i.e., nocturnal emissions in boys and menstruation in girls). Thus, a marriage between a fifteen-year-old girl who had entered puberty and a prepubescent ten-year-old boy would be understood as a marriage between an adult female and a male child in Islamic law. Similarly, a marriage between two individuals, aged fifteen, would be considered a marriage of two adults if both individuals had already entered puberty. However, both situations would be considered child marriages within many contemporary legal systems.

9. Hugh Cunningham, "Review Essay: Histories of Childhood," *American Historical Review* 103, no. 4 (1998): 1202.

10. The same is true for enslaved people, who can also be compelled into marriage. For more on this, see the previous chapter.

11. Philippe Aries, *Centuries of Childhood: A Social History of Family Life* (New York: Vintage, 1965).

12. Cunningham has argued, however, that this is a fundamental misunderstanding of Aries's argument owing to the way it was translated from French to English (Cunningham, "Review Essay," 1197).

13. Colin Heywood, *A History of Childhood: Children and Childhood in the West from Medieval to Modern Times* (Cambridge: Polity Press, 2001), chapter 1.

14. Anver Giladi, *Children of Islam: Concepts of Childhood in Medieval Muslim Society* (Basingstoke: Macmillan, 1992).

15. Najmabadi, "Crafting an Educated Housewife."

16. Kueny, *Conceiving Identities*, 52.

17. Zahra Ayubi, "Rearing Gendered Souls: Childhood and the Making of Muslim Manhood in Pre-Modern Islamic Ethics," *Journal of the American Academy of Religion* 87 (2019): 1–31.

18. Qur'an 17:23.

19. Al-Bukhari, *Sahih al-Bukhari*, 7138.

20. Ahmad b. Muhammad b. Hanbal, *Musnad al-Imam Ahmad ibn Hanbal*, Beirut: Mu'assasat al-Risalah, 1993–2001, 7073.

21. Mansour Shaki, "Children iii. Legal Rights of Children in Sasanian Period," in *Encyclopaedia Iranica*, 4:407–10 (New York: Ehsan Yarshater for Iranian Studies, 1996). New York, 1996), https://www.iranicaonline.org/articles/children-iii.

22. As Carolyn Baugh has noted, paternal power in Islamic law largely ended when the child came of age (*Minor Marriage*, 30).

23. Al-Kasani, *Badai' al-Sana'i'*, 3:367.

24. In Islamic law, the bride receives a dower from the husband upon/at the time of the marriage. The woman is at liberty to negotiate whatever amount she wishes; nonetheless, jurists have ruminated on the appropriate amount of dower in case it came under contestation. Legally, the dower was based on the class background and status of the woman's family, particularly the dower amount of the women of the paternal family.

25. Hanafi jurists do often talk about nocturnal emissions as a sign of puberty for girls as well. See al-Kasani, *Badai' al-Sana'i'*, 16:50.

26. See also Ayubi ("Rearing Gendered Souls," 6), who notes this in relation to Islamic ethical discourse as well.

27. For more on this, see juristic discussions in the book *Kitab al-Hajr* in al-Kasani's *Bada'i' al-Sana'i'*.

28. Al-Kasani, *Badai' al-Sana'i'*, 16:46–47.

29. In male children, this state is based on physiological markers: the prepubescent male child can achieve an erection (that the law construes as desire-bearing) but is not yet able to ejaculate. For the female child, entrance into this liminal stage is not gauged by physiological markers of her desire, but of her desirability to men (Al-Sarakhsi, *al-Mabsut*, 9:55). For a more detailed discussion of this liminal stage across the Sunni legal schools, see *Al-Mawsu'ah al-fiqhiyya al-Kuwaitiyah* (Kuwait: Kuwait Ministry of Awqaf and Islamic Affairs, 1983), 36:338. For more on the different stages of human development between childhood and adulthood, see Oğuzhan Tan, "Childhood and Child Marriage in Islamic Law," *Cumhuriyet Ilahiyat Dergisi* 22, no. 2 (2018): 783–805.

30. For more on the distinction between these two forms of acquisition, see the section on legal capacity in the introduction.

31. Despite this legal incapacity, the Hanafis considered the possibility of mature male minors (*al-sabi al-'aqil*) contracting their own marriages. In such a situation, they held, the contract was suspended until the minor's guardian consented to the marriage, as discussed below; see also al-Kasani, *Badai' al-Sana'i'*, 3:329–30.

32. Despite the more expansive definition, Hanafis distinguished between the father and paternal grandfather and other agnate relatives. While the child had the option at puberty to rescind a marriage contracted by agnate relatives, a marriage contracted by the father or paternal grandfather was binding.

33. Whereas a male child is considered a minor (*katan*) until age thirteen, a female's minority has a few more gradations. She is considered a minor (*ketannah*) until she is twelve, at which point she reaches legal majority. However, she is considered a *na'arah* until she is twelve and six months and a *bogeret* at twelve and a half plus one day. The distinction is important, in that a *na'arah* must have the father's consent in order to contract a marriage. Furthermore, the father of a *ketannah* or a *na'arah* can negotiate her betrothal (*kiddushin*)

without her consent. See Ben Zion Schereschewsky and Menachem Elon, "Child Marriage," in *Encyclopedia Judaica*, ed. Michael Beck (Jerusalem: Encyclopedia Judaica, 1972), 616–17.

34. Roughly 50–500 CE. The Mishnah and halakhic Midrash were the key scholarly productions from the years 50–135 CE, and the Palestinian Talmud, the Aggadic Midrash, and the Babylonian Talmud from 220 to 500 CE.

35. Baugh, *Minor Marriage*, 26.

36. Schereschewsky and Elon, "Child Marriage," 616.

37. Baugh, *Minor Marriage*, 28.

38. See Baugh, *Minor Marriage*, 28; M. K. Hopkins, "The Age of Roman Girls at Marriage," *Population Studies* 18 (1965): 309–27; and Brent D. Shaw, "The Age of Roman Girls at Marriage: Some Reconsiderations," *Journal of Roman Studies* 77 (1987): 30–46.

39. Angeliki E. Laiou, "Sex, Consent, and Coercion in Byzantium," in *Consent and Coercion to Sex and Marriage in Ancient and Medieval Societies*, ed. Angeliki E. Laiou (Washington, DC: Dumbarton Oaks, 1993), 109–219.

40. Shaki, "Children iii."

41. Leslie Peirce, *Morality Tales: Law and Gender in the Ottoman Court of Aintab* (Berkeley: University of California Press, 2003), 129–42.

42. For more information on child marriage from a sociolegal perspective, see Judith E. Tucker, *In the House of Law: Gender and Islamic Law in Ottoman Syria and Palestine* (Berkeley: University of California Press, 1998). Legal opinions from that period also demonstrate that consummation of the marriage when the female child had not entered puberty was an exceptional practice. See Mahmoud Yazbak, "Minor Marriages and Khiyār al-Bulūgh in Ottoman Palestine: A Note on Women's Strategies in a Patriarchal Society," *Islamic Law and Society* 9, no. 3 (2002): 395.

43. Tucker, *In the House of Law*, 148.

44. See Maya Shatzmiller, *Her Day in Court: Women's Property Rights in Fifteenth-Century Granada* (Cambridge, MA: Harvard University Press, 2007), Chapter 1.

45. 'Aisha's age is, of course, hotly contested. While the pre-modern legal texts uniformly describe her age as six at the time of the marriage contract and nine at the time of consummation, modern Muslim discourse has disputed these claims. Some thinkers argue that she was twelve at the age of consummation, while others assert that she was eighteen. Some have even proposed that she was twenty-one. In her extensive survey of early juristic discussions on minor marriage, Baugh argues that the incident of 'Aisha's marriage is rarely brought up in early legal compendiums (*Minor Marriage*, 61). For more on the contestations around 'Aisha's age, see Kecia Ali, *Sexual Ethics and Islam: Feminist Reflections on Qur'an, Hadith, and Jurisprudence* (Oxford: Oneworld Academic, 2006), chapter 8; Kecia Ali, *Lives of Muhammad* (Cambridge, MA: Harvard University Press, 2014), chapter 5; and Jonathan Brown, *Misquoting Muhammad: The Challenge and Choices of Interpreting the Prophet's Legacy* (London: Oneworld Academic, 2014), Chapter 4.

46. For a more detailed account of these early narratives, see Baugh, *Minor Marriage*.

47. Al-Kasani, *Badai' al-Sana'i'*, 3:355.

48. Al-San'ani, *Al-Musannaf*, 6:163, no. 10352. In another narration, she is described as a young girl (*jariya*) who played with other young girls (al-San'ani, *Al-Musannaf*, 6:162–63, no. 10351).

49. Another tale in the *Al-Muṣannaf* describes ʿUmar's desire to marry Umm Kulthum as motivated not by his sexual desire ("inni lam atazawwaj min nishat bi") but because he wanted to link his lineage to the Prophet's (al-Sanʿani, *Al-Musannaf*, 6:163, no. 10354). While he was already linked to the Prophet through marriage (his daughter Hafsa was among the wives of the Prophet), marrying Umm Kulthum (the daughter of Ali, the Prophet's cousin) would allow him to link his lineage to that of the Prophet.

50. Al-Sanʿani, *Al-Musannaf*, 10352.

51. For more on the line of succession in guardianship see al-Shaybani, *Al-Hujja ʿala Ahl al-Madina*, 3:7. For more on the minor's right of rescission see al-Shaybani, 3:140.

52. For more on this, see Baugh, *Minor Marriage*, chapters 4 and 5.

53. al-Shaybani, *Al-Hujja ʿala Ahl al-Madina*, 3:140–42.

54. Al-Kasani, *Badaiʿ al-Sanaʾiʿ*, 3:345; al-Marghinani, *Al-Hidaya*, 1:193.

55. See Maya Shatzmiller, *Her Day in Court: Women's Property Rights in Fifteenth-Century Granada* (Cambridge, MA: Harvard University Press, 2007).

56. al-Shaybani, *Al-Hujja ʿala Ahl al-Madina*, 3:98.

57. The *Hujja* first states her name as Qariʿa, but later it appears as Fariʿa, so her name is under dispute. Baugh notes that she has searched for more information on her with no success. Ali has chosen the name Qurayʿa, whereas Baugh has chosen the name Fariʿa. I have listed both names here to stay close to the text of *al-Hujja*. See Ali, *Marriage and Slavery*, 29, and Baugh, *Minor Marriage*, 89.

58. al-Shaybani, *Al-Hujja ʿala Ahl al-Madina*, 3:117.

59. See, for example, Judith E. Tucker, "Questions of Consent: Contracting a Marriage in Ottoman Syria and Palestine," in *The Islamic Marriage Contract: Case Studies in Islamic Family Law*, ed. Asifa Quraishi and Frank E. Vogel (Cambridge, MA: Harvard University Press, 2008), 123–35, and Yazbak, "Minor Marriages."

60. As Baugh notes, while some jurists state that Ibn Shubrumah took a position against minor marriage, others (such as al-Marwazi and Ibn ʿAbd l-Barr) argued that he supported it (see Baugh, *Minor Marriage*, chapter 2).

61. Ibn ʿAbd al-Barr reports that Ibn Shubrumah held that a minor had the right to rescind the marriage after the onset of puberty but still affirmed the right of any guardian to contract the marriage of a minor. See Carolyn Baugh, "An Exploration of the Juristic Consensus (*ijmaʿ*) on Compulsion in the Marriages of Minors," *Comparative Islamic Studies* 5 (2011): 58n84.

62. Qurʾan 4:6.

63. Al-Sarakhsi, *Al-Mabsut*, 4:212.

64. Both ʿUthman al-Batti and Ibn Shubrumah were prominent jurists who were contemporaries of Abu Hanifa.

65. Al-Kasani, *Badaiʿ al-Sanaʾiʿ*, 2:354.

66. Al-Sarakhsi, *Al-Mabsut*, 4:212.

67. See the previous chapter.

68. As the Hanafis were the only ones who granted the right of compulsion to legal guardians more broadly, perhaps they refused the right of rescission for the father and paternal grandfather in order to distinguish between the guardianship of the family patriarchs and other adult guardians. Or perhaps they made this distinction in order to safeguard the right of the father and paternal grandfather over the members of the family. I suspect it was both.

69. Al-Marghinani, *Al-Hidaya*, 1:194. Al-Marghinani makes this comment in the broader context of explaining why rescission requires the intervention of a judge in contrast to the annulment of marriage at the emancipation of an enslaved woman. His explanation centers around the nature of the harm caused to these two individuals (the child and the enslaved woman) as a result of being compelled into marriage. In minor marriage, he argues, the harm caused to the child is not obvious (*khafi*) and is thus difficult to decipher, requiring the intervention of the judge. In the case of the enslaved woman, he argues, the evident (*jali*) harm is owing to the additional dominion under which she becomes bound by her enslaver (i.e., the dominion of enslavement and marriage). Thus, upon emancipation, she has the right to decide whether to remain under the dominion of her husband, a relationship she was compelled into by her enslaver. For more on the marriage of enslaved women see the previous chapter.

70. Al-Sarakhsi, *Al-Mabsut*, 4:212–13.

71. The idea of compatibility here is understood as based on particular markers of social ranking. For more on this, see the following section on the marriage of virgin and non-virgin women.

72. Al-Sarakhsi, *Al-Mabsut*, 4:212–13.

73. "Al-lati yujama' mithluha" (al-Sarakhsi, *Al-Mabsut*, 5:148).

74. Later Hanafi jurists began to define female desirability through both fixed age markers and physical attributes. Almost three hundred years after al-Sarakhsi, 'Uthman b. 'Ali al-Zayla'i, a famous fourteenth-century Hanafi jurist, argued that a girl over the age of nine was considered desirable and a girl under the age of five was categorically undesirable. For medieval Hanafis, the desirability of the female child was ambivalent between the ages of six and eight, when the ability to endure penetration had to be determined, often by her plumpness. Late Hanafism maintained the same position. In his expansive legal commentary *Hashiyat Radd al-Muhtar*, Ibn 'Abidin, a nineteenth-century Hanafi jurist, also defines the minor girl as one who has not yet reached nine years of age. See Muhammad Amin ibn 'Umar Ibn 'Abidin, *Hashiyat Radd al-Muhtar 'ala al-durr al-Mukhtar* (Beirut: Dar al-Fikr, 1992), 1:306.

75. The classical jurists define "valid privacy" to be when the spouses are alone in each other's company and no other individual would enter that space without their permission. The assumption is that in the moment of such privacy, sexual intercourse would take place. See Salah Muhammad Abu al-Hajj, *Subul al-wifaq fi ahkam al-zawaj wa al-talaq* (Amman: al-Warraq, 2005), 151.

76. Al-Sarakhsi, *Al-Mabsut*, 5:150. See also Al-Kasani, *Badai' al-Sana'i'*, 6:26.

77. Al-Kasani, *Badai' al-Sana'i'*, 6:26.

78. Islamic law holds that if a man marries and has sexual intercourse with a woman, then certain female relatives of the wife become permanently prohibited to him in marriage (the woman's mother, for example). These are called "prohibitions of consanguinity."

79. "Wa tab' al-'uqala' la yamilu ila wat' al-saghirah al-lati la tushtaha wa la tahtamil al-jima'" (al-Sarakhsi, *Al-Mabsut*, 9:75).

80. Jurists also considered the possibility of physical harm in sex with adult women. Both al-Kasani and al-Sarakhsi have extended discussions about the legal implications of a man or husband causing physical harm, particularly perineal tearing, to the woman or wife during sex. See al-Kasani, *Badai' al-Sana'i'*, 17:90–92.

81. Third-degree perineal lacerations are a tear in the vaginal tissue, perineal skin, and perineal muscles that extend into the anal sphincter. Fourth-degree lacerations are the most severe in that the tear goes through the anal sphincter. Al-Sarakhsi refers to this as the inability of the female child to control her bowels due to the tearing (*la tastamsik al-bawl*). For more on perineal tearing, see Ryan Goh, Daryl Goh, and Hasthika Ellepola, "Perineal tears—A Review," *Australian Journal of General Practice* 47, nos. 1–2 (2018): 35–38.

82. Al-Sarakhsi, *Al-Mabsut*, 9:75–76.

83. The Hanafi conception of sexual intercourse as vaginal penetration is most apparent in the juridical conversation around "actual intercourse" (*haqiqat al-wat'*) and its importance in determining whether financial compensation is due to the wife. The term "actual intercourse" is an expression used often in relation to the question of physical harm caused to the girl, the term refers to the act of penetration. Thus, should the act of penetration cause injury to the minor child, the husband was liable to pay recompense. In contrast to this phrase, we also find reference to "nonvaginal intercourse" (*al-jima' fi ma dun al-farj*.) Here, the jurists bring into discussion the necessity of maintenance (*nafaqa*) for the minor bride who is not yet capable of enduring sex.

84. "la yujami' mithluhu" (al-Kasani, *Badai' al-Sana'i'*, 6:26, section "Fasl bayan ma yata'akkad bihi al-mahr"). While the verb *jama'a* is used for prepubescent boys and girls alike, I interpret the phrase as a passive participle (*yujama'*) for the prepubescent girl and as an active participle for the prepubescent boy: i.e., "the one, the like of I has sexual intercourse" (*sabi al-ladhi yujami' mithluhu*). Premodern Arabic texts do not provide diacritical marks and thus the active and passive participles require interpretation on the part of the reader. My choice here is justified by the gendered usage of the verb (*j-m-'*). As Kecia Ali notes, the verb "to have intercourse" (*j-m-'*) in Arabic takes a direct object and not a prepositional phrase (i.e., the man sexes the woman rather than having sex with her) (Ali, *Marriage and Slavery*, 141). While the verb itself does not stipulate a particular gender as the subject, jurists do not use the female as the subject who performs sex. Thus, when using the verb "to have intercourse," the jurists never use the phrase, "she performs sex on him," but always, "he performs sex on her." Al-Sarakhsi, for example, always speaks of the boy as the active subject of sexual intercourse. In the section on the legal definition of sexual intercourse in chapter 1, we saw that al-Sarakhsi linguistically describes illicit sexual intercourse between an adult woman and a prepubescent boy as the active agency of the boy in penetration and the passive agency of the woman in making herself available. Given the gendered usage of the verb "to have sexual intercourse" and its direct object, I have chosen to read the phrase used to describe the prepubescent girl as a passive participle and the phrase used to describe the prepubescent boy as an active participle. See also al-Sarakhsi, *Al-Mabsut*, 5:148; al-Jassas, *Ahkam al-Qur'an*, 4:196, from section "bab ma yuhram min al-nisa in surah nisa"; and al-Farghani, *Fatawa Qadikhan fi Madhhab al-Imam al-A'zam Abi Hanifa al-Nu'man* (Beirut: Dar al-Kutub al-'Ilmiyah, 2009), 1:346 for the use of the same terminology.

85. Al-Sarakhsi, *Al-Mabsut*, 6:52.

86. In Islamic law, the unilateral right of divorce (*talaq*) is granted only to the husband; it does not require the wife's consent and can be either revocable (*raj'i*) or irrevocable (*ba'in*). In a revocable divorce, the husband can rescind the pronouncement of divorce during the waiting period (*'iddah*) of three menstrual cycles, or, if the wife is pregnant, during the entire gestational period (regardless of the woman's consent). If the divorce is finalized after

the end of the waiting period and the couple wishes to reconcile, they must marry again under a new marriage contract. If the divorce is irrevocable, however, the husband may not rescind the utterance of divorce, and at the end of the waiting period the couple is permanently divorced. In order for the couple to remarry in this situation, the wife must marry another man, consummate the marriage, and get a divorce before remarriage. The interim marriage that makes remarriage to the first husband possible is referred to as *zawaj al-tahlil*. For more on *zawaj al-tahlil* as well as controversies over social practices around this form of marriage, see Ali, *Marriage and Slavery*, 84–85, and Yossef Rapoport, *Marriage, Money and Divorce in Medieval Islamic Society* (Cambridge: Cambridge University Press, 2005).

87. The hadith is found in *Sahih al-Bukhari* and refers to a woman who came to the Prophet complaining about her sexual dissatisfaction with her husband. In her complaint, she told the Prophet that she was previously married to a man who had divorced her, after which she married her second husband. When she attributed her sexual dissatisfaction to the diminutive size of her husband's penis, the Prophet perceived her complaint to be an excuse to return to her first husband, to which he responded by stipulating that this would be possible only after her second marriage was consummated (*hatta yadhuq 'usaylataki wa tadhuqi 'usaylatahu*). See al-Bukhari, *Sahih al-Bukhari*, 7, book 68, hadith 10, sunnah.com, accessed October 15, 2023, https://sunnah.com/bukhari:5260. (This passage is also quoted in al-Sarakhsi, *Al-Mabsut*, 5:148.) Additionally, the act of penetration that makes the woman permissible to her first husband is described as "the penetrative act of the boy" (*dukhul al-sabi*) (al-Sarakhsi, *Al-Mabsut*, 5:148).

88. Interestingly, while al-Sarakhsi's argument is predicated on the woman's sexual pleasure, he does not provide any markers for determining its presence. The fulfillment of her desire is simply assumed.

89. Al-Sarakhsi, *Al-Mabsut*, 5:148.

90. Al-Sarakhsi also uses the phrases "the action of the boy" (*fi'l al-sabi*) or "the sex act of the boy" (*bi wat' al-sabi*) to describe sexual intercourse between the adult woman and the boy (*Al-Mabsut*, 5:148).

91. I am grateful to the reviewer of my book for urging me to critically examine this juristic assumption.

92. In his study of marriage and divorce in medieval Cairo and Damascus, Rapoport mentions that there was a practice involving individuals who would perform the role of *muhallil*; i.e., the man who would marry, have sexual intercourse, and then divorce the wife so that she could remarry her previous husband. Rapoport claims that elite households commonly employed such a professional *muhallil* in order to preserve the family's honor. While Rapoport does not mention the use of prepubescent boys by their families for such a purpose, it is possible they might have, given that serving as a *muhallil* could be a means for earning an income (*Marriage, Money, and Divorce*, chapter 5).

93. Baugh, *Minor Marriage*, 148.

94. See, for example, Harald Motzki, "Child Marriage in Seventeenth-Century Palestine," in *Islamic Legal Interpretation, Muftis and their Practices*, ed. Muhammad Khalid Masud, Brinkley Morris Messick, and David Stephan Powers (Cambridge, MA: Harvard University Press, 1996), 129–40; Yazbak, "Minor Marriages"; Tucker, "Questions of Consent"; and Tucker, *In the House of the Law*.

95. I am referring here to the unrestricted *legal* right granted to the adult male. In practice, families probably played a significant role in arranging the marriages of both their male and female children, whether minor or legal adult.

96. While the Hanafis allow a free woman to contract her own marriage, legal texts often assumed the presence of the guardian. Al-Sarakhsi argued, in fact, that it is recommended (*mustahab*) for the guardian to contract the marriage on the woman's behalf (*Al-Mabsut*, 5:12). For more on the different legal considerations regarding the guardian's role in contracting women's marriages, see Kecia Ali, "Marriage in Classical Islamic Jurisprudence: A Survey of Doctrines," in *The Islamic Marriage Contract: Case Studies in Islamic Family Law*, ed. Asifa Quraishi and Frank E. Vogel (Cambridge, MA: Harvard University Press, 2008), 40–44.

97. Al-Kasani, *Badai' al-Sana'i'*, 3:358.

98. Al-Sarakhsi, *Al-Mabsut*, 4:197; al-Kasani, *Badai' al-Sana'i'*, 5:358.

99. Suitability (*kafa'a*) was measured according to six considerations: lineage, religion, occupation, freedom, good character, and wealth. Thus, if a woman married a man who was not her equal based on these six considerations, her father and paternal grandfather reserved the right to challenge and void the marriage. For more information, see Siddiqui, "Law and the Desire."

100. al-Sarakhsi, *Al-Mabsut*, 5:10. See also al-Marghinani, *Al-Hidaya*, 1:191.

101. al-Sarakhsi, *Al-Mabsut*, 5:13.

102. The guardian, however, could not compel her into marriage, as the ultimate decision to accept or reject a marriage lay with the adult bride. See Siddiqui, "Law and the Desire," 52–53.

103. See al-Sarakhsi, *Al-Mabsut*, 5:12–13; al-Kasani, *Badai' al-Sana'i'*, 3:360; al-Marghinani, *Al-Hidaya*, 1:192.

104. In an oft-quoted hadith, 'Aisha asks the Prophet if women's consent for marriage should be sought. When the Prophet replies in the affirmative, she asks further regarding the virgin woman, who might feel shy in expressing her consent openly. To this, the Prophet replied that her silence is her consent. See Al Bukhari, *Sahih al-Bukhari*, 9: book 89, hadith 79, sunnah.com, accessed October 15, 2023, https://sunnah.com/bukhari:6946.

105. "Fa innahu la yastahyi min al-raghbah fi al-nisa'" (al-Sarakhsi, *Al-Mabsut*, 5:6).

106. Al-Sarakhsi, *Al-Mabsut*, 5:6

107. It is important to note that virginity in legal texts was not always understood as physiological or anatomical; rather, it was constructed as a sociolegal status. Hanafi jurists state, for example, that women who "lost their virginity" towing to leaping, menstruation, or injury would be considered legally a virgin with regard to consent. For a woman who had committed fornication, the Hanafis held two positions. The first, held by Abu Yusuf, maintained that such a woman would acquire the legal status of a nonvirgin. Al-Sarakhsi justified this position by claiming that it would be inappropriate for this woman to inhabit the shyness of a virgin, which would come across as flippant instead of praiseworthy. He asked: how can a woman who did not shy away from expressing desire for a man in the most abominable of ways shy away from expressing her desire in the best of ways? (al-Sarakhsi, *Al-Mabsut*, 5:11). The other position was held by Abu Hanifa, who stated that she was still legally considered a virgin as she was read socially as a virgin. For the law to demand that she verbalize her consent as a nonvirgin would make her vulnerable to social censure and

rebuke. See also al-Kasani, *Badai' al-Sana'i'*, 3:363, and al-Marghinani, *Al-Hidaya*, 1:192. For more on virginity as a construct, see Kelto-Lillis, *Virgin Territory*.

108. Katz, *Women in the Mosque*, 101.

109. Al-Sarakhsi, *Al-Mabsut*, 4:197.

110. "Fa in kanat al-bikr qad dakhalat fi al-sin fa ijtumi'a laha ra'yuha wa 'aqluha" (al-Sarakhsi, *Al-Mabsut*, 5:213).

111. Al-Sarakhsi, 5:207.

112. Al-Sarakhsi, 5:208. As mentioned earlier, al-Sarakhsi takes as precedent the Prophet's marriage to 'Aisha when she was six and its consummation when she was nine. However, since the Hanafi jurists insist that a daughter return to the custodial care of her father at age twelve, we can perhaps extrapolate that girls were far more likely to be married at the age of twelve or beyond rather than at younger ages (as the mention of 'Aisha would seem to indicate). My thanks to Elizabeth Urban for helping me recognize this point.

113. Al-Sarakhsi, 5:208. Al-Sarakhsi's reasoning for why the young boy enters into the father's custodial care has more to do with the socialization into the masculinity appropriate for a free man. If a boy were to remain with his mother, al-Sarakhsi claimed, the company of women would make him effeminate.

114. Ishita Pande, "'Listen to the Child': Law, Sex, and the Child Wife in Indian Historiography," *History Compass* 11 (2013): 687.

115. Gauri Viswanathan, *Outside the Fold: Conversion, Modernity, and Belief* (Princeton, NJ: Princeton University Press, 1998), 107.

116. Pande, "Listen to the Child," 697; my emphasis.

117. Ali, *Marriage and Slavery*, 32.

4. GENDER AND LEGAL PERSONHOOD IN HANAFI LAW

1. Jamal A. Badawi, *Gender Equity in Islam: Basic Principles* (Plainfield, IN: American Trust, 1995).

2. See Muslim Association of Canada—Calgary, "Dr Jamal Badawi at Al-Salam Centre speaking about gender equality and equity, a normative Islamic perspective," Facebook, April 21, 2019, https://www.facebook.com/MACCalgary/videos/383704515818900/.

3. Badawi, *Gender Equity in Islam*, n. 1; author's emphasis.

4. Badawi, n. 1; author's emphasis.

5. It is worth mentioning that Badawi has a conflicted relationship throughout the book with the historical Islamic legal tradition. In his introductory note, he emphasizes that he is returning to the primary sources of Islam (the Qur'an and Sunnah) to make his claims; however, he insists that one should not be beholden to particular jurists' conclusions if they contradict these primary sources. Badawi makes arguments for women's legal rights that come from the legal schools. He does not, however, explicitly cite the legal schools when it comes to staking these claims. Badawi's attitude is consistent with revivalist engagements with Islamic law, which tend to read the law selectively. The legal schools are relied on as authoritative when the author agrees with them but are rejected when they contradict the author's claims. For more on this sort of cherry-picking, see Kecia Ali, "Progressive Muslims and Islamic Jurisprudence: The Necessity for a Critical Engagement with Marriage and Divorce Law," in *Progressive Muslims: On Justice, Gender and Pluralism*, ed. Omid Safi (Oxford: Oneworld Academics, 2003), 163–89.

6. Seyyed Hossein Nasr, *Traditional Islam in the Modern World* (London: K. Paul International, 1990), 47.

7. Nasr, 49.

8. Chaudhry, *Domestic Violence.*

9. Omaima Abou-Bakr, "Turning the Tables: Perspectives on the Construction of 'Muslim Manhood,'" *Hawwa* 11 (2014): 89–107.

10. Fatima Seedat, "Sitting in Difference: Queering the Study of Islam," *Journal of Feminist Studies in Religion* 34 (2018): 149–54.

11. The full verse reads: "And as for those of you who, owing to circumstances, are not in a position to marry free believing women, [let them marry] believing maidens from among those whom you rightfully possess. And God knows all about your faith; each one of you is an issue of the other. Marry them, then, with their people's leave, and give them their dowers in an equitable manner—they being women who give themselves in honest wedlock, not in fornication, nor as secret love-companions. And when they are married, and thereafter become guilty of immoral conduct, they shall be liable to half the penalty to which free married women are liable. This [permission to marry slave-girls applies] to those of you who fear lest they stumble into evil. But it is for your own good to persevere in patience [and to abstain from such marriages]: and God is much-forgiving, a dispenser of grace." (Qur'an 4:25)

12. Abu Bakr Ahmad b. 'Ali al-Razi Al-Jassas, *Ahkam al-Quran* (Beirut: Dar al-Fikr, 2008), 2:239.

13. Katz, *Women in the Mosque*, chapter 1.

14. In practice, these hierarchies were complicated by hierarchies of enslavement. Muslim practices of enslavement had elite, domestic, and plantation slavery. Thus, an enslaved woman who was a concubine to a noble or the mother of a caliph would certainly command tremendous respect, above and beyond many free women in society. Overwhelmingly, however, legal discussions pertain to domestic slavery.

15. Kimberlé Crenshaw, "Demarginalizing the Intersection of Race and Sex: A Black Feminist Critique of Antidiscrimination Doctrine, Feminist Theory, and Antiracist Politics," *University of Chicago Legal Forum* 140, no. 1 (1989): 314–43. While Crenshaw is often credited with coining the term "intersectionality," it is important to note that intersectional analysis predates Crenshaw. As Patricia Hill Collins and Sirma Bilge have argued, intersectionality existed as a critical inquiry and critical praxis well before its naming and introduction into the academy in the 1990s. They cite the work of Toni Cade Bambara, Frances Beal, and "A Black Feminist Statement" by the Combahee River Collective (CRC) as articulations of intersectionality among Black feminists. Collins and Bilge also describe the work of Chicana feminists like Gloria Anzaldúa, Indigenous feminists, Asian American feminists, and postcolonial feminists engaged in intersectional analysis. See Collins and Bilge, *Intersectionality*, chapter 3 for more information and the sources mentioned above.

16. Crenshaw, "Demarginalizing the Intersection," 321.

17. Patricia Hill Collins, *Intersectionality as Critical Social Theory* (Durham, NC: Duke University Press, 2019), 26.

18. Katz, "Gender and Law."

19. Seedat, "Sex and the Legal Subject," 245–46.

20. Collins, *Intersectionality as Critical Social Theory*, 227–28. An additive approach, Collins argues, disrupts the logic of segregation that is assumed in the analysis of social

relations, an analytical approach that presumes that each entity has only one place in relation to other places (229).

21. Collins, 229.

22. Collins, 241.

23. Collins argues that the desire to dissect and tease apart is emblematic of the Western logic of segregation. This analytical approach is unable to contend with complexity and therefore tries to dissect and break down entities into individual parts that can be observed and analyzed (Collins, 227–28 and 243–44).

24. Ngaire Naffine, "Can Women Be Legal Persons?," in *Visible Women: Essays on Feminist Legal Theory and Political Philosophy*, ed. Susan James and Stephanie Palmer (London: Hart, 2013), 75.

25. Naffine, 73.

26. Naffine, *Law and the Sexes*, 54.

27. Baugh, *Minor Marriage*, 148.

28. Al-Kasani, *Badai' al-Sana'i'*, 3:330.

29. Al-Kasani, 16:46–47.

30. Al-Kasani, 16:51.

31. For a more detailed discussion of this, see chapter 1.

32. Hall, *Familiar Stranger*, 16.

33. Collins and Bilge, *Intersectionality*, 167.

34. For more on the juristic assumptions about marriage and the position this created for the wife, see Ali, *Marriage and Slavery*.

35. Ali, 13–15.

36. Ali, 13–15.

37. Bray, "Men, women and slaves in Abbasid society," 146.

38. Jones-Rogers, *They Were Her Property*, xiii.

39. See Julia Bray's article for a similar discussion for a similar discussion in the context of urban Abbasid society.

40. See, for example, "Kitab al-Hajar" in al-Kasani, *Badai' al-Sana'i'*, 16:40.

41. For more on this, see Nebil Husayn, "*Aḥkām* concerning the *ahl al-bayt*," *Islamic Law and Society* 27 (2019): 145–84, and Razan Idris, "Is the Ex-Slave Equal to the Free Arab in Marriage? Debating Lineage, Race, and Freedom in Mālikī Muslim History" (bachelor's thesis, Duke University, 2018).

42. For more on intersexuality in Islamic law, see Indira Gesink, "Intersex in Islamic Medicine" and "Intersex Bodies."

43. Joan Wallach Scott, "Gender: A Useful Category of Historical Analysis," *American Historical Review* 91, no. 5 (1986): 1053–75.

44. Scott, 1055.

45. Scott, 1059.

46. Scott, 1064.

47. Scott, 1067.

48. Scott, 1067–68.

49. American Historical Association, "Introduction," *American Historical Review* 113, no. 5 (2008): 1344–45.

50. Jeanne Boydston, "Gender as a Question of Historical Analysis," *Gender and History* 20, no. 3 (2008): 563.

51. Boydston, 563.

52. Boydston, 563–64.

53. Boydston, 560.

54. Boydston, 572.

55. Boydston, 577.

56. Boydston, 573.

57. Oyeronke Oyèwùmí, "Conceptualizing Gender: The Eurocentric Foundations of Feminist Concepts and the Challenge of African Epistemologies," *JENDA: A Journal of Culture and African Women Studies* 2, no. 1 (2002): 1.

58. Oyeronke Oyèwùmí, *The Invention of Women: Making an African Sense of Western Gender Discourses* (Minneapolis: University of Minnesota Press, 1997), xii.

59. Oyèwùmí, ix.

60. Oyèwùmí, "Conceptualizing Gender," 2.

61. Oyèwùmí, *Invention of Women*, xiii.

62. Oyeronke Oyèwùmí, "Visualizing the Body: Western Theories and African Subjects," in *African Gender Studies: A Reader*, ed. Oyeronke Oyèwùmi (New York: Palgrave Macmillan, 2005), 11.

63. Oyèwùmí, *Invention of Women*, 13.

64. Asfaneh Najmabadi, "Beyond the Americas: Are Gender and Sexuality Useful Categories of Historical Analysis?" *Journal of Women's History* 18, no. 1 (2006): 17 and 14.

65. Najmabadi, 12.

66. For a broader critique of Orientalist methods in the study of gender and Islamic law, see Annelies Moors, "Debating Islamic Family Law," in *Social History of Women and Gender in the Modern Middle East*, ed. Margaret L. Meriwether and Judith E. Tucker (Boulder, CO: Westview Press, 1999), 141–75.

67. For a more detailed account of social histories of Islamic law and gender, see Yacoob, "Islamic Law and Gender."

68. Yacoob, 82–83.

69. Yacoob, 83–86.

70. Ali, *Marriage and Slavery*.

71. Ali, 8.

72. Ali, 47.

73. Tucker, *Women, Family, and Gender*, 149.

74. As noted in previous chapters, of the four Sunni legal schools, only the Hanafis allowed a free adult virgin woman to contract her own marriage. However, the patriarch retained the right to contest the marriage if he deemed the match incompatible. For more information, see also Siddiqui, "Law and the Desire."

75. Tucker, *Women, Family, and Gender*, 173.

76. Katz, "Gender and Law."

77. Katz, 3.

78. Johansen, "Valorization," 71.

79. Johansen, 72.

80. Johansen, 82.

81. Seedat, "Sex and the Legal Subject," 262.

82. Yacoob, "Islamic Law and Gender."

83. Najmabadi, "Beyond the Americas," 18–19.

84. Ayubi, *Gendered Morality*, 176–77.

85. Sara Abdel-Latif, "Narrativizing Early Mystic and Sufi Women: Mechanisms of Gendering in Sufi Hagiographies," in *The Routledge Handbook on Sufism*, ed. Lloyd Ridgeon (London: Routledge, 2020), 132–45.

86. [Ash] Geissinger, "Applying Gender and Queer Theory to Pre-Modern Sources," in *The Routledge Handbook of Islam and Gender*, ed. Justine Howe (London: Routledge, 2021), 104.

87. Geissinger borrows the term "internally fractured" from Afsaneh Najmabadi. See Geissinger, *Gender and Muslim Constructions*, 26.

88. Serena Tolino, "Locating Discourses on the Gender Binary (and beyond) in Pre-Modern Islamicate Societies," in *Sex and Desire in Muslim Cultures: Beyond Norms and Transgression from the Abbasids to the Present Day*, ed. Aymon Kreil, Lucia Sorbera, and Serena Tolino (London: I. B. Tauris, 2021), 36.

89. Najmabadi, "Beyond the Americas," 14.

90. Jones-Rogers, *They Were Her Property*, xviii.

91. Myrne, "A *Jariya's* Prospects," 64.

92. Abu al-Husayn Ahmad b. Muhammad al-Baghdadi al-Quduri, *Mukhtasar al-Quduri*, (Beirut: Mu'assasat al-Rayan, 2008), 349.

93. Myrne, "A *Jariya's* Prospects," 55.

94. Myrne, 55.

95. Seedat, "Sex and the Legal Subject," 249.

96. Shaikh, *Sufi Narratives of Intimacy*, 211.

97. For more on Shaikh's critique of Sachiko Murata and Seyyed Hossein Nasr, see Shaikh, *Sufi Narratives*, chapter 7.

BIBLIOGRAPHY

PRIMARY SOURCES

al-Bayhaqi, Ahmad b. al-Hussain b. 'Ali. *Sunan al-Bayhaqi al-Kubra*. 10 vols. Mecca: Maktaba Dar al-Baz, 1994.

al-Bukhari, Muhammad b. Ismail. *Sahih al-Bukhari*. Translated by Muhammad Muhsin Khan. 9 vols. Riyadh: Dar-us-Salaam, 1997.

Ibn Abi Shayba, Abu Bakr 'Adallah b. Muhammad b. Ibrahim. *Al-Kitab al-Musannaf fi Ahadith wa al-Athar*. 7 vols. Riyadh: Maktaba al-Rushd, 1988.

Ibn 'Abidin, Muhammad Amin b. 'Umar. *Hashiyat Radd al-Muhtar 'ala al-durr al-Mukhtar*. 6 vols. Beirut: Dar al-Fikr, 1992.

Ibn Hanbal, Ahmad b. Muhammad. *Musnad al-Imam Ahmad ibn Hanbal*. 50 vols. Beirut: Mu'assasat al-Risalah, 1993–2001.

Ibn Nujaym, Zayn al-Din b. Ibrahim b. Muhammad. *Al-Bahr al-Ra'iq: Sharh Kanz al-Daqa'iq*. 8 vols. Beirut: Dar al-Kutub al-'Ilmiyyah,1997.

al-Jaṣṣaṣ, Abu Bakr Ahmad b. 'Ali al-Razi. *Ahkam al-Quran*. 3 vols. Beirut: Dar al-Fikr, 2008.

———. *Mukhtasar Iktilaf al-Ulama*. 5 vols. Beirut: Dar al-Basha'ir al-Islamiyah, 1995.

———. *Sharh Mukhtasar al-Tahawi*. 8 vols. Medina: Dar al-Siraj, 1983.

al-Kasani, 'Ala al-Din Abu Bakr b. Mas'ud. *Badai' al-Sana'i' fi tartib al-Shara'i'*. 10 vols. Lubnan: Dar al-Kutub al-'Ilmiyah: 2010.

al-Marghinani, Burhan al-Din. *Al-Hidaya fi Sharh Bidayat al-Mubtadi'*. 4 vols. Beirut: Dar al-Ihya' al-Turath al-'Arabi: 1995.

Qadi Khan, Fakhr al-Din al-Hasan b. Mansur al-Farghani. *Fatawa Qadikhan fi Madhhab al-Imam al-A'zam Abi Hanifa al-Nu'man*. 3 vols. Beirut: Dar al-Kutub al-'Ilmiyah, 2009.

al-Quduri, Abu al-Husayn Ahmad b. Muhammad al-Baghdadi. *Mukhtasar al-Quduri*. Beirut: Mu'assasat al-Rayan, 2008.

al-San'ani, Abu Bakr 'Abd al-Razzaq b. Hammam. *Al-Musannaf.* 12 vols. Beirut: Al-Maktab al-Islami, 1983.

al-Sarakhsi, Muhammad b. Ahmad. *Kitab al-Mabsut.* 31 vols. Beirut: Dar al-Ma'rifa, 1989.

———. *Usul al-Sarakhsi.* 30 vols. Beirut: Dar al-Ma'rifa, 1997.

al-Shafi'i, Muḥammad b. Idris. *Kitab al-Umm.* 7 vols. Al-Qahirah: al-Dar al-Miṣriyah lil Ta'lif wa al-Tarjamah, 1966.

al-Shaybani, Muhammad b. al-Hasan. *Al-Jami' al-Saghir.* Karachi, Pakistan: Idarat al-Quran wa al-Ulum al-Islamiyah, 1990.

———. *Kitab al-Asl.* 4 vols. Lahore: Dar al-Ma'arif al-Nu'maniyah, 1981.

———. *Kitab al-Hujja 'ala ahl al-Madina.* 4 vols. Beirut: 'Alam al-Kutub, n.d.

SECONDARY SOURCES

Abdel-Latif, Sara. "Narrativizing Early Mystic and Sufi Women: Mechanisms of Gendering in Sufi Hagiographies." In *The Routledge Handbook of Sufism*, edited by Lloyd Ridgeon, 132–45. London: Routledge, 2020.

Abou-Bakr, Omaima. "Turning the Tables: Perspectives on the Construction of 'Muslim Manhood'." *Hawwa* 11 (2014): 89–107.

Abu al-Hajj, Salah Muhammad. *Sabil al-Wusul ila 'ilm al-usul.* Amman: Dar al-Faruq, 2007.

———. *Subul al-wifaq fi ahkam al-zawaj wa al-talaq.* Amman: al-Warraq, 2005.

Ahmed, Leila. *Women and Gender in Islam: Historical Roots of a Modern Debate.* New Haven, CT: Yale University Press, 1993.

Ali, Kecia. "'The best of you will not strike': Al-Shafi'i on Qur'an, Sunnah, and Wife-Beating." *Comparative Islamic Studies* 2, no. 2 (2006): 143–55.

———. "Concubinage and Consent." *International Journal of Middle East Studies* 49 (2017): 148–52.

———. *Lives of Muhammad.* Cambridge, MA: Harvard University Press, 2014.

———. *Marriage and Slavery in Early Islam.* Cambridge, MA: Harvard University Press, 2010.

———. "Marriage in Classical Islamic Jurisprudence: A Survey of Doctrines." In *The Islamic Marriage Contract: Case Studies in Islamic Family Law*, edited by Asifa Quraishi and Frank E. Vogel, 11–45. Cambridge, MA: Harvard University Press, 2008.

———. "Progressive Muslims and Islamic Jurisprudence: The Necessity for Critical Engagement with Marriage and Divorce Law." In *Progressive Muslims: On Justice, Gender and Pluralism*, edited by Omid Safi, 163–89. Oxford: Oneworld Academic, 2003.

———. *Sexual Ethics and Islam: Feminist Reflections on Qur'an, Hadith, and Jurisprudence.* Oxford: Oneworld Academic, 2006.

American Historical Association. "Introduction." *American Historical Review* 113, no. 5 (2008): 1344–45.

Aries, Philippe. *Centuries of Childhood: A Social History of Family Life.* New York: Vintage, 1965.

Asad, Muhammad, trans. *The Message of the Qur'an: The Full Account of the Revealed Arabic Text Accompanied by Parallel Transliteration.* London: Book Foundation, 2003.

Ayalon, David. *Eunuchs, Caliphs, and Sultans: A Study in Power Relationships.* Jerusalem: Magnes Press, 1999.

Ayubi, Zahra. *Gendered Morality: Classical Islamic Ethics of the Self, Family, and Society.* New York: Columbia University Press, 2019.

———. "Rearing Gendered Souls: Childhood and the Making of Muslim Manhood in Pre-Modern Islamic Ethics." *Journal of the American Academy of Religion* 87 (2019): 1–31.

Azam, Hina. *Sexual Violation in Islamic Law: Substance, Evidence, and Procedure.* New York: Cambridge University Press, 2015.

al-Azem, Talal. *Rule-Formulation and Binding Precedent in the Madhhab-Law Tradition: Ibn Quṭlubghā's Commentary on* The Compendium of Qudūrī. Leiden: Brill, 2017.

Badawi, Jamal A. *Gender Equity in Islam: Basic Principles.* Plainfield, IN: American Trust, 1995.

Baugh, Carolyn. "An Exploration of the Juristic Consensus (*ijma'*) on Compulsion in the Marriages of Minors." *Comparative Islamic Studies* 5 (2011): 33–92.

———. *Minor Marriage in Early Islamic Law.* Leiden: Brill, 2017.

Boyarin, Daniel. "Are There any Jews in 'The History of Sexuality'?" *Journal of the History of Sexuality* 5, no. 3 (1995): 333–55.

Boydston, Jeanne. "Gender as a Question of Historical Analysis." *Gender and History* 20, no. 3 (2008): 558–83.

Bray, Julia. "Men, women and slaves in Abbasid society." In *Gender in the Early Medieval World: East and West, 300–900,* edited by Leslie Brubaker and Julia M. H. Smith, 121–46. Cambridge: Cambridge University Press, 2004.

Brown, Jonathan. *Misquoting Muhammad: The Challenge and Choices of Interpreting the Prophet's Legacy.* London: Oneworld Academic, 2014.

———. *Slavery and Islam.* London: Oneworld Academic, 2019.

Brunschvig, Robert. "Abd." In *Encyclopedia of Islam,* edited by P. Bearman, Th. Bianquis, C. E. Bosworth, E. van Donzel, and W. P. Heinrichs. 2nd ed. https://referenceworks .brillonline.com/entries/encyclopaedia-of-islam-2/abd-COM_0003?s.num=0&s.f.s2 _parent=s.f.book.encyclopaedia-of-islam-2&s.q=abd.

Burton, J. "Muḥṣan." In *Encyclopedia of Islam,* edited by P. Bearman, Th. Bianquis, C. E. Bosworth, E. van Donzel, and W. P. Heinrichs. 2nd ed. https://referenceworks.brillonline .com/entries/encyclopaedia-of-islam-2/muhsan-SIM_5435?s.num=0&s.f.s2_parent=s.f .book.encyclopaedia-of-islam-2&s.q=Mu%E1%B8%A5%E1%B9%A3an.

Butler, Judith. *Gender Trouble: Feminism and the Subversion of Identity.* 1989. Reprint, New York: Routledge, 2007.

Calder, Norman. "Al-SaraKẖsī." In *Encyclopedia of Islam,* edited by P. Bearman, Th. Bianquis, C. E. Bosworth, E. van Donzel, and W. P. Heinrichs. 2nd ed. https://referenceworks .brillonline.com/entries/encyclopaedia-of-islam-2/al-sarakhsi-SIM_6620?s.num=0&s.f .s2_parent=s.f.book.encyclopaedia-of-islam-2&s.q=al-Sarakh%CC%B2s%C4%AB.

Chaudhry, Ayesha S. *Domestic Violence and the Islamic Tradition.* Oxford: Oxford University Press, 2014.

Collins, Patricia Hill. *Intersectionality as Critical Social Theory.* Durham, NC: Duke University Press, 2019.

Collins, Patricia Hill, and Sirma Bilge. *Intersectionality.* 2nd ed. Cambridge: Polity Press, 2021.

Connell, R. W. *Masculinities.* 1993. Reprint, Berkeley: University of California Press, 2005.

Connell, R. W., and James W. Messerschmidt. "Hegemonic Masculinity: Rethinking the Concept." *Gender and Society* 19 (2005): 829–59.

Coulson, Noel. *A History of Islamic Law*. Piscataway, NJ: Transaction, 2011.

Crenshaw, Kimberlé. "Demarginalizing the Intersection of Race and Sex: A Black Feminist Critique of Antidiscrimination Doctrine, Feminist Theory, and Antiracist Politics." *University of Chicago Legal Forum* 140, no. 1 (1989): 314–43.

Crone, Patricia. *Roman, Provincial, and Islamic Law: The Origins of the Islamic Patronate*. Cambridge: Cambridge University Press, 1987.

Cunningham, Hugh. "Review Essay: Histories of Childhood." *American Historical Review* 103, no. 4 (1998): 1195–208.

Dallal, Ahmad. "Sexualities: Scientific Discourses, Premodern." In *Encyclopedia of Women and Islamic Cultures*, edited by Joseph Suad Joseph, 401–7. Vol. 3. Leiden: Brill, 2006.

de Bellefonds, Y. Linant. "Fāsid wa Bāṭil." In *Encyclopedia of Islam*, edited by P. Bearman, Th. Bianquis, C. E. Bosworth, E. van Donzel, and W. P. Heinrichs. 2nd ed. https://referenceworks.brillonline.com/entries/encyclopaedia-of-islam-2/fasid-wa-batil-COM_0215?s.num=0&s.f.s2_parent=s.f.book.encyclopaedia-of-islam-2&s.q=%E2%80%9CF%C4%81sid+wa+B%C4%81%E1%B9%ADil%2C%E2%80%9D.

Fausto-Sterling, Anne. *Sex/Gender: Biology in a Social World*. London: Routledge, 2012.

Finley, Moses. *Ancient Slavery and Modern Ideology*. London: Chatto and Windus, 1980.

Fonrobert, Charlotte. "The Semiotics of the Sexed Body in Early Halakhic Discourse." In *How Should Rabbinic Literature Be Read in the Modern World*, edited by Matthew A. Kraus, 79–104. Piscataway, NJ: Gorgias Press, 2006.

Foucault, Michel. *The History of Sexuality*. Vol. 1, *The Will of Knowledge*, edited by Frédéric Gros, translated by Robert Hurley. New York: Pantheon Books, 1978.

Freamon, Bernard K. *Possessed by the Right Hand: The Problem of Slavery in Islamic Law and Muslim Cultures*. Leiden: Brill, 2019.

———. "Definitions and Conceptions of Slave Ownership in Islamic Law." In *The Legal Understanding of Slavery: From the Historical to the Contemporary*, edited by Jean Allain, 40–60. Oxford: Oxford University Press, 2012.

Freeland, Cynthia. "Nourishing Speculation: A Feminist Reading of Aristotelian Science." In *Engendering Origins: Critical Feminist Readings of Plato and Aristotle*, edited by Bat-Ami Bar On, 145–87. Albany: State University of New York Press, 1994.

Geissinger, [Ash]. "Applying Gender and Queer Theory to Pre-Modern Sources." In *The Routledge Handbook of Islam and Gender*, edited by Justine Howe, 101–15. London: Routledge, 2021.

———. "'Are Men the Majority in Paradise, or Women?': Constructing Gender and Communal Boundaries in Muslim B. Al-Ḥajjāj's (d. 261/875) *Kitāb Al-Janna*." In *Roads to Paradise: Eschatology and Concepts of the Hereafter in Islam*, edited by Sebastian Günther and Todd Lawson, 442–73. Leiden: Brill, 2017.

———. *Gender and Muslim Constructions of Exegetical Authority: A Rereading of the Classical Genre of Qur'ān Commentary*. Leiden: Brill, 2015.

———. "'Umm al-Dardā' Sat in *Tashahhud* Like a Man': Towards the Historical Contextualization of a Portrayal of Female Religious Authority." *Muslim World* 103 (2003): 305–19.

Gesink, Indira. "Intersex Bodies in Premodern Islamic Discourse: Complicating the Binary." *Journal of Middle East Women's Studies* 14 (2018): 152–73.

———. "Intersex in Islamic Medicine, Law, and Activism." In *The Routledge Handbook of Islam and Gender*, edited by Justine Howe, 116–29. London: Routledge, 2021.

Giladi, Anver. *Children of Islam: Concepts of Childhood in Medieval Muslim Society*. Basingstoke: Macmillan, 1992.

Goh, Ryan, Daryl Goh, and Hasthika Ellepola. "Perineal tears—A Review." *Australian Journal of General Practice* 47, nos. 1–2 (2018): 35–38.

Hall, Stuart. *Familiar Stranger: A Life Between Two Islands*. Edited by Bill Schwarz. Durham, NC: Duke University Press, 2017.

Hallaq, Wael. *The Origins and Evolution of Islamic Law*. Cambridge: Cambridge University Press, 2005.

Hallet, Judith P., and Marilyn B. Skinner, eds. *Roman Sexualities*. Princeton, NJ: Princeton University Press, 1998.

Halperin, David. *How to Do the History of Homosexuality*. Chicago: University of Chicago Press, 2002.

Hathaway, Jane. *The Chief Eunuch of the Ottoman Harem: From African Slave to Power-Broker*. Cambridge: Cambridge University Press, 2020.

Heywood, Colin. *A History of Childhood: Children and Childhood in the West from Medieval to Modern Times*. Cambridge: Polity Press, 2001.

Hopkins, M. K. "The Age of Roman Girls at Marriage." *Population Studies* 18 (1965): 309–27.

Horowitz, Maryanne Cline. "Aristotle and Woman." *Journal of the History of Biology* 9 (1976): 183–213.

Husayn, Nebil A. "*Aḥkām* Concerning the *Ahl al-bayt*." *Islamic Law and Society* 27 (2019): 145–84.

Idris, Razan. "Is the Ex-Slave Equal to the Free Arab in Marriage: Debating Lineage, Race and Freedom in Mālikī Muslim History." Bachelor's thesis, Duke University, 2018.

Jane, Emma. "'Dude . . . stop the spread': Antagonism, Agonism, and #manspreading on Social Media." *International Journal of Cultural Studies* 20, no. 5 (2017): 459–75.

Jankowiak, Marek. "What Does the Slave Trade in the Saqaliba Tell Us about Early Islamic Slavery?" *International Journal of Middle East Studies* 49 (2017): 169–72.

Johansen, Baber. "The Valorization of the Human Body in Muslim Sunni Law." In Devin J. Stewart, Baber Johansen, and Amy Singer, *Law and Society in Islam*, 71–112. Princeton, NJ: Markus Wiener, 1996.

Jones-Rogers, Stephanie. *They Were Her Property: White Women as Slave Owners in the American South*. New Haven, CT: Yale University Press, 2019.

Kadi, Wadad. "The Primordial Covenant and Human History in the Qur'ān." *Proceedings of the American Philosophical Society* 147, no. 4 (2003): 332–38.

Karras, Ruth Mazo. "Active/Passive, Acts/Passions: Greek and Roman Sexualities." *American Historical Review* 105, no. 4 (2000): 1250–65.

———. "Prostitution and the Question of Sexual Identity in Medieval Europe." *Journal of Women's History* 11, no. 2 (1999): 159–77.

———. *Slavery and Society in Medieval Scandinavia*. New Haven, CT: Yale University Press, 1988.

Katz, Marion. "Gender and Law." In *Encyclopedia of Islam*, edited by Kate Fleet, Gudrun Krämer, Denis Matringe, John Nawas, and Devin J. Stewart. 3rd ed. https://referenceworks.brillonline.com/entries/encyclopaedia-of-islam-3/gender-and-law-COM_27397?s.num=0&s.f.s2_parent=s.f.book.encyclopaedia-of-islam-3&s.q=gender+and+law.

———. *Prayer in Islamic Thought and Practice*. Cambridge: Cambridge University Press, 2013.

———. "Textual Study of Gender." In *Islamic Studies in the Twenty-First Century: Transformations and Continuities*, edited by Leon Buskens and Annemarie van Sandwjik, 87–107. Amsterdam: Amsterdam University Press, 2016.

———. *Women in the Mosque: A History of Legal Thought and Social Practice*. New York: Columbia University Press, 2014.

Kelto-Lillis, Julia. *Virgin Territory: Configuring Female Virginity in Early Christianity*. Oakland: University of California Press, 2022.

Kennedy, Hugh. *When Baghdad Ruled the Muslim World: The Rise and Fall of Islam's Greatest Dynasty*. Cambridge, MA: Da Capo Press, 2006.

Khan, Akhtar Hamid. *Komila se Aurangi Tak: Mushahidat-o-Tasurat*. Karachi: City Press Book Shop, 1998.

Kueny, Kathryn. *Conceiving Identities: Maternity in Medieval Muslim Discourse and Practice*. Albany: State University of New York Press, 2013.

Laiou, Angeliki E. "Sex, Consent, and Coercion in Byzantium." In *Consent and Coercion to Sex and Marriage in Ancient and Medieval Societies*, edited by Angeliki E. Laiou, 109–219. Washington, DC: Dumbarton Oaks, 1993.

Lane, Edward William. *Arabic-English Lexicon*. Lahore: Islamic Book Centre, 1978. https://catalog.hathitrust.org/Record/006790012.

Laqueur, Thomas W. *Making Sex: Body and Gender from the Greeks to Freud*. Cambridge, MA: Harvard University Press, 1990.

Marchal, Joseph. *Appalling Bodies: Queer Figures before and after Paul's Letters*. Oxford: Oxford University Press, 2019.

Marin, Manuela. "Women, Gender and Sexuality." In *The New Cambridge History of Islam, Vol. 4: Islamic Cultures and Societies to the End of the Eighteenth Century*, edited by Robert Irwin, 355–80. Cambridge: Cambridge University Press, 2010.

Marlow, Louise. *Hierarchy and Egalitarianism in Islamic Thought*. Princeton, NJ: Princeton University Press, 1997.

Marmon, Shaun. *Eunuchs and Sacred Boundaries in Islamic Society*. New York: Oxford University Press, 1995.

Maududi, Seyed Abu'l 'ala. *Purdah shar'i aur ijtima'i nuqta-e-nigah se*. Punjab: Maktaba Jamat-e-Islami, 1959.

Al-Mawsu'ah al-fiqhiyya al-Kuwaitiyah. 45 vols. Kuwait: Kuwait Ministry of Awqaf and Islamic Affairs, 1983.

Melchert, Christopher. *The Formation of the Sunni Schools of Law, 9th–10th centuries C.E.* New York: Brill, 1997.

Meron, Ya'akov. "The Development of Legal Thought in Hanafi Texts." *Studia Islamica* 30 (1969): 73–118.

Metcalf, Barbara. *Perfecting Women: Maulana Ashraf 'Ali Thanawi's Bihishti Zewar*. Berkeley: University of California Press, 1992.

Moors, Annelies. "Debating Islamic Family Law." In *Social History of Women and Gender in the Modern Middle East*, edited by Margaret L. Meriwether and Judith E. Tucker, 141–75. Boulder, CO: Westview Press, 1999.

Motzki, Harald. "Child Marriage in Seventeenth-Century Palestine." In *Islamic Legal Interpretation, Muftis and their Fatwas*, edited by Muhammad Khalid Masud, Brinkley Morris Messick, and David Stephan Powers, 129–40. Cambridge, MA: Harvard University Press, 1996.

Muslim Association of Canada—Calgary. "Dr Jamal Badawi at Al-Salam Centre speaking about gender equality and equity, a normative Islamic perspective." Facebook. April 21, 2019. https://www.facebook.com/MACCalgary/videos/383704515818900/.

Myrne, Pernilla. "A *Jariya's* Prospects in Abbasid Baghdad." In *Concubines and Courtesans: Women and Slavery in Islamic History*, edited by Matthew Gordon and Kathryn A. Hain, 52–74. New York: Oxford University Press, 2017.

Naffine, Ngaire. "Can Women Be Legal Persons?" In *Visible Women: Essays on Feminist Legal Theory and Political Philosophy*, edited by Susan James and Stephanie Palmer, 69–90. London: Hart, 2013.

———. *Law and the Sexes: Explorations in Feminist Jurisprudence*. Sydney: Allen & Unwin, 1990.

Najmabadi, Afsaneh. "Beyond the Americas: Are Gender and Sexuality Useful Categories of Analysis?" *Journal of Women's History* 18, no. 1 (2006): 11–21.

———. "Crafting an Educated Housewife in Iran." In *Remaking Women: Feminism and Modernity in the Middle East*, edited by Lila Abu-Lughod, 91–125. Princeton, NJ: Princeton University Press, 1998.

———. "Genus of Sex or the Sexing of *Jins*." *International Journal of Middle East Studies* 45 (2013): 211–31.

Nash, Jennifer. "Intersectionality and Its Discontents." *American Quarterly* 69 (2017): 117–29.

Nasr, Seyyed Hossein. *Traditional Islam in the Modern World*. London: K. Paul International, 1990.

Okin, Susan Moller. *Women in Western Political Thought*. Princeton, NJ: Princeton University Press, 1979.

Omar, Sara. "From Semantics to Normative Law: Perceptions of *Liwāṭ* (Sodomy) and *Siḥāq* (Tribadism) in Islamic Jurisprudence (8th to 15th Century CE)." *Islamic Law and Society* 19 (2012): 222–56.

Oyèwùmi, Oyeronke. "Conceptualizing Gender: The Eurocentric Foundations of Feminist Concepts and the Challenge of African Epistemologies." *JENDA: A Journal of Culture and African Women Studies* 2, no. 1 (2002).

———. *The Invention of Women: Making an African Sense of Western Gender Discourses*. Minneapolis: University of Minnesota Press, 1997.

———. "Visualizing the Body: Western Theories and African Subjects." In *African Gender Studies: A Reader*, edited by Oyeronke Oyèwùmi, 3–21. New York: Palgrave Macmillan, 2005.

Pande, Ishita. "'Listen to the Child': Law, Sex, and the Child Wife in Indian Historiography." *History Compass* 11 (2013): 687–701.

Paret, R. "Istiḥsān and Istiṣlaḥ." In *Encyclopedia of Islam*, edited by P. Bearman, Th. Bianquis, C. E. Bosworth, E. van Donzel, and W. P. Heinrichs. 2nd ed. https://referenceworks.brillonline.com/entries/encyclopaedia-of-islam-2/istihsan-and-istislah-COM_0395?s.num=0&s.f.s2_parent=s.f.book.encyclopaedia-of-islam-2&s.q=Isti%E1%B8%A5s%C4%81n+and+Isti%E1%B9%A3la%E1%B8%A5.

Peirce, Leslie. *Morality Tales: Law and Gender in the Ottoman Court of Aintab.* Berkeley: University of California Press, 2003.

Peters, Rudolph. "Capacity (*Ahliyya*)." In *The Oxford International Encyclopedia of Legal History*, edited by Stanley N. Katz. Oxford: Oxford University Press, 2009.

———. *Crime and Punishment in Islamic Law.* Cambridge: Cambridge University Press, 2006.

Quraishi-Landes, Asifa. "A Meditation on *Mahr*, Modernity and Muslim Marriage Contract Law." In *Feminism, Law and Religion*, edited by Marie A. Failinger, Elizabeth R. Schlitz, and Susan J. Stabile, 173–95. Farnham: Ashgate, 2013.

Rabb, Intisar. *Doubt in Islamic Law: A History of Legal Maxims, Interpretation, and Islamic Criminal Law.* Cambridge: Cambridge University Press, 2014.

Rapoport, Yossef. *Marriage, Money and Divorce in Medieval Islamic Society.* Cambridge: Cambridge University Press, 2005.

Robinson, Chase. "Slavery in the Conquest Period." *International Journal of Middle East Studies* 49 (2017): 158–63.

Rosenthal, Franz. *The Muslim Concept of Freedom Prior to the Nineteenth Century.* Leiden: Brill, 1960.

El-Rouayheb, Khaled. *Before Homosexuality in the Arab-Islamic World, 1500–1800.* Chicago: University of Chicago Press, 2009.

Rowson, Everett. "The Categorization of Gender and Sexual Irregularity in Medieval Arabic Vice Lists." In *Body Guards: The Cultural Politics of Gender Ambiguity*, edited by Julia Epstein and Kristina Straub, 50–79. New York: Routledge, 1991.

———. "Homoerotic Liaisons among the Mamluk Elite in Late Medieval Egypt and Syria." In *Islamicate Sexualities: Translations across Temporal Geographies of Desire*, edited by Kathryn Babayan and Afsaneh Najmabadi, 204–38. Cambridge, MA: Harvard University Press, 2008.

———. "The Traffic in Boys: Slavery and Homoerotic Liaisons in Elite ʿAbbāsid Society." *Middle Eastern Literatures* 11 (2008): 193–204.

Rubin, Gayle. "The Traffic in Women: Notes on the 'Political Economy' of Sex." In *Toward an Anthropology of Women*, edited by Rayna R. Reiter, 157–210. New York: Monthly Review Press, 1975.

Sanders, Paula. "Gendering the Ungendered Body: Hermaphrodites in Medieval Islamic Law." In *Women in Middle Eastern History: Shifting Boundaries in Sex and Gender*, edited by Nikki R. Keddi and Beth Baron, 74–95. New Haven, CT: Yale University Press, 1992.

Schacht, Joseph. *An Introduction to Islamic Law.* New York: Clarendon Press, 1964.

Schereschewsky, Ben Zion, and Menachem Elon. "Child Marriage." In *Encyclopedia Judaica*, edited by Michael Beck, 616–17. Jerusalem: Encyclopedia Judaica, 1972.

Scott, Joan Wallach. "Gender: A Useful Category of Historical Analysis." *American Historical Review* 91, no. 5 (1986): 1053–75.

Seedat, Fatima. "Gender and the Study of Islamic Law: From Polemics to Feminist Ethics." In *The Routledge Handbook of Islam and Gender*, edited by Justine Howe, 138–42. London: Routledge, 2020.

———. "Sex and the Legal Subject: Women and Legal Capacity in Hanafi Law." PhD diss., McGill University, 2014.

———. "Sitting in Difference: Queering the Study of Islam." *Journal of Feminist Studies in Religion* 34 (2018): 149–54.

———. "When Islam and Feminism Converge." *Muslim World* 103 (2013): 404–20.

Shaikh, Sa'diyya. *Sufi Narratives of Intimacy: Ibn 'Arabī, Gender, and Sexuality*. Chapel Hill: University of North Carolina Press, 2012.

Shaki, Mansour. "Children iii. Legal Rights of Children in Sasanian Period." In *Encyclopaedia Iranica*, 4:407–10. New York: Ehsan Yarshater for Iranian Studies, 1996. https://www.iranicaonline.org/articles/children-iii.

Shakry, Omnia. "Schooled Mothers and Structured Play: Child Rearing in Turn-of-the-Century Egypt." In *Remaking Women: Feminism and Modernity in the Middle East*, edited by Lila Abu-Lughod, 126–70. Princeton, NJ: Princeton University Press, 1998.

El Shamsy, Ahmed. *The Canonization of Islamic Law: A Social and Intellectual History*. New York: Cambridge University Press, 2013.

Shatzmiller, Maya. *Her Day in Court: Women's Property Rights in Fifteenth-Century Granada*. Cambridge, MA: Harvard University Press, 2007.

Shaw, Brent D. "The Age of Roman Girls at Marriage: Some Reconsiderations." *Journal of Roman Studies* 77 (1987): 28–46.

Siddiqui, Mona. "Law and the Desire for Social Control: An Insight into the Hanafi Concept of *Kafa'a* with Reference to the Fatawa 'Alamgiri (1664–1672)." In *Feminism and Islam: Legal and Literary Perspectives*, edited by Mai Yamani, 49–68. New York: New York University Press, 1996.

Skinner, Marilyn B. *Sexuality in Greek and Roman Culture*. Oxford: Blackwell, 2005.

Spellman, Elizabeth. "Aristotle and the Politicization of the Soul." In *Discovering Reality: Feminist Perspectives on Epistemology*, edited by Sandra Harding and Merrill B. Hintikka, 17–30. Dordrecht: Kluwer Academic, 1983.

Strassfeld, Max. *Trans Talmud: Androgynes and Eunuchs in Rabbinic Literature*. Oakland: University of California Press, 2022.

Sukava, Tyson. "Blending Bodies in Classical Greek Medicine." In *Exploring Gender Diversity in the Ancient World*, edited by Jennifer Surtees and Jennifer Dyer, 43–53. Edinburgh: Edinburgh University Press, 2020.

Tan, Oğuzhan. "Childhood and Child Marriage in Islamic Law." *Cumhuriyet Ilahiyat Dergisi* 22, no. 2 (2018): 783–805.

Tolino, Serena. "Locating Discourses on the Gender Binary (and beyond) in Pre-Modern Islamicate Societies." In *Sex and Desire in Muslim Cultures: Beyond Norms and Transgression from the Abbasids to the Present Day*, edited by Aymon Kreil, Lucia Sorbera, and Serena Tolino, 23–45. London: I. B. Tauris, 2021.

Tucker, Judith E. *In the House of Law: Gender and Islamic Law in Ottoman Syria and Palestine*. Berkeley: University of California Press, 1998.

———. "Questions of Consent: Contracting a Marriage in Ottoman Syria and Palestine." In *The Islamic Marriage Contract: Case Studies in Islamic Family Law*, edited by Asifa Quraishi and Frank E. Vogel, 123–35. Cambridge, MA: Harvard University Press, 2008.

———. *Women, Family, and Gender in Islamic Law*. Cambridge: Cambridge University Press, 2008.

Urban, Elizabeth. *Conquered Populations in Early Islam: Non-Arabs, Slaves and the Sons of Slave Mothers*. Edinburgh: Edinburgh University Press, 2020.

Vishanoff, David. *The Formation of Islamic Hermeneutics: How Sunni Legal Theorists Imagined a Revealed Law*. New Haven, CT: American Oriental Society, 2011.

Viswanathan, Gauri. *Outside the Fold: Conversion, Modernity, and Belief.* Princeton, NJ: Princeton University Press, 1998.

Walters, Jonathan. "Invading the Roman Body: Manliness and Impenetrability in Roman Thought." In *Roman Sexualities*, edited by Judith P. Hallett and Marilyn B. Skinner, 29–44. Princeton, NJ: Princeton University Press, 1997.

Wheeler, Brannon. *Applying the Canon in Islam: The Authorization and Maintenance of Interpretive Reasoning in Ḥanafī Scholarship.* Albany: State University of New York Press, 1996.

Williams, Craig. *Roman Homosexuality: Ideologies of Masculinity in Classical Antiquity.* Oxford: Oxford University Press, 1999.

Witt, Charlotte. "Form, Normativity and Gender in Aristotle: A Feminist Perspective." In *Feminist Reflections on the History of Philosophy*, edited by Lilli Alanen and Charlotte Witt, 117–36. Dordrecht: Kluwer Academic, 2004.

Yacoob, Saadia. "Islamic Law and Gender." In *The Oxford Handbook of Islamic Law*, edited by Anver M. Emon and Rumee Ahmed, 75–101. Oxford: Oxford University Press, 2018.

Yazbak, Mahmoud. "Minor Marriages and Khiyār al-Bulūgh in Ottoman Palestine: A Note on Women's Strategies in a Patriarchal Society." *Islamic Law and Society* 9, no. 3 (2002): 386–409.

Zahraa, Mahdi. "The Legal Capacity of Women in Islamic Law." *Arab Law Quarterly* 11 (1996): 245–63.

———. "Legal Personality in Islamic Law." *Arab Law Quarterly* 10 (1995): 193–206.

Ze'evi, Dror. *Producing Desire: Changing Sexual Discourse in the Ottoman Middle East, 1500–1900.* Berkeley: University of California Press, 2006.

Zilfi, Madeline C. *Women and Slavery in the Late Ottoman Empire: The Design of Difference.* New York: Cambridge University Press, 2010.

al-Zuhayli, Wahbah. *Usul al-fiqh al-Islami.* 2 vols. Damascus: Dar al-Fikr, 2008.

Founded in 1893,
UNIVERSITY OF CALIFORNIA PRESS
publishes bold, progressive books and journals
on topics in the arts, humanities, social sciences,
and natural sciences—with a focus on social
justice issues—that inspire thought and action
among readers worldwide.

The UC PRESS FOUNDATION
raises funds to uphold the press's vital role
as an independent, nonprofit publisher, and
receives philanthropic support from a wide
range of individuals and institutions—and from
committed readers like you. To learn more, visit
ucpress.edu/supportus.